NECESSARY DREAMS

NECESSARY DREAMS

AMBITION IN WOMEN'S CHANGING LIVES

ANNA FELS

PANTHEON BOOKS, NEW YORK

Owing to space limitations, permissions will be found following the index.

Pantheon Books and colophon are registered trademarks of Random House, Inc.

Library of Congress Cataloging-in-Publication Data

Fels, Anna.
Necessary dreams : the vital role of ambition in women's changing lives / Anna Fels.
p.   cm.
Includes bibliographical references and index.
ISBN 0-679-44244-8
1. Women—Psychology.   2. Women in the professions.   3. Working mothers.
4. Ambition.   5. Sex role.   I. Title.

HQ1206.F35 2004   305.4—dc22   2003062422

www.pantheonbooks.com

Book design by M. Kristen Bearse

Printed in the United States of America
First Edition
2   4   6   8   9   7   5   3   1

FOR
JIM, MOLLY, AND WILL

What happens when Olivia—this organism that has been under the shadow of the rock this million years—feels the light fall on it, sees coming her way a piece of strange food—knowledge, adventure, art. And she reaches out for it . . . and has to devise some entirely new combination of her resources, so highly developed for other purposes, so as to absorb the new into the old.

—VIRGINIA WOOLF, *A Room of One's Own*

ACKNOWLEDGMENTS

I realized, as I began to write these acknowledgments, that this project actually started many years ago, but then lay dormant for decades. As an undergraduate, I worked with Matina Horner, one of the earliest and most influential researchers in the area of women and achievement. Her research posed questions that I and many other women in the following decades, endlessly revisited and struggled with throughout our lives and that ultimately led to the writing of this book.

Many years later an informal discussion of these issues with Linda Healey, then an editor at Pantheon, led her to suggest that I write a book on the subject. Her confidence that I could successfully produce a book on the daunting subject of women and ambition launched this project. Sarah Chalfant, my agent, shepherded the book through its initial stages and also was a discerning and enthusiastic reader. My editor, Shelley Wanger, patiently followed the book through its many incarnations, helping me to shape it and carefully guiding it though the complex process of publication. Sydney Johnson tracked down the diverse and sometimes obscure references that inform this work.

While writing the manuscript, I have had the advice as well as the insights of many friends. A study group of my colleagues, Dr. Leonard Groopman, Dr. Richard Friedman, Dr. Minna Fyer, Dr. Alan Barasch, and Dr. Scott Goldsmith, generously critiqued some of the hypotheses that I formulated in the book's early stages. My writing group, including Wendy Gimbel and Mac Griswold, lent me their support and guidance. Susan Grace Galassi, also a member of this group, has done more than I can ever repay by her encouragement throughout the writing process, keeping up my morale during the most difficult moments.

Exploratory conversations with several distinguished women including Eve Ensler, Nancy Evans, and Leslie Stahl, raised important issues that I have tried to address. Friends who provided the lively discussions and continued support without which this book could not have been completed include Cynthia Farrar, Jonathan Galassi, Dr. Edward Hallowell, Dr. Judith Tanenbaum, and Randolyn Zinn. Barbara Strauch at *The New York Times* encouraged me, while I was working on the book, to write columns for the Science Times section, which served as a much-needed counterbalance to the longer project. Throughout the intense periods of writing, while continuing my full-time practice, I could not have survived without the memorable expeditions as well as friendships provided by Pamela McCarthy and Elizabeth Bailey.

When I think of my own "necessary dreams"—my evolving plans and career—I am well aware that they could never have developed without the love and encouragement of my husband, who pitched in to help me with everything from child care to copyediting. Finally, my two children, Molly and Will, have made it all seem worthwhile, even in those moments when finding some balance in life seemed like a crazy pipe dream.

CONTENTS

Acknowledgments   ix

Introduction   xiii

PART ONE   *Women and Ambition*

1   What Is Ambition?   3

2   Distorted Ambitions   19

PART TWO   *Recognition and Ambition in Women's Lives*

3   Avoiding Attention   35

4   Femininity   47

5   Why Is Recognition So Important for Ambition?   72

6   Unequal Rewards   99

7   Pseudo-Recognition: Historical and Contemporary   106

8   Parents, Mentors, Institutions, and Peers   118

PART THREE   *Women and Mastery*

9   Developing Skills   141

10   Combining Femininity and Mastery   162

PART FOUR   *Careers, Marriage, and Family*

11   The Current Dilemma   201

12   Careers   205

13   Marriage   220

14   Children and Careers   237

Conclusion   252

Notes   257

Index   281

INTRODUCTION

A young professional woman who came to see me several years ago for a psychiatric consultation left me sitting in my office late that afternoon as puzzled by her predicament as she was. Alice had arrived at my office looking strikingly elegant in an understated way, but tired and demoralized. She was a lawyer who had recently finished law school, filled with visions of an engrossing and even distinguished career. She had begun working at a small but prestigious law firm. In her wry, articulate style, Alice filled me in on her family background. She was an only child who had grown up in southern California in the 1970s. Her parents, both ex-hippies, had had an "open marriage" and later had separated when she was a teenager. Her mother, a smart woman who had never finished her education, resented her academically successful daughter. But school was Alice's lifeline—the place where she could get adult attention and praise—and she was always at the head of her class no matter what went on at home. Her father, a self-absorbed, moderately successful real estate developer, had largely ignored his daughter except for rare visits when he would inappropriately pour out his heart to her about his business problems and love life. The first time he had shown real pride in her was when she told him about her new job and her impressive salary.

At the high-powered law firm where she worked, Alice was performing well, but she was increasingly miserable. There were only two women in the upper ranks of the firm. The woman Alice worked most closely with had an annoyingly detail-oriented, fastidious style; she was referred to as "the librarian." Meanwhile, a middle-level woman lawyer at the firm who had befriended Alice had just gotten pregnant and was planning to quit. The male partner my patient worked directly for was encouraging about her work, but he had started to confide his personal problems to her during their weekly meetings—shades of her father. To make matters worse, Alice's fiancé had recently been made partner in his law firm. Now that he had some control over his hours, he was understanding but frustrated that Alice was often unavailable because of work. And in truth, she often had to work around the clock on no notice. As Alice succinctly put it, career success did not seem worth the price. Somehow the equation of hard work producing desirable rewards—a sense of self-worth, pleasure, independence, and competence—seemed to have run amok in some baffling way.

I had barely begun to mull over some of the issues that my session with Alice had raised when forty-five minutes later another, slightly older woman lawyer arrived in my office for a consultation, or as she put it, "just for some advice. I don't want the therapy thing." Katherine was a colorful presence, literally. She wore a crisp navy suit with red piping, buttons, and shoes. Her speech was vivid and unselfconscious. She had come to see me about a problem with a colleague whose drug use was creating conflicts in the office. But what struck me that afternoon, as Katherine sketched in a picture of her workplace, was how much she enjoyed her work. She, too, was in a stodgy firm and, like Alice, did not particularly admire the partners she worked with. But Katherine had just made a multimedia presentation (something apparently rarely done at legal conferences) to much acclaim. It had set her thinking about the possibility of starting a law-media firm sometime in the future. Her husband, also a lawyer but an entrepreneur wannabe, was encouraging, if somewhat envious. There was no question that this woman had found a work situation in which she thrived.

There were certainly differences in these two women's situations, but there were also many similarities: in particular, both had started out with nearly identical legal ambitions. Yet one was blossoming in her career, while the other felt more and more depleted. I found myself mulling over their parallel work lives. What specific elements had combined to make the work a pleasure for one but stressful and discouraging for the other? Were there missed clues right from the start that things would work for Katherine and not for Alice, or was the outcome due to a set of unpredictable circumstances? And if the latter was the case, what were the key elements in their respective situations that had invigorated one and left the other feeling anxious and listless?

The question was not altogether a new one for me, although seeing these two young women lawyers back to back certainly put it in bold relief. Like both of them, I had known from adolescence that I wanted my own profession. In my early teens, my father had died, leaving my mother financially insecure and socially adrift—a position I had vowed never to be in. But in my thirties, deep into a medical career, struggling to see patients and do research, married with two children, I realized that the various parts of my life didn't add up to a whole that I wanted. After much painful soul searching I left internal medicine for psychiatry, and even later I discovered that I enjoyed writing about psychiatric issues in addition to seeing patients. But finding the right combination of elements in my life had been a long, tortuous journey. It left me wondering how I could have made better choices earlier.

In my psychiatric practice, I frequently encounter women who made very different choices from those of us who went into professions, yet who end up facing similar issues. These are women who chose to be full-time mothers. Some thought of themselves as career women, only to discover that they hadn't the slightest desire to return to work after having children. Others, who had predicated their lives on establishing a family, came to therapy devastated to discover that the domestic life they had always dreamed of felt deadly: lonely and boring. Somehow, as these women had imagined their futures, something crucial had been missed, left out, or ignored—as they discovered to their dismay. But what?

Planning for the future is difficult under the best of circumstances. But for contemporary women it is both harder and more necessary than at any time in the past. Up until the last fifty years, women were largely excluded from universities, professions, clubs, politics, and jobs, even from written history. The paucity of their life choices undoubtedly impoverished the quality of their lives, but their roles, constricted though they were, were clearly delineated. At the beginning of the twenty-first century, however, middle-class women have access to training in virtually every profession. Their rights to education and employment—without which relatively few ambitions can be realized—have largely been won. Progress has been made. Yet the availability of these choices has taken women only part of the way—the opportunities as well as the obstacles facing women have become more varied and subtle. The feminist movement, advances in reproductive biology, cultural changes such as the increased divorce rate, and the economic forces that necessitate the two-income family have all disrupted the traditional roles assigned to women.

Women, more than men, need to actively imagine themselves into their futures because so little is mapped out for them at this historical moment. Unlike men, women have few accepted roles in our society—or more accurately, they have too many: innovative professional, devoted mother, competent employee, sexually attractive "babe," supportive wife, talented homemaker, and independent wage earner, to name a few. It falls nearly entirely on the individual woman to carve out a life for herself with adequate meaning and satisfactions—not an easy task for anyone, let alone an impressionable young person. For each woman life must be a creation of sorts and also an assertion of values, priorities, and identity, because no role is accepted unquestioningly.

The earliest and most intensely studied step in the process of creating a life amid the intense and often conflicting pressures that girls experience is imagining a desired future. This goal or ambition can be thought of as a highly gratifying role lying on the borderline between realistic planning and fantasies informed by our wishes and needs. It contains within it a conversation between one's past and future that forms a crucial part of our ideas about ourselves—our identities. Wishes and needs have histories—they arise from our past relationships and experiences. But they are about the creation of a specific and satisfying future. The projection of ourselves into our futures, made of our hopes and plans, can be thought of as a guide that allows us to travel toward its realization. The first step in creating a future is to imagine it.

Unfortunately, psychological theories have largely ignored the subject of the creation and vicissitudes of ambitions for the future, focusing intently and nearly exclusively on the past. It has been tacitly assumed that, if the past can be sorted out, the future will take care of itself. Asking for a patient's earliest memory, for example, is a standard question at the beginning of any therapy. Creating a coherent narrative of the patient's past is thought to be a major therapeutic goal. But very little is written or asked about a narrative of the future, as if this were not at least as important in understanding a patient's sense of him- or herself.

As I began to interview young women and ask them what they would like to be doing in five and ten years, I discovered that the answers were all over the map. Some drew a complete blank. Others described totally diffuse ambitions: "I could see being on television, like maybe a newscaster, but I could also see being a writer or politician." Some women voiced clear ambitions and then undercut them with self-deprecating comments: "I'd love to be one of those Jane Goodall types in Africa or maybe study bears in Alaska, but with my luck I'd probably end up in the local petting zoo." And there were women with cogent and seemingly practicable goals. A young woman who had worked summers during college in Washington researching health care issues wanted to get an M.D. and work overseas for the World Health Organization. Another woman, who did freelance photography and was assembling her first book of pictures, wanted to become a famous photographer, the next Cindy Sherman.

What became clear, listening to these wildly diverse scenarios, was that the liveliness and pleasure with which the women told their stories often corresponded closely to their level of self-esteem and general sense of well-being. The more diffuse or undeveloped the story, the more anxious or joyless was the person sitting across from me. The goal might be overly ambitious and unachievable at one extreme or uninspiring and unchallenging on the other. These people's images of their future were as clear an indicator of the coherence and vitality of their lives as any information I could glean from their histories. And in fact ego strength—that amorphous psychological entity that includes coping skills, understanding of reality, and sense of self-worth—has been shown to be higher in women with well-defined future plans than in those with vague or nonexistent ones.

This is not to say that everyone always has to have a final plan for the future. What I think it does say is that people, and particularly women, need to imagine themselves into their future since so little is mapped out for them. Trying out different stories or scenarios, picturing themselves in different lives, is a necessary prelude to investigating them in the real world. The future is a significant part of who we believe ourselves to be. Without an imagined future we have a sense of helplessness and passivity about our fate.

As has been amply documented, adolescent girls, unlike boys, encounter myriad difficulties as they begin to form their ambitions. Carol Gilligan in *Making Connections,* Mary Pipher in *Reviving Ophelia,* and Peggy Orenstein in *School Girls,* among others, have written eloquently about this problematic stage in girls' development—the lack of encouragement they receive, the discrimination in both academic and nonacademic settings, the conflicting cultural pressures. These and other groundbreaking writings have sensitized educators and the public alike to many of the important issues. Multiple initiatives have been designed that seek to address them. In the early years of their academic life, girls and young women receive more support than at any time previously. And encouragingly, evidence is now accumulating that young women are becoming more active, self-confident, and purposeful about imagining goals for themselves.

But an even more fraught period, in which ambitions must be reconsidered or reshaped, occurs after women complete their education, enter the workforce, and begin to make decisions about relationships and family. It is these women, in their twenties, thirties, and early forties, who I find coming to see me for psychiatric consultations, perplexed and self-doubting as they face painful decisions about their lives. Should they relocate for their husband's job, have children without a spouse, take a job that involves travel, stay home with their children, work more hours to satisfy their boss? The pressures and reevaluations that women face at each juncture of their career development are graphically outlined by their attrition rates. In physics, for example, girls make up 37 percent of classes in high school, 22 percent in college; 15 percent of female college students receive a degree in the subject; women are 10 percent of the Ph.D.'s, 7 percent of the assistant professors in the field, and 3 percent of the full professors. The flip side of these figures is that 63 percent of boys take physics in high school and presumably from this pool 97 percent of physics professors are ultimately chosen. Clearly, for a higher proportion of women than for men, the decision to pursue an interest is reconsidered repeatedly and often abandoned. Young women's goals for the future are far from definitive; they are a necessary but not sufficient element for realizing an ambition.

In my experience, it is extremely rare for men to come for a psychiatric consultation to deal with questions similar to those posed by women. For women, negotiating the adult stages of life remains problematic in ways that simply have no parallel in men's lives. When similar issues arise in men's lives, they feel less urgency because there is much more cultural consensus about their roles and because men continue to participate only marginally in child care. Although some data suggest that men are starting to assume a slightly greater share of household and child-care tasks, studies also indicate that men still both define themselves and evaluate other men primarily on the basis of their work. Particularly for middle-class men, work remains their primary source of identity and self-worth. As a consequence, they prioritize decisions in a predictable and largely unconflicted manner.

Having a husband who worked at home for a year and did more than his share of child care, I can tell you that men who deviate from this career trajectory elicit a certain patronizing humor and incredulity. He would inevitably be the only father at the nursery school or playground during the workday. Equally revealing of how anomalous others found his position was the frequent, overly effusive praise he got for his role. It was so *wonderful* to see a father in the park or on the field trip. Much was made of the fact that he took our daughter to school—although I too had a full-time job and took her to school three out of five days. And no one ever took me aside to say how *wonderful* it was that I was supporting the family.

Clearly, a father taking care of his child is still considered something of note. Movies like *Three Men and a Baby, Big Daddy,* and *Daddy Day Care,* in which men care for infants or children, are all comedies. Each of them is a two-hour gag about the hilarity of such a role reversal. For men the social imperatives are more clearly defined, for better or worse. Certainly men can have life crises, and they can question their decisions and change their direction, but these choices are not built inevitably into the very structure of their lives as they are for women. The choices do not have to be made as early or as repeatedly.

It is women in the midst of their adult lives, not men, who are faced with continuous pressures to reevaluate and reshape their lives. Unfortunately, nearly all the books and studies on adult women's ambitions are narrowly focused on highly specific situations—mentoring in graduate school, career choices in science, barriers to advancement in the business environment, women's political careers. There are also many books and studies that focus on the crucial issue of continuing discrimination against women in the workplace—the problem is enormously important and requires ongoing investigation. But what is lacking in the literature is an overarching view of the process by which women create, realize, reconfigure, and abandon goals. We need to know how this process differs for men and women and, most important, whether there are more useful ways of framing and understanding women's choices.

My research began with interviews of friends—men and women, acquaintances, and several women of unusual accomplishment. I read profiles, biographies, and autobiographies of women and many of the new books on "women's studies." I reflected back on the lives of some of my women patients and, in a few cases, asked their permission to use parts of their stories in disguised form in this book. Ultimately, however, my questions led me to the research literature, including studies from clinical psychology, experimental psychology, occupational behavior research, sociology, learning theory, and even neurophysiology. I am not an academic; nor is this book intended for an academic audience. But I believe that the available research regarding ambition must anchor any discussion of this complex, sprawling subject.

From these diverse sources, surprisingly specific factors emerged as essential to the vitality and satisfaction of women's as well as men's lives. This book is an attempt to define these core elements and trace them through the various stages and pressures that exist in women's lives. My hope is that it will provide a template that women can use to analyze their decisions and make more-informed choices. The ultimate goal is for women to be able to create coherent and satisfying lives in this tumultuous period of change.

PART ONE

WOMEN AND AMBITION

CHAPTER ONE

WHAT IS AMBITION?

I wondered, before I came here, whether I was going to confess to you this secret I've had since I was seven. I haven't even told my husband about it." The woman across from me, a journalist in her forties, paused and looked at me intently, trying to decide whether she should reveal her secret. Sitting there under her worried gaze, I wasn't sure where we were going. As a psychiatrist, I'm used to hearing the most improbable and even lurid of personal secrets. But this woman was not a patient. She was a friend of a friend, who had kindly agreed to let me interview her. It was actually the very first of a series of exploratory discussions that I had scheduled to start my research on ambition in women's lives, and I already found myself in unfamiliar territory. How had my seemingly straightforward question about childhood goals elicited a long-hidden secret?

The journalist looked at me uncertainly but continued. "When I was about seven, I had a notebook at school, and I would write poems and stories and illustrate them. I was going to write and illustrate children's books. They were clearly based on the books I loved. And I had this acronym that was like magic, like a secret pact with myself. I didn't even tell my sisters its meaning. It was IWBF—I Will Be Famous." She broke out into nervous laughter. "Oh my God, I can't believe I told you. You must understand, I didn't want to be recognized in the streets. My pact was tied up with writing and being recognized for it. I'm sure it was tied up with my father's approval and the literary world he operated in."

This was the long-withheld secret? Not sex, lies, or videotapes, but an odd incantation from childhood? It was the first of what were to be many lessons for me on how hidden and emotionally fraught the subject of ambition is for women. I soon came to realize that although the articulate, educated group of women I interviewed could talk cogently and calmly about topics ranging from money to sex, when the subject of ambition arose, the level of intensity and anxiety took a quantum leap.

It was hard to know what to make of the often long-winded, evasive, contradictory, and confused responses this subject elicited. A woman editor of a popular magazine vehemently denied that she was ambitious and produced an astounding string of euphemisms about pursuing "her personal best," "self-realization and understanding," and enlightenment, sounding more like a Zen master than an executive in the midst of the bustling, highly commercial magazine world. A choreographer who had recently started a career as a playwright gave me the following reply when asked about her ambitions: "I don't have any ambition. Well, I'm interested in creativity and in my work. I've been working on a one-act play and a screenplay. I guess one could say, 'That sounds ambitious,' but the fact is, what I don't want to do is promote myself. I do work." A woman in her forties who had started but then left a fledgling business to be at home with her children said emphatically, "I'm just thrilled that I didn't spend my twenties or thirties trying to grow my business and be a star in that world. I have a close friend who was also in a start-up, for a very hot product. They got a lot of attention. But she spent seven years at it, took too much cocaine, had an abortion, and by thirty-nine had no children or life or job." Yet toward the end of the interview the same woman suddenly revealed her continuing fantasy of returning to a career and making a success of it. A young woman who works on math textbooks announced, before I so much as asked a question, that she felt troubled by her lack of ambition. "I think it's all tied up with this business of goals. There needs to be some target out there. At work every year we have this development discussion, and we meet with our supervisors. And they ask, 'What are your short- and long-term goals?' I always put something down, but it's nothing I feel passionate about, it's usually some small project." The absence of ambition seemed no less fraught than its presence.

The women I interviewed hated the word *ambition* when applied to their own lives. One woman executive began by stating, "That word is not one I've used much in my vocabulary. On previous occasions when asked whether I was ambitious, I would tend to say no. I would describe myself as purposeful." For these women ambition necessarily implied egotism, selfishness, self-aggrandizement, or the manipulative use of others for one's own ends. Despite the fact that women are currently more career-oriented than at any time in history—and often more clearly ambitious—there is something about the concept that makes them distinctly uncomfortable. These women's denial of their own ambitiousness was particularly striking in contrast to the men I interviewed, who assumed that ambition was a necessary and desirable part of their lives. They often chided themselves for lacking sufficient amounts of it. Perhaps even more surprising, the very women who deplored ambition in reference to their own lives freely admitted to admiring it in men. If ambition was, by definition, self-serving and egotistical, why was it not only acceptable but desirable for men?

As I tried to sort through the diverse responses to my questions and to home in on the aspect of ambition that made women so uncomfortable, I realized that I needed to backtrack. I needed to understand what ambition consists of—for men and for women. But the more I tried to pin down its meaning, the blurrier it got. When I asked people to define ambition, nearly all of them, after a few attempts, finally resorted to examples: "Take Bill Gates . . ." There was something elusive about ambition. Everyone seemed intuitively to know what it was, but no one could articulate it.

In psychiatry, as in most branches of science, the study of a complex phenomenon often begins by tracing it to its earliest, simplest form. So I decided to review the childhood ambitions recalled by the women I had interviewed. Perhaps in this embryonic form I would find clues to its most basic elements. And indeed, compared to the wordy, ambivalent responses that these women had given about their current ambitions, their answers concerning childhood were direct and clear. They had a delightfully naïve and unapologetic sense of grandiosity and limitless possibility. As a child, each of the women had pictured herself in an important role: a great American novelist, an Olympic figure skater, a famous actress, a president of the United States, a fashion designer, a rock star, an international diplomat. "My fantasies about what I wanted to be? I think they were very ordinary, like being a ballerina. I took dancing lessons for seven years. I think of those kinds of fantasies as being common. Or maybe I'd be an artist—being anything that I did well. I wanted to be the best. I thought everyone had those kinds of fantasies, but I haven't really thought about this." "When I was a kid, we had a summer home in rural Maryland and on the way there we'd see signs saying, 'Impeach [Supreme Court Justice] Earl Warren.' And my mother or one of my siblings would say, 'One day that sign is going to say "Impeach Jenny Fenlow." ' Oh God, it's hard to believe, but that's what I thought I'd be, a Supreme Court justice." "Oh, my ambitions? They were very pedestrian. I was going to be either a brilliant writer or an actress. I had a very specific picture of being an actress. I wanted to be Sarah Bernhardt; I mean, I was extremely ambitious. I wrote a musical when I was in eighth grade that was produced at school. When I look back on it, I think, I wrote that?"

In nearly all the childhood ambitions, two undisguised elements were joined together. One was a special skill: writing, dancing, acting, diplomacy. But the childhood ambitions recalled were not just about developing a talent or expertise. The images of future accomplishment virtually always included a large helping of attention in the form of an appreciative audience. In each picture of the future self, the woman-to-be was front and center; she was the star of her own story. Public recognition was either included explicitly or, more often, implied by the very nature of the endeavor chosen. Special talent was assumed. In part, it was this open celebration of their specialness that made their childhood ambitions seem so silly or even embarrassing to the women who recalled them, that made them laugh and then ask me nervously if I thought their ambitions were normal.

Looking through developmental studies of both boys and girls, I noticed that they virtually always identified the same two components of childhood ambition. There was a (at least theoretically) practicable plan that involved a real accomplishment requiring work and skill. And then there was an expectation of approval: fame, status, acclaim, praise, honor. Each ambition was a narrative about a wished-for future, and in each story the child projected him- or herself into an adult life as a productive, admired member of society.

Of the two aspects of ambition, or at least of childhood ambition, the first seemed nearly incontrovertible. Without an element of mastery, after all, a picture of the future is not an ambition; it's simply wishful thinking. It's about luck or fate—you are merely a passive recipient of whatever fortune comes your way. You may desperately want to win the lottery, but that wish is not an ambition. Ambition requires an imagined future that can be worked toward by the development of skills and expertise.

Long ago the scientific community embraced the notion that there is a powerful and innate pleasure in mastery. Approximately half a century after Freud postulated his "drive theory" of motivation based on sex and aggression, researchers and theoreticians alike realized that a huge portion of behavior simply could not be explained in these terms. By the 1960s workers in the fields of animal behavior, child development, and even psychoanalysis accepted the existence of a powerful drive to explore, manipulate, and control the environment—in other words, to develop mastery.

Jean Piaget and other developmental psychologists who focused on children's need to master both intellectual and motor tasks discovered that children would repeat a task over and over until they could predict and determine the outcome. Theorists such as Erik Erikson began to posit a human need to "be able to make things and make them well and even perfectly: this is what I call a sense of industry." Researchers even turned their attention to "the addiction to bridge or solitaire, vices whose very existence depends upon the level of difficulty of the problem presented." Robert White, at the time a Harvard professor of psychology and one of the seminal investigators of motivation, named this drive to mastery "effectance." In describing such behavior he noted, "It is characteristic of this particular sort of activity that it is selective, directed, and persistent, and that instrumental acts will be learned for the sole reward of engaging in it." Mastery has its own powerful, built-in motivational engine. And there is no evidence to date that the intensity of this motivation differs between girls and boys, women and men.

The delight with which children describe their ambitions derives in no small part from the pleasure they foresee in developing this mastery. Children, as well as adults, passionately engage in learning skills—a fact so obvious that at times its significance is overlooked. There are few people whose lives do not include multiple areas of mastery—at home, at work, at play. People who strive to improve their professional skills often greatly enjoy their evolving expertise. But just as often they work at perfecting their avocations. Think of the intensity with which people practice their golf or tennis strokes—hardly key survival skills—or pursue bird watching, heading out to the woods and fields at dawn.

In Frank Conroy's classic memoir of his childhood, *Stop-Time,* he captures the sheer joy that children, like adults, take in mastery. The young Conroy becomes fascinated with the yo-yo and painstakingly works his way through a book of tricks, standing hour after hour practicing in the woods across from his house:

> The greatest pleasure in yo-yoing was an abstract pleasure—watching the dramatization of simple physical laws, and realizing they would never fail if a trick was done correctly. . . . I remember the first time I did a particularly lovely trick. . . . My pleasure at that moment was as much from the beauty of the experiment as from pride. Snapping apart my hands I sent the yo-yo into the air above my head, bouncing it off nothing, back into my palm.
>
> I practiced the yo-yo because it pleased me to do so.

Doing a thing well is an end in and of itself. The delight provided by the skill easily repays the effort of learning it.

The wish for mastery is undoubtedly a key component of ambition. But the pursuit of mastery virtually always requires a specific context: an evaluating, encouraging audience must be present for skills and talents to develop. Frank Conroy, in the same childhood scene, rushes off to show his new yo-yo expertise to his friends and to two particularly proficient older boys, Ramos and Ricardo. He seeks their acknowledgment of his ability. Like the young Conroy, we all need our efforts and accomplishments to be recognized. Without such earned affirmation, long-term learning and performance goals are rarely reached.

As the term is used here, *recognition* means being valued by others for qualities that we experience and value in ourselves; it involves appreciation by another person that feels accurate and meaningful to the recipient. Because recognition affirms a person's individual experience or accomplishment, it is different from other forms of attention.

Attention can perhaps best be pictured on a graph. On one axis attention goes from positive to negative; on the other from personal to generic. If you rob a bank and are caught, you will likely receive attention that is both negative and highly specific to you personally. If you win your local bingo tournament, the attention will be positive but generic; no particular individual skill or quality was involved.

One area of the diagram would represent attention that is at once individualized and affirming. It is this combination that defines recognition. The attention is specific, accurate, and positive. It might be praise for a series of photographs you have displayed, for the furnishings of your home, or for a program you designed for your computer. It could be admiration expressed for work in the local environmental group, or recognition for being a steady friend or for a presentation at work. The affirmation elicited is particular to the person; most likely no one else would have done these things in exactly the same way.

Attention received purely for an accepted, societal role such as being a minister, policeman, doctor, scholar, parent, or teacher is usually affirming but only moderately individualized. In my own life, for example, I receive a certain amount of recognition for being a psychiatrist. And indeed being a psychiatrist represents a personal accomplishment— I got through medical school and residency. However, it is also a role that I share with many others and that elicits a response that is, to that extent, positive but slightly impersonal. There are lots of psychiatrists out there. Recognition for belonging to a specific group can overlap with recognition that is highly individualized—as it might be if I were praised for my skills by one of my patients. Both types of recognition are central to the formulation of an ambition.

As will be discussed further on, virtually every area of research into human behavior, from sociology to clinical psychology, from occupational behavioral studies to investigations of learning, has concluded that we are constantly motivated and shaped by this type of response. Many investigators have postulated that the need for approval is a powerful innate drive in humans. Attention is a key currency in all human interactions, and recognition is its most valued specie. Throughout life, recognition by others defines us to ourselves, energizes us, directs our efforts, and even appears to alter mood.

It's important to emphasize that recognition is not synonymous with praise. Unlike recognition, praise is often given for a trait or an accomplishment that we don't care about. I can recall as a young child receiving an award for my penmanship and, even in that pre-computer era, thinking that it was an utterly useless skill and therefore a meaningless prize. Receiving the prize was a nonevent. I would probably not even recall it if I had not recently come upon the certificate in a box (and thrown it out).

Praise, in contrast to recognition, can be experienced as false—in which case it has no impact. Humans are endowed with an uncanny ability to discern fake, unspontaneous emotions. Undoubtedly that is why acting is such a difficult art; it's hard to put one over on us if you're not Sir Laurence Olivier. On a more humble note, when parents *ooh* and *ahh* over a child's every drawing of spindly figures under a line of blue sky, no one is fooled. Nor are we credulous when we give a bad presentation at work and our friends tell us that it was just fine. Praise qualifies as recognition only if its content feels meaningful, deserved, and accurate.

As noted previously, ambitions are about goals that require work and the acquisition of skills. It is precisely for such mastery that we desire to be recognized. The wish to be recognized as a descendant of a *Mayflower* family is not an ambition, because it is (or is not) a historical fact irrespective of any individual effort. It is an attribute that may be admired by others, but it is passively acquired. Equally important to an ambition is the expectation that one's efforts will be affirmed outside an immediate circle of family and friends. Ambitions involve a public arena, even if that arena is as small as a classroom or an office. When we acknowledge an ambition, we are admitting to a desire to act and be appreciated within this larger sphere. You will rarely, if ever, hear people say that their ambition is to write a novel that they can share with a few friends before putting it in a drawer or to do scientific research but not present their findings to a scientific forum. Ambitions assume participation in and recognition from a community larger than one's intimate social circle.

The fact that ambitions develop within a community has several important and beneficial consequences. At the most obvious level, it permits a larger quantity and range of response; the audience is more diverse and populous than one's buddies and family. A community also allows there to be more objective criteria for evaluating skills. Realization of an ambition usually depends on work and talent as much as or more than attractiveness and likability. Whether the ambition is to be a rock star, a caterer, a nurse, a lawyer, a landscape architect, or a dress designer, the criteria by which your accomplishment is evaluated extend beyond the personal. If you are a broker whose bottom line is bad, a lawyer who loses cases, or a musician who frequently misses notes, it's unlikely that you will thrive professionally no matter how affable you are. Social skills may be important, but they are rarely sufficient. Effort and work, things over which we have some control, are the sine qua non of realizing an ambition.

The motivations behind ambitions—to practice skills and be appreciated for them in "the real world"—are powerful and essentially inseparable. In one revealing survey, for example, accomplished scientists were asked whether they would rather make a great discovery or receive the Nobel Prize. Most of them found it hard to come up with an answer—splitting off recognition from mastery hugely diminished the discovery's value for them.

If we are to pursue an ambition, we must have both the wish for mastery and a potential audience, along with an expectation that we can reach the desired end point. When these elements combine and we achieve a goal, even on a small scale, the impact can be huge. In fact, the effect of experiences in which our accomplishments are recognized can hardly be exaggerated; they are often remembered for a lifetime. When, in the course of my interviews, I asked women to tell me a favorite memory from childhood, every single one recalled an experience of unusual recognition. Here is a typical memory:

> We used to put on productions at the beach we visited each summer. One summer when I was around ten, we put on this amazing production with old songs like "Strolling Through the Park One Day"—all these songs from the 1920s and 1930s. It just stands out. I think actually the other thing I remember was another production. [Starts laughing.] Maybe I should have become an actress or a singer! In sixth grade we put on *HMS Pinafore.* I was the star.

The findings from my unscientific, anecdotal interviews are backed by more rigorous research. In one study in which twelve hundred successful women were asked this same question about a favorite memory, the author notes that the most frequently cited memory was success in a competition. "Furthermore," she adds, "four of the other frequently mentioned positive experiences [were] awards in a talent field, exhibitions of work at high school, elective office, and publication of written work." High-recognition events are both intensely pleasurable and vividly recalled. They can become virtually iconic memories.

They are also highly formative. The impact of such moments is repeatedly described in the biographical literature. Willa Cather, for example, whose ambition as a young woman was to be a doctor, abandoned that vocation after an unexpected event: "Cather went off to Lincoln, home of the University of Nebraska," wrote Joan Acocella in *The New Yorker:*

> The following spring, for her English class, she wrote a theme on Thomas Carlyle which so impressed her teacher that, behind her back, he submitted it to Lincoln's foremost newspaper, the *Nebraska State Journal.* One day soon afterward, Cather found herself in print. The effect, she later said, was "hypnotic." She was no longer going to be a doctor; she was going to be a writer.

Clearly, a single event such as this, as powerful as it is, doesn't suffice to create an identity or a career. There must be a context—in this case Cather's relationship with her enthusiastic teacher. And there must be ongoing successes: eventually she became a regular columnist for the *State Journal*.

Ambitions necessarily include the expectation of recognition for our accomplishments. The recognition may come as applause, a raise, a pat on the back, a change in title, a compliment by a boss or colleague, a good grade. In some cases it may even be experienced as coming from someone in our past who we have "internalized" and kept alive within us. Embedded within ambition is often a kind of dialogue between past and future figures in our lives. The dialogue can take many forms, such as the belief that someone in the past would have affirmed the present accomplishment: "He would have been so proud." "I know she is watching me now, wherever she is, and is thrilled."

Ambitions can even be fueled by the wish to receive recognition retroactively from an important figure who previously withheld it—a critical, doubting parent is a common example. A parent's withholding of affirmation, particularly in childhood, can create in a child a lifelong need to "prove them wrong" and finally receive the wished-for acknowledgment of one's talents or worth. There is a fantasy of finally receiving recognition long denied: "He never thought I could do this. I'd have loved to see the look on his face now."

The famous composer Igor Stravinsky once poignantly described this type of driving need for retroactive recognition:

I am convinced that it was my misfortune that my father was spiritually very distant from me and that even my mother had no love for me. When my oldest brother died unexpectedly (without my mother transferring her feelings from him onto me) I resolved that one day I would show them. Now this day has come and gone. No one remembers this day but me, who am its only remaining witness.

Clearly such internalized figures from the past can add an important dimension to ambitions. They can strengthen or resonate with current goals. Ideally a sustaining dialogue between past and present sources of recognition can be established. But unless we expect real, continuing

recognition—either by these same figures or new ones—our ambitions
cannot be sustained.

An anecdote in the writer Jamaica Kincaid's autobiographical book
My Brother beautifully captures the complex and reinforcing interplay
of past and present, internal and external experiences of recognition.
She describes her relationship with the famous editor of *The New
Yorker* William Shawn:

> For many years I wrote for a man named William Shawn. Whenever I
> thought of something to write, I immediately thought of him reading
> it, and the thought of this man, William Shawn, reading something I
> had written only made me want to write it more; I could see him sit-
> ting (not in any particular place) and reading what I had written and
> telling me if he liked it, or never mentioning it again if he didn't, and
> the point wasn't to hear him say that he liked it (though that was bet-
> ter than anything in the whole world) but only to know that he had
> read it. . . . Almost all my life as a writer, everything I wrote I expected
> Mr. Shawn to read.

After Shawn's death, Kincaid reflects:

> The perfect reader has died, but I cannot see any reason not to write
> for him anyway, for I can sooner get used to never hearing from him—
> the perfect reader—than to not being able to write for him at all.

But such internalized sources of recognition, powerful though they
may be, are rarely sufficient without additional, real, external sources.
Kincaid herself notes that as she writes, she also imagines the approval
and praise of her future readers: "For is it not a desire of people who
on writing books allow them to be published and exposed to the public: that people who do not know them, absolute strangers, will buy
the book and read it and then like it?" Kincaid's pleasure in writing is
inextricably fused with her expectation that it will be recognized.

Mastery and recognition here, as in virtually all cases, are the twin
emotional engines of ambition. Yet ambition has a bad name because
it includes within it an acknowledgment of this need, this dependence

on the approval of others, which makes us all feel vulnerable. We wish to dissociate ourselves from such needs and believe that we are autonomous and independent—an ideal that the sociologist Robert Bellah has termed "radical individualism." We are like the kids on the playground who put down the child who is "showing off" or "just trying to get attention."

And in truth, some people have needs for recognition that are exaggerated and nearly insatiable, and require constant infusions of admiration to maintain their tenuous sense of self-worth. In psychiatry such individuals are called *narcissists*. If there is an imbalance between the need for recognition and the need for mastery, an ambition can deteriorate into an overly pressing need for affirmation or a pure fantasy of fame and fortune divorced from reality. But when these two elements are balanced, they are healthy and productive forces. If we are to meet our needs and realize our ambitions, both of these elements must be in play. Without an element of mastery, we have little control over our destiny. Without recognition, we feel isolated and, ultimately, demoralized.

Social structures in which we can reliably obtain recognition provide the armature of our lives; it is hard to overestimate their importance. And it is not simply a matter of having a multiplicity of affiliations or "connections" or roles. The accuracy, breadth, and specificity of the recognition we receive as well as the control we have over obtaining it are crucial.

Creating relationships in areas where we have some control, where the recognition is based on a talent or skill or hard work—rather than on appearance, sexual availability, pure social skills, or subservience—is the essence of ambition. Evaluating the variety and depth of such structures tells us volumes about the quality of a person's life.

AMBITIONS IN MEN VERSUS WOMEN

The exercise of expertise within a public arena has historically been the great divide that separated the ambitions of men from those of women. It was here that—until very recently—male and female visions of the future parted ways. For men, work outside the home was not only a financial necessity but the cornerstone of identity and self-worth—as it remains today. Virtually every study of ambition in men has confirmed this basic fact.

Women, on the other hand, were defined by their role (or lack of role) as an adjunct to and provider for others within the private sphere. As mother, mistress, or wife, women's social designation implied exactly whom they were expected to provide for and what they were supposed to provide. Private relationships represented women's sole source of identity and affirmation. As a consequence, they carefully developed the skills required to maximize their narrowly defined opportunities. A huge premium was placed on physical attractiveness, sensitivity, and service to others. At times these qualities provided women with a richness of social connections unavailable to most men. Women valued and nurtured their relationships.

But the exclusive focus on the interpersonal as a source of self-worth also entailed a huge loss of control for women. To a large extent, women cannot control their looks, particularly as they age, and they often cannot control the people with whom they have relationships. Husbands can have midlife crises; women friends can relocate thousands of miles away; children grow up; friends with demanding jobs or families may become unavailable. A woman's own efforts in maintaining important connections may have little to do with the final outcome. The private sphere has its pleasures and benefits but also its limitations and risks.

Yet until recently virtually all types of work that could garner public recognition were forbidden to women. Even skills such as writing, which could be done within the home but might be admired beyond the domestic sphere, were largely proscribed until the eighteenth century. Dorothy Wordsworth—the sister of William Wordsworth and now, after being "discovered," a respected poet in her own right— went to enormous lengths to deny her "worldly" accomplishments. Writing to a close friend to whom her brother had read two of her poems, Dorothy Wordsworth clearly tried to deflect the disapproval she expected for her efforts:

I'm truly glad that my Brother's manuscript poems give you so much pleasure. . . . Do not think that I was ever bold enough to hope to compose verses for the pleasure of grown-up persons . . . even if I had the gift of language and numbers, that I could have the vanity to suppose I could be of any use beyond your own fireside, or to please, as in your case . . . but I have no command of language, no power of expressing my ideas. . . . As for those two little things which I did write, I was very unwilling to place them beside my Brother's poems, but he insisted upon it, and I was obliged to submit; and though you have been pleased with them I cannot but think that was chiefly owing to the spirit which William gave them in the reading and your kindness for me.

Even granting that some of her demurral was social etiquette, the very fact that Dorothy knew such a disavowal was required tells us a great deal about the limits placed on her ambitions.

By the early twentieth century middle-class women were freer to participate in genteel occupations that kept them in or close to the home, and women writers in particular were increasingly accepted, but occupations for women outside of the home were still pitifully limited. In *A Room of One's Own,* Virginia Woolf has her female protagonist describe the jobs available to women of her era:

Before that I had made my living by cadging odd jobs from newspapers, by reporting a donkey show here or a wedding there; I had earned a few pounds by addressing envelopes, reading to old ladies, making artificial flowers, teaching the alphabet to small children in a kindergarten. Such were the chief occupations that were open to women before 1918.

In what has undoubtedly been one of the most far-reaching revolutions in human history, throughout the nineteenth and twentieth centuries women gradually won access to a broad range of educational and work opportunities. By the mid-twentieth century, women were allowed to work outside the home—not only at menial labor, poorly paid factory jobs, or domestic chores, but in a few professions as well. The first of the two parts of ambition, developing an expertise that could be practiced in the public sphere, was finally becoming an option for women.

CHAPTER TWO

DISTORTED AMBITIONS

D espite middle-class women's steady if slow movement into new educational and work environments, by the mid-twentieth century an odd phenomenon persisted. For women, receiving attention for their accomplishments remained highly problematic. The fact that women could become skilled in various fields did not mean that they could reap the rewards those skills were supposed to obtain. Surprisingly, the prohibition against women gaining access to this core part of ambition persisted despite their having acquired skills—as if it tapped into a yet deeper cultural prejudice. They were now able to develop expertise, but only if their goals were "selfless." Someone else had to be front and center.

This phenomenon was noted first by writers and then, later, by research psychologists: women marginalized themselves within their own lives and ambitions. When they imagined a future within the larger community, it had to be primarily as an adjunct to a man. They were not encouraged to be, nor did they envision themselves as, individuals working directly toward a personal goal. Women continued, as in the past, to remove themselves from their own narratives of accomplishment within the larger society—they left the role of the protagonist to someone or something else and moved into supporting, peripheral positions.

Simone de Beauvoir first called attention to this deformation of ambition in women in the 1950s when she published *The Second Sex*. She famously described women functioning primarily as the "Other"—the object rather than the subject in their life stories. De Beauvoir primarily singled out women's auxiliary role to men, observing that

"humanity is male and man defines woman not in herself, but as relative to him; she is not regarded as an autonomous being. . . . For the
young woman . . . there is a contradiction between her status as a real
human being and her vocation as a female." De Beauvoir lamented that
women relinquished their sense of agency and centrality in their lives
and subordinated themselves to men.

Despite her feminist insights, Simone de Beauvoir was herself a
prime example of the very phenomenon she so accurately described.
Her status as one of the seminal thinkers of the twentieth century is
undisputed. From the present vantage point, her contributions are
arguably more important than those of her lifelong companion and
lover, the philosopher Jean-Paul Sartre. Yet de Beauvoir places Sartre
near the center of her autobiography. Both he and she see him as
the dominant, shaping force in their lives. "From now on, I'm going
to take you under my wing," he announced at the beginning of the
romance, after he told her that they had both passed their examina-
tions. She breathlessly acceded: "But what he himself recognized as a
true superiority over me, and one which was immediately obvious to
myself, was the calm and yet almost frenzied passion with which he
was preparing for the books he was going to write. . . . And indeed
when I compared myself with him, how lukewarm my feverish ambitions appeared!" This from a woman who went on to write more than
a dozen major books.

In contrast, Sartre's autobiography, *The Words,* does not even mention de Beauvoir. There is no question as to who is the protagonist,
star, and mastermind of his successes: "At the age of thirty, I executed
the masterstroke of writing in *Nausea*—quite sincerely, believe me—
about the bitter unjustified existence of my fellowmen and of exonerat-
ing my own [*sic*]. . . . Dogmatic though I was, I doubted everything
except that I was the elect of doubt. I built with one hand what I
destroyed with the other, and I regarded anxiety as the guarantee of my
security; I was happy."

Despite de Beauvoir's occasional romantic backsliding, her brilliant
polemic had a huge impact. Nearly forty years after the publication
of *The Second Sex,* her insights were still being rediscovered, mined,
and elaborated. Carolyn Heilbrun, in her book on women's literary

representations of their lives, *Writing a Woman's Life,* noted that for women "identity is grounded through relation to the chosen other." Endorsing de Beauvoir's position, she rhetorically asked in the late 1980s, "What does it mean to be unambiguously a woman? It means to put a man at the center of one's life and to allow to occur only what honors his prime position. Occasionally women have put god or Christ in the place of man; the results are always the same: one's own desires and quests are always secondary."

Heilbrun pointed out that by removing themselves from a central role in their own lives, women become storyless; their own needs, motives, and accomplishments are reduced or rendered nearly invisible. She bleakly summarized her vision of the lives of women whose ambitions are subsumed by those of another: "For a short time, during courtship, the illusion is maintained that women, by withholding themselves, are central. . . . And courtship itself is, as often as not, an illusion: that is, the woman must entrap the man to ensure herself a center for her life. The rest is aging and regret."

Although, from our present vantage, Heilbrun's conclusions may seem unnecessarily grim and overstated, research on girls' and women's ambitions from the decades preceding her work largely supports her analysis. Even as women were beginning to have increased opportunities, for most girls and women depending on a skill for obtaining social affirmation remained too conflicted and risky. A relationship to a man represented the safest source of social approval, necessitating that a woman's personal ambition be subordinated to that of her husband. It was a realistic, if costly, strategy.

In the 1960s Elizabeth Douvan and Joseph Adelson, in one of the most extensive studies of adolescents ever carried out, recorded in-depth interviews with 3,500 girls and boys. They reported a dramatic split between the genders with regard to ambition—in fact, they singled it out as their most striking finding. "The clearest form in which the sex difference appears in our interviews is in the degree of coherence between fantasy and reality conceptions of future adulthood." Adolescent boys, they discovered, integrated the two main aspects of ambition—skill and the expectation of social affirmation—into a coherent and largely realistic plan. They pictured themselves working at tasks that would bring them recognition and status. Their self-esteem was closely tied to their projection of future accomplishment in the work world.

In adolescent girls, by contrast, ambitions commonly fragmented into their two separate parts. The wish for mastery, so evident in their childhood ambitions, dropped out or became relatively insignificant. Specific skills were rarely mentioned. This left the need for social affirmation, which is so intense during adolescence, detached from any specific expertise. It became diverted to personal characteristics over which the girls had little control. "[The adolescent girl's] 'talents' are relatively vague—beauty, charm, and 'personality.' Her opportunities are also obscure—an unknown boy of unknown quality and unknown future." Not surprisingly, with no future goal toward which they could actively work, many of the girls retreated to daydreaming of glamour, affluence, and celebrity. It was at this moment of their lives that their picture of a role for themselves in the greater world faded. Their aspirations became attached instead to the accomplishments of a future, unknown mate to whom they would play a supportive, subordinate role.

Why the adolescent girls of this era focused on relationships rather than achievements is not hard to surmise. This landmark study, published in 1966, reflects a cultural climate in which its authors did not hesitate to label as socially deviant all girls who did not choose marriage as the vehicle for their "ambitions":

This group includes all girls in the sample who say they do not want to marry. The American adolescent girl who consciously rejects the feminine goal of marriage is, we think, deviant in a number of senses. First, she takes a position that is statistically very rare. Only 5% of adolescent girls do not want to get married. More important, she is deviant in that she rejects a status prescribed as the single most important goal for women, the only status aside from the religious life which assures a woman acceptance in our society. Realization of her feminine nature in child-bearing is legitimately available only to the woman who marries, and a woman's access to conventional social circles depends on being married or having been married. To reject the goal of marriage then implies a turning against society and its regulated rewards. We suspected that it might also signal a fairly severe personal pathology, since it means in most cases that the girl is giving up the idea of feminine realization. Unless these are all very young girls, their rejection of marriage would, we thought, indicate a rejection of, an alienation from, the self.

These researchers were not reactionary. They accurately reported on their contemporary culture. Five percent of the adolescent girls interviewed—the girls who rejected marriage—represented such a small portion of the group that it was accurate to label them as "deviant." Seeing these "deviant" girls as pathological or disturbed was a cultural assumption of the era that the authors honestly identified as only a hypothesis and not a fact.

The dependence on men to affirm their specialness and create their place in society effectively removed these girls from the center of their own ambitions. The areas in which they could glean affirmation—as friends, as mates, and as sexual partners—were ones over which they had relatively little control. The areas where they could work toward goals—in the home, in relatively low-paying jobs, or in professions where they constituted a small, barely tolerated minority—provided little in the way of recognition. Girls and women who deviated from the cultural norm were perceived as pathological.

The wonderful thing about well-designed research is that the findings do not always conform to cultural beliefs and expectations. Despite the huge social forces during the 1960s pushing women out of the public sphere and into the private marital and domestic arena, Douvan and Adelson found (to their surprise) that the small subgroup of "personally mobile" girls who wanted to be upwardly mobile via their own achievements—and not by way of a husband's status—were the most psychologically well adjusted. "The 'personally mobile' [girls] show statistical differences from others. . . . They are more eager to reach adulthood, are more self-confident, self-accepting, and poised . . . they more often dream of individual achievement. . . . Not a single one of the personally mobile girls chose a movie star or other 'glamour figure' as an adult model." For this small group of girls the pieces of ambition—specific achievement and social affirmation for that achievement—were still integrated. They had retained a sense of a future which they could work toward and for which they could receive affirmation.

In a fascinating aside, the authors of the study noted that the girls who bucked the social constraints and opted for pursuing their own achievements were from lower-middle-class backgrounds. One could speculate that they had either a less rigid gender socialization and/or less faith in the upward mobility of their potential mates. In any case, the study was one of the first to notice a surprising phenomenon that would later reappear in numerous research reports: middle- and upper-middle-class white girls and women exhibit more anxiety and ambivalence about ambition than their "less privileged" white peers or their black and Hispanic counterparts.

Seen from a different angle, however, the fact that 5 percent of the girls interviewed by Douvan and Adelson in the 1960s entertained realizable professional ambitions was a huge step forward. Throughout the first two-thirds of the twentieth century a small but growing number of women did in fact actively pursue cultural, professional, and political careers. Yet despite their daring and innovative historical roles, the paradigm of the selfless narrative persisted.

THE DENIAL OF PERSONAL ACCOMPLISHMENT

The growing number of women who had personal achievements often chose to present their accomplishments in highly traditional terms. These women adamantly, at times desperately, denied that they pursued or took pleasure in the acclaim or power that their work produced. Women, to a greater extent than ever before, were allowed to develop expertise outside the domestic sphere—the first part of ambition. The second part, however, remained taboo: openly working toward and taking pleasure in the recognition their achievements provided. Women continued to experience themselves and/or present themselves as being in passive, serving roles. Their subordinate roles, however, now often centered on a cause rather than a man.

In autobiographies, profiles, and interviews, women of immense achievement—such as Eleanor Roosevelt, Golda Meir, Mary McCarthy, and more recently, Katharine Graham—had enormous difficulty acknowledging that they created or enjoyed their public successes. They grasped after alternative explanations for their prominent positions that bordered (unintentionally) on the comic. Golda Meir, for example, demurely disclaimed any personal agency in attaining her position as Israeli head of state: "I became prime minister because that is how it was." The writer Mary McCarthy, in her memoirs, describes her nervy political activism as a kind of muddled passivity: "I let my name stay [on the Trotskyite petition]—a pivotal decision, perhaps the pivotal decision in my life. Yet I had no sense of making a choice; it was as if the choice had been thrust on me." Even her decision to marry the eminent, well-connected critic Edmund Wilson is presented as if she were simply a perplexed observer and not an ambitious young woman actively making her way: "To this day, I can't make out whether I 'really' wanted to marry Wilson or prayed to be spared it." Or again: "The logic of having slept with Wilson compelled the sequence of marriage if that was what he wanted." One could hardly guess from this prim passage that McCarthy was so promiscuous that in her memoir she described once sleeping with three men in a twenty-four-hour period. In her denials of self-determination, it's hard not to hear the distant refrain of Dorothy Wordsworth's elaborate disclaimers echoing down the centuries.

In telling their stories, these women of accomplishment used two main, well-worn narrative devices. One was the story in which the successful woman starts as a young innocent and is waylaid by circumstances and somehow bamboozled into her present, utterly surprising success. The alternative narrative is one in which the drive and organizing skills are acknowledged, but all of the female protagonist's efforts are on behalf of others—whether they be the poor, the Jews, the Catholic Church, the blind, or children. These are highly admirable lives, but somehow in these stories the "cause" is front and center and the richness of the personal narrative gets lost. The memoirist's ambition is nowhere to be found. The unspoken fear is that admitting to ambition will make her seem selfish and egotistical, as if personal and altruistic goals were incompatible.

These women's narratives tended to be bleached out or tamped down or reconfigured to disguise the underlying personal motivation. The active pursuit of achievement was hidden or denied. Their groundbreaking lives were refashioned into stories that had powerful actions without powerful actors. Ambitions were buried so deep under layers of denial that one virtually needed an archaeological dig to bring them into the light of day. One can see that they are there—like those aerial shots of fields in which the outlines of ancient cities are discernible—but they are fuzzy and incomplete.

It is illuminating to compare the autobiographical writings of these groundbreaking women to those of their male counterparts. The difference in self-presentation is stark. Mary McCarthy, whom I previously quoted, described her radical political decisions as virtually avolitional, stating that she had no sense of "making a choice"—as if the choice had been "thrust on" her. Her soon-to-be husband, Edmund Wilson, writing in his diaries around the same time, forthrightly saw himself as the agent of his own actions: "I shall vote for the Communist candidates because they seem to me to understand the crisis better than the other candidates in the field. I believe that they are fundamentally right."

Skipping ahead several decades to another pair of autobiographies by a man and a woman linked throughout lives of unusual accomplishment, we can again get the male and female take on shared events. Here is how Katharine Graham, publisher of the *Washington Post,* described her risky, highly principled stand on the Watergate political crisis, in which she chose to publish information despite potentially severe legal repercussions: "I have often been credited with courage for backing our editors in Watergate. The truth is that I never felt there was much choice. Courage applies only when there is choice. . . . Once I found myself in the deepest water in the middle of the current, there was no turning back." Her editor, Ben Bradlee, who did not have to make the ultimate decision or take responsibility for publishing the Watergate story, expressed no such compunction. He felt free to take pleasure in and credit for his role in the events: "We went after Woodward and Bernstein like prosecutors, demanding to know word for bloody word what each source had said in reply to what questions, not the general meaning but the exact words. Then I finally said, 'Go.' It was October 24, for the issue of October 25, 1972."

When Bradlee is lionized for his role in the Watergate episode, he happily and appropriately takes credit: "All of us seek evidence of our effectiveness, and when that evidence turns public, it is hard to pretend that it doesn't feel good." For Graham the same publicity provoked only intense anxiety and ambivalence. When Robert Redford made his famous film about Watergate, *All the President's Men,* she noted with puzzlement: "I should have been pleased and interested to meet Redford, but we didn't get along, thanks partially to my own defensive crouch—the results of all my concerns, however real or imagined." When the film appeared without mention of her—as she had requested—she observed wistfully, "Redford imagined that I would be relieved, which I was, but, to my surprise, my feelings were hurt by being omitted altogether."

Are these accomplished, powerful women being coy or purposefully misleading? Do they truly experience themselves as passive or inferior or bit players? Are they really so self-effacing, or is there an element of calculation—in other words, are they covering their tracks? Probably some of each. After all, they had to live with the old cultural stereotypes, even as they forged new templates for women's ambitions. Their odd combination of achievement with self-denigrating storylines awkwardly attempts to bridge the divide.

Twenty-five or more years have now passed since pioneering women broke through the cultural and legal barriers that had denied them access to public forms of achievement. Much has changed. Large numbers of women now acquire professional skills, and women are beginning to assume more socially prominent roles. Certainly nothing like equality has been achieved; one look at the sea of men in black suits that "represents" us in the Senate and Congress will dispel that notion. Sexual harassment has been documented at every level of the armed services and in many major corporations. More women than men are poor, and women make significantly less money than men in equivalent work positions.

The progress, nonetheless, is real and continuing. In fact, women ironically now face overwhelming economic and social pressures to enter the workplace. Women on average bear less than half the number of children they did at the turn of the century and live over thirty years longer—including many decades past the childbearing and child-rearing years. Whereas in the 1970s, the U.S. Census Bureau notes, one paycheck supported a family, in the 1990s two were needed. Married women with working husbands need to help support the family. For most of the 42.1 percent of women in the United States who are single—divorced, never married, or widowed—jobs are crucial to sustaining a decent standard of living. The many divorced spouses with child custody and delinquent partners (overwhelmingly mothers) collect less than 20 percent of court-ordered alimony. Basically, they are financially on their own.

Not surprisingly, new pressures to join the workforce in combination with new opportunities available to women have had a decided impact on how girls imagine their futures and describe their ambitions. In Carol Gilligan's study of white, middle-class adolescent girls in the 1980s, *Making Connections,* the findings are strikingly different from those of Douvan and Adelson twenty years earlier:

> Without exception, the girls interviewed express interest in having careers that would enable them to do interesting work. Most mention wanting to be "successful" as very important to their image of themselves in the future. While most are vague about particular careers, relationships, and life-styles they envision, there tends to be greater clarity and concreteness concerning their future work than future marriages and families. For most of the girls it is easier to imagine living as an adult with a job than it is to imagine living a married life.

Broader and more scientific studies than Gilligan's support her finding of increased career orientation in young women. By the mid-1980s over 90 percent of college men and women expected "to work full-time most of their adult lives," and over two-thirds of college men and women endorsed "equal emphasis on children and career." Other researchers found that "there has been an increase in the value young women place on status-attainment goals. Concerning the goal of being an authority in [one's] field, 72% of female freshmen in 1984 indicated that the goal was important to them compared to 54% in 1969." In high school and college, these young women place themselves at the center of their own future.

But exactly how such early goals play out, for both women and men, at later life stages is another question. The rapid expansion of educational opportunities for women has pushed many decisions about career and family further into adulthood. Despite the fact that college men now verbalize a wish to put "equal emphasis on children and career," there is little evidence that they participate anywhere near equally in child care. One recent study of 138 men found only twelve who spent as much time parenting as their wives did. For women, early aspirations do not necessarily translate into their pursuit. At many junctures in their lives, women must reevaluate the meaning and value of their ambitions and decide how intensely to pursue them. Sociologists who have compared middle-class girls' and women's goals to their actual situations in midlife have found the correlation to be surprisingly weak. As one author summarized her findings: "Women are only slightly more likely to follow the paths they expect to [early on] than not. The effects of adolescent plans are real but not overwhelmingly powerful." Many factors intervene to divert, reshape, or undermine women's ambitions as they proceed through their adult lives.

One possible clue to the pressures that contemporary women experience around their ambitions can be found in the stories that unusually successful women tell about their lives. These are women who must face whatever cultural constraints exist at full force, in their most intense and stark form. Tensions or social expectations that may be so subtle that most of us sense and respond to them without even being aware of it stand out in bold relief in these outsize lives. Conflicts that can be avoided by women who quietly downsize their ambitions here remain exposed for all to see.

Disturbingly, contemporary women of accomplishment in the pub-

lic eye often repeat the anxiety-laden, self-abnegating stance of the earlier women of achievement. In general, self-deprecation is somewhat
less common in women from occupations that are largely female, such
as models or ballerinas. But in gender-integrated occupations, despite
the massively transformed work landscape, we still hear the same self-
effacing, self-doubting sagas. For these women, who have to compete
with men, something remains deeply confusing about acknowledging
their pursuit of and pleasure in their achievements. In their best-selling
1999 book *See Jane Win: The Rimm Report on How 1,000 Successful
Girls Became Successful Women,* Sylvia Rimm and her coauthors, after
offering a profile of a state senator, remark with puzzlement, "[The
senator], like many of the women of our study, attributes much of her
success to luck." In another chapter they quote an eminent chairman
of a department of medicine as concluding, "Everything has been rather
serendipitous. None of what I've described to you was planned. . . . I
was able to get good positions and good things just happened."

One could chalk up these demurrals to women's innate modesty or
even see them as a manipulative, sly way of highlighting their achievements. But the level of fear, at times verging on panic, that women express when they are personally recognized for their work belies this
interpretation. And as psychiatrists and other therapists have long
known, anxiety is the signal emotion that indicates unresolved issues
in people's lives. Like a Geiger counter that begins to tick as it ap-
proaches a radioactive hot spot, anxiety tends to show up at the point
where there are problematic unresolved issues.

Anxiety-drenched narratives by successful contemporary women
are ubiquitous. These magazine interviews with the two most successful American women architects are typical. The first is from a *Vogue*
magazine interview with Laurinda Spear, cofounder and director of the
highly influential architectural firm Architectonica:

Laurinda Spear is concerned with her image. Worried about her public
profile. Nervous that people will get the wrong idea. Actually Laurinda Spear is so riddled with anxiety about the way she might come
across in print that she endlessly repeats the same self-deprecating
refrain—over dinner at Nemo in South Beach, over drinks at home in

Coconut Grove, over a series of borderline-obsessive calls to New York from her car, her office, her cellular. "In no way am I some sort of superwoman," Spear says not once or twice or three times but so often it becomes a kind of mea culpa mantra. And then she adds, on the off chance that her unrelenting attempts to adequately belittle herself have failed, "Can't you just say that I'm this totally bumbling person?"

In case you think that Spear is anomalous, here is a magazine profile of her youthful contemporary Maya Lin, the architect of the Vietnam Memorial:

It is perhaps worth noting that in keeping with the low-profile tack she has attempted to maintain since catapulting to national attention in 1981, Lin panicked at the prospect of sitting for a formal portrait. "You don't need to look at a picture of me," she said. "I'm over-exposed." Her anxiety about facing the camera seemed to stem from the recent news that the American Film Foundation's 104-minute documentary of her career, "Maya Lin: A Strong Clear Vision," had been nominated for an Academy Award. . . .

"In a way I'm lucky, because I'm five foot two and three-quarters and weigh 96 pounds. And people tend not to see you if you're small. . . . Besides, I'm not a celebrity. The work is famous, not me."

Maya Lin's wish for privacy is in many ways understandable and admirable. What is somewhat less clear is why she would agree to have a documentary film made of her and then be surprised and anxious when it was seen and praised. It is also unclear why she would agree to an interview, plead not to have her picture taken for the interview, and then apparently agree to have it taken. (It accompanies the article.) In the photo Lin stares miserably into the camera, her hair covering much of her face, her anxiety and discomfort about receiving this attention readily apparent. One can't help wondering if her palpable unhappiness serves as a kind of preemptive strategy: if she's already cringing with discomfort and pain, no one else need criticize her for being self-promoting or egotistical.

Here is a similar passage from an interview of a woman of unusual achievement, this time a politician, ex-congresswoman Pat Schroeder. It recounts the origin of her career as told to a reporter:

> It was [her husband] who went into politics first. . . . Pat's own candidacy two years later was almost an afterthought. The Democrats were faced with a seemingly hopeless race for Congress against a strong incumbent Republican. Jim Schroeder asked one man who turned down the nomination, "What about your wife?" To which the fellow shot back, "What about yours?" Everyone had a good laugh. . . ." Schroeder didn't much agonize about getting into the race, "because people thought I would surely lose," she recalls.

What is the intense need these women feel to remove themselves from the picture (literally and figuratively) or to belittle their own ambitions? Why must the work or accomplishment stand alone, orphaned, without a creator or as a purely unwilled or chance occurrence? In my own interviews with women of all levels of accomplishment, the constant refrain was "It's not me; it's the work." "It's not about me; it's about helping children." "I hate to promote myself. I'd rather be in my workshop alone." "It's the group. I hardly contributed a thing." "I really did it because my husband got sick of the work, and I just sort of carried on." You could chalk these comments up to social convention or mere window dressing if it weren't for two facts. Men simply do not talk this way—can you picture a famous male architect begging not to have his picture taken and explaining how thankful he is to be so tiny that he is never noticed? How many congressmen would declare that they happily ran for office because they assumed they would lose? And these disclaimers are not tossed off casually. The women seem deeply worried. As one woman CEO said to me, "I've never met a [career] woman who doesn't feel scared of something—they can always fill in the blank: scared that they're not smart enough, scared that they will talk out of turn, scared they'll be punished, scared they won't be listened to, scared that the role is too grandiose. The list goes on and on." Clearly these accomplished women are caught up in some sort of fear. But of what?

PART TWO

RECOGNITION AND AMBITION
IN WOMEN'S LIVES

Life is an endless recruitment of witnesses.
—CAROL SHIELDS, *The Stone Diaries*

What men need is men's approval.
—DAVID MAMET, *The New York Times*

CHAPTER THREE

AVOIDING ATTENTION

Women are afraid to say that they will be changed by outside recognition. The truth is that you are radically changed by it. For a long time I tried to pretend it was fine that success was eluding me. It was only after I got a bit of it that I realized how profound outside recognition can be in letting one know that she matters.

—EVE ENSLER, playwright, author of
The Vagina Monologues

It seems paradoxical. Women have now gained hard-won access to training in nearly all fields, and this type of expertise brings with it enormous pleasures. We all, men and women, spend our lives seeking out and mastering skills for the sheer delight and sense of competence they provide us; whether we are baking a featherweight pie crust, throwing a pot on a pottery wheel, writing a business proposal, or diagnosing a patient, there is a satisfaction inherent in putting our learning and talents to use. But far from celebrating their achievements in newly available professions, women fearfully seek to deflect attention from themselves. They refuse to claim a central, purposeful place in their own stories, eagerly shifting the credit elsewhere and shunning recognition. In effect, they shut themselves out of their own stories. Is it any wonder that Hollywood has trouble finding scripts for women when women themselves often believe that their narratives must be hidden or denied and are of no import or interest to others?

It's easy to minimize such disclaimers and interpret them simply as a superficial, becoming modesty of no significance. But they take on a more profoundly problematic quality when you realize that recognition, far from being a pleasant but largely inessential human response, is in fact one of the most basic of human requirements. As I will discuss in greater detail in Chapter 4, the absence of recognition effectively prevents the development of expertise required for pursuing any ambition. By contrast, the recognition of one's skills within a community creates a sense of identity, personal worth, and social inclusion—basic cornerstones in any life, but ones that are particularly hard to come by in the mobile and unstable social structures of our present culture.

Outstanding women of achievement have often solved this problem by getting sufficient private recognition to sustain their work—from personal relationships or special mentors or encouraging bosses or unusually supportive husbands. But they are savvy enough to realize that in public they need to appear totally uninterested in such affirmation: they "voluntarily" relinquish the larger rewards. It is all about working for the benefit of others.

Furthermore, it emerges on close inspection that it is not only women of achievement who anxiously work to relinquish recognition—virtually all women do. The daily texture of women's lives from childhood on is infiltrated with microencounters in which quiet withdrawal, the ceding of available attention to others, is expected, particularly in the presence of men.

I recently had a casual but illuminating experience that brought home to me the gendered economics of recognition. At a professional meeting a friend introduced me to a colleague visiting from France. He did not speak English well, and so I gave it a go in my halting, high school French. I introduced myself and made some brief pleasantry about his trip. Encouraged by this tentative linguistic foray, he spoke nearly nonstop for fifteen or twenty minutes. I would occasionally murmur, *"Ah, oui?"* but said nothing further, largely because I could only vaguely catch the drift of what he was saying. Several days later my friend called to say that her French acquaintance had found me *"charmante"* and had said that my French was exquisite. I mulled this over in puzzlement and eventually realized that my near-silence had been irrelevant. As far as my new French friend was concerned, we were "conversing"—in exquisite French.

This minor incident was interesting to me not because it revealed a kind of male egotism or even because it highlighted the unspoken convention that states that he was well within his rights in expecting to dominate the conversation with a woman he knew nothing about. What was more disturbing and even sinister, as I reflected on this microevent, was that I received high praise for being silent and attending to him. And absurd though it was, I enjoyed being called *"charmante."* Silence was the venue for receiving the scant "recognition," distorted though it might be, that was available.

This kind of silence is a subtle but pervasive element in women's struggles with ambition. It is not always literal silence, of course. It is the silencing of a woman's wish for and expectation of direct and accurate affirmation—recognition that is not always refracted through the needs of others (as the affirmation of me was refracted through the Frenchman's own wish for recognition). Studies of speech, the most ubiquitous medium for soliciting recognition, have amply documented that women tend to take on the role of listener. In classes, faculty meetings, business gatherings, conferences, or just conversations where men are present, women speak less than their male counterparts. And they speak more softly, apologetically, and more tentatively, drawing less attention to themselves and their contributions.

Women have difficulties presenting themselves in a favorable light even in interviews where presumably they wish to impress. The law professor and journalist Susan Estrich has described how women being considered for professorships at Harvard Law School would anxiously undercut their own candidacies:

To get a job as a law professor, candidates must give a presentation before the faculty about the scholarly work they are doing, which is then subject to extensive discussion and dissection in faculty meetings. Sitting in on those meetings at Harvard throughout the 1980's, I became aware that there were certain words used, disparagingly, to critique the presentations of these women. *They were tentative, not ambitious enough, not far enough advanced; they didn't break enough new ground, their work was too limited in scope.* . . . The irony was that the substance of the presentations did not break down so neatly along gender lines: In fact, the women were often more ambitious than the men, taking on bigger issues, trying to do harder things than fit together a dozen cases or apply well-established economic principles to new areas of the law.

What was going on? It wasn't what they were doing. It was what they said they were doing. Women would come in and apologize before they began; downplay their goals; admit to the limitations of their accomplishments.

Eventually Estrich and some female colleagues realized that they needed to coach women candidates on self-presentation if Harvard was ever going to have more than a token number of female law professors. When you understand that the women Estrich was describing were already accomplished enough to be considered for, arguably, the most sought-after position in their profession, you get some sense of the strength of the anxiety women experience when asking for deserved acknowledgment of their work.

Conveying their strengths and attainments to others is so far from the expected female style of self-effacement that women experience it as "bragging"—in other words, socially unacceptable boastfulness. The linguist Deborah Tannen, in her book on language and gender, *Talking from Nine to Five,* concluded that soliciting or even accepting recognition is heavily proscribed: "For middle-class American women, the constraint is clear: talking about your own accomplishments in a way that calls attention to yourself is not acceptable. . . . Girls are supposed to be 'humble'—not try to take the spotlight, emphasize the ways they are just like everyone else, and de-emphasize the ways they are special."

Venues for seeking recognition other than speech are equally uncomfortable for women. When women wield power, they try to do it indirectly so that it will not come to the attention of their colleagues. Women even tend to minimize their physical presence, sitting rather than standing to speak, speaking from the audience instead of moving to the front of a room, not gesturing or even relaxing into open or sprawled positions that might call attention to themselves. They even tell fewer jokes. The unspoken social dictum is that girls and women must forgo this pleasurable, motivating, and highly sought-after emotional response—without which ambitions cannot be sustained.

The "difference feminists," with their rigid emphasis on "connectedness" in every type of relationship, whether intimate or professional, have unwittingly endorsed this taboo. Judith Jordan, director of the Women's Network at McLean Hospital and assistant professor of psychiatry at Harvard Medical School, observes:

> The desire . . . to move people, to become engaged in relationship [sic] is not the same as trying to impress people, or to manage self-presentation in order to receive approval or accolades. In the management of images and self-presentation in order to gain praise or rewards, one, in fact, moves into inauthentic, deadening exchanges.

She could hardly be more damning about the negative consequences of openly seeking "praise or rewards"—innocent and universal enough wishes, one would think. But in Jordan's view, this necessary and ubiquitous activity is narcissistic, inauthentic, and deadening. The naïve, pleasurable fantasies of fame and fortune that characterize little girls' early ambitions take on, for her, a dark, pathological quality.

The prohibition against openly seeking recognition is deeply ingrained. One sociologist who interviewed forty-five senior management women remarked with amazement, "None of them talked of the need for visibility. . . . No one seemed to recognize that if one is not 'seen' by others as a kind of person who should have a particular job, that all the competence in the world would not get it for them." And then when the system didn't spontaneously reward these women for their work purely on its merits, they were "helplessly disappointed." The researcher went on to note, "Women see career as personal growth and self-fulfillment. . . . While men indubitably want these things too, they visualize the career as a path leading upward with recognition and the reward implied."

One can't help wondering if "growth and self-fulfillment" are not code words meant to assure male colleagues that career women are not competing for coveted social rewards. "Don't worry about us," they seem to say: "We're off in a corner doing our own thing." It comes as no surprise that women scientists more frequently than their male counterparts have been found to take a "niche approach," working on their own small areas of expertise rather than on large issues where they would have to compete with male colleagues.

The message is all too clear: if others are vying for the available recognition, women must simply forgo it, even when it is appropriate for their accomplishment. Typically, women find it harder than their male peers to ask for deserved promotions or pay increases—the most generic forms of recognition in the workplace. I once had a woman patient who discovered, after receiving a long-overdue promotion, that her new position upset the male colleague under whom she had amicably worked for six years. She was now at the same level as he. Feeling a mixture of bewilderment and guilt, as if she'd done something mean-spirited or selfish by being promoted, she actually went to the head of the division and requested that her promotion be rescinded! The director listened to her in stupefaction and then, to his credit, simply ignored her request.

It's tempting to conclude, as many have, that women aren't actually deferring to others when they remove themselves from the spotlight; they're just intrinsically different in their needs and style. This is how they choose to work. Women, after all, may just be less interested in personal attention than men. Or maybe they simply don't care about the types of recognition that men strive for. It has been suggested, for example, that women have a greater capacity for empathy than men, making it more painful for them not to gratify the wishes of others or relinquish coveted resources. And recognition is nothing if not a coveted social resource.

The belief that women's deferential behavior with regard to recognition is "natural" has not held up well in the massive research literature on gender that has evolved since the 1970s. Over the last few decades multiple studies have sought to clarify whether women's deferential behavior is a constant or whether it is elicited only by certain social cues. By and large, the literature has suggested that to a significant degree such behavior is not a constant but varies according to the social context: girls and women change their behaviors when their interactions involve men. They more openly seek and compete for affirmation when they are with other women—for example, in sports or in all-girls academic institutions. They have no difficulty aggressively pursuing roles that complement rather than compete with males (trying out for a female acting part, a modeling career, or a singing group).

Women also have much less difficulty soliciting recognition when they believe that their actions will not be known by male peers. Women's self-effacing style is elicited in specific settings—and virtually without exception the most anxiety-provoking situations are those in which males and females are vying for the available recognition, such as a meeting, a class, a casual phone call, or a conversation on a date.

In these situations women have devised brilliant strategies to reassure their male counterparts that they will not compete for recognition. A recent newspaper profile of a highly respected woman scientist reads like a case study in such placating behavior. The scientist, Dr. Marguerite Vogt, "worked for years with Dr. Renato Dulbecco of the Salk Institute on groundbreaking studies that proved essential to the development of a polio vaccine," according to *The New York Times:*

> But while Dr. Dulbecco eventually won a Nobel Prize for his research, Dr. Vogt has yet to be awarded a single significant prize, or even to gain membership in the prestigious National Academy of Sciences. Not that you would hear a grumble of bitterness or complaint from Dr. Vogt. "I'm happy not to have been bothered," she said. "When you get too famous, you stop being able to work."

Her eminent (male) colleagues are delighted to take Dr. Vogt at her word and look no further:

> Dr. David Baltimore, the president of Caltech, said: "Marguerite is just a deeply devoted scientist who worked very hard, loved what she did and was uninterested in the professional side of the business, or in being recognized for what she did. She didn't try to establish herself in that way, or to get out there and tell her story . . . in the case of the work she did with Renato, he was the spokesman for the pair of them."

What an admirable, dedicated, selfless woman, working for the betterment of mankind! Undoubtedly this version of the story has much truth to it; Dr. Vogt is without question an exceptional and impressive woman. But it doesn't take a lot of imagination to realize what is left out of this tale. In a brief aside at the end of the piece, Dr. Vogt quietly gives the lie to the idea that such self-effacement is voluntary: "There have to be many more of us [women] around. . . . Maybe then it will be hard to ignore us."

The research literature has elegantly documented that girls' and women's withdrawal from the pursuit of recognition occurs only in specific social settings. One small, rather charming study, done in the early 1980s, which used a spelling bee as a paradigm, set out to clarify girls' behavior in competition with males for academic praise (winning the spelling bee). Spelling was chosen as a task "appropriate" for both sexes. A baseline was obtained to determine individual spelling skills, and the children were divided into high- and low-skill groups. The girls and boys were then asked to compete against each other in the spelling contest. In the experimental condition in which the high-skill girls competed with the low-skill boys—in other words, the condition in which the boys were likely to lose—the girls' performances deteriorated. They actually performed below their proven level of competence, thereby avoiding taking the laurels from the boys or at least humiliating them. Even when they knew the answer, they would refrain from volunteering it:

> The typical Chicago [group] high-skill girl response was to back off, let the boy misspell the word, and then spell the word correctly

herself. This amounted to winning by default, and one wonders what would have happened if the girl had not been given the opportunity to spell the word after the boy's effort. Actually, three low-skill girls in Chicago showed the lowest possible level of competitiveness; they refused to try to spell the words even after their boy opponents failed.

The authors concluded: "It seems that females alter their behavior when moving from female opponents to male opponents."

In an equally vivid if somewhat more complex investigation, seventy-two male and female subjects were given a task to perform in either a mixed-sex, same-sex, or solitary situation. Unbeknownst to the subjects, the task—digit memorization—was set up so that they would always fail. Before the test the subjects were asked to predict how well they would perform. After the test they were asked to give themselves a financial reward commensurate with the quality of their work.

In the mixed-sex situations, the women "had lower expectations than the men, performed worse, rewarded themselves less, and attributed their poor performance to lack of ability more than men did." Perhaps more revealing, however, was that in single-sex and solitary situations, the women's expectations and self-rewards did not differ from those of the men. In fact, the only way in which the single-sex groups differed was that the women outperformed the men. Clearly something about the presence of male participants led the women—consciously or unconsciously—to reduce their public assessment of their skills and performance. The available social recognition for accomplishment was ceded to men.

The conclusions arrived at in these research investigations are borne out in the real world. Girls' and women's performances deteriorate when males are present; girls do better in math classes if most of the students and the teacher are female; girls in single-sex parochial schools do the best academically, despite the fact that their schools have lower funding per student than parochial coed schools or boys' schools. Studies of college graduates have found that "the correlation between women achievers and both men students and the total number of men in the college environment were statistically significant and negative. Men students accounted for the major input to the negative correlation." Women from women's colleges are more likely to enter high-status male professions than those from coed institutions.

In other words, in any given educational institution the more men are around, the lower the accomplishments of the girls and women and the less their chance to achieve. Women in mixed-sex groups, in sociologist-speak, "tend to have less influence over group decisions, re-act more in socio-emotional categories of behavior rather than proact in task-oriented ones, are more deferential, and, in agreement with men, hold lower expectations for their task performance." To trans-late: in mixed-gender situations, women lower their self-expectations, defer to men more, and affirm the men's ideas.

Although these researchers don't mention it, one possibility sug-gested by their work is that the most "high-skill" girls—those who have been most motivated to learn or have natural abilities—are most at risk for having to deny or disguise their accomplishments, since they are the ones most likely to "rob" their male peers of praise. And indeed, studies of teenagers make it clear why academically successful girls might chose to underperform. When girls persist in being high achievers, they are subtly penalized by their teachers. They actually receive less attention from their teachers than any of the other student types—less than high-achieving boys, less than low-achieving boys, and less than low-achieving girls. They have been shown to pay a heavy price socially as well. It should come as no surprise that in a 1985 study of women who as high school girls had been identified as intel-lectually "gifted," the women were loath to acknowledge the distinction and insisted (often cheerfully) that they were "normal." A substantial number even wrote ad hoc denials on the questionnaire they were sent, such as, "I don't believe that I am gifted."

Women underperform in structured, competitive situations in which they might receive public recognition coveted by male peers. Even in work situations they alter their style in face-to-face encounters with men, becoming more "sensitive" and responsive to male colleagues—but not to female colleagues. In the interpersonal aspect of careers, women are as deferential and supportive of male emotional needs as they are in their private relationships.

Sensitivity to others' feelings has been frequently cited as a prime

cause of girls' and women's distaste for competition. It has been assumed that taking resources (including emotional ones) from others is
antithetical to women's nature. Numerous studies have looked at this
issue, and the jury is still out. One review of thirty studies of empathy
concluded that there were no proven gender differences. Another review of seventy-five studies concluded that women are better than
men at assessing nonverbal cues. However, many of these studies have
been questioned; it is often unclear whether the observed "sensitivity" reflects an innate capacity or women's general subordinate
status. It has been demonstrated that those in subordinate statuses
are more sensitive—aware and responsive to others—than those who
are not.

There is also an issue about the validity of some of these investigations: studies that suggest that women are more sympathetic than
men are largely based on self-report questionnaires. When investigators use more objective measures, such as facial expressions, gestures,
or vocal changes, differences between the sexes tend to disappear. A
review article on this subject concluded, "No sex differences were evident when the measure of empathy was either physiologic or unobtrusive observation of nonverbal reactions to another's emotional state."
The phrase "unobtrusive observation" is the key here; the women did
not know that they were being watched.

Women's empathic behavior appears, at the very least, to be heavily
modified by social cues. Women's "sensitivity," like their competitiveness, waxes and wanes depending on the specific social context. In as
simple an activity as playing dodgeball, research has shown that girls
act less "girlish" when no boys are around. They play better and more
competitively.

One investigator compared the responses that occurred in male-
female, male-male, and female-female pairs in which a member of each
couple was assigned the teacher (dominant) role and the other the student (subordinate) role. The sensitivity of each participant was mea-
sured by comparing their assessment of the other's feelings with that
person's self-report; the sensitivity score is a measure of awareness of
another person's variation in emotions over time.

The highest sensitivity ratings, as you might predict, were found in the women in the male-female pairs—irrespective of whether the woman was in the teacher or student role. More unexpected, however, was the finding that the women in the female-female pairs were less sensitive to their female partners than the males were with their male or female partners. As the author succinctly summarized the findings: "When leadership-subordinate role was crossed with sex, women showed *no* advantage over men in sensitivity to others."

Perhaps we should not be surprised that to a significant extent the empathic qualities associated with women are elicited by specific social contexts and are reversed when those social conditions no longer exist. Intuitively we know this is true. Ellen Fein and Sherrie Schneider, authors of the best-selling book *The Rules: Time-Tested Secrets for Capturing the Heart of Mr. Right,* advise women, "Don't be a loud, knee-slapping, hysterically funny girl. This is O.K. when you're alone with your girlfriend. But when you're with a man you like, be quiet and mysterious, cross your legs and smile. Don't talk so much. . . . You may feel that you won't be able to be yourself, but men will love it." We immediately understand what they are saying. When the authors tell women to "look into his eyes, be attentive and a good listener so he knows you are a caring being—a person who would make a supportive wife," we get it. Both the authors and the readers assume that the womanly, supportive behavior recommended can be turned off and on. The very title of the book tells us that these are not deep-seated propensities; they are the "rules" that must be learned and applied chiefly to one situation: when women are with men. If the empathic, self-effacing, nurturing behaviors that the *Rules* authors advocate in women come naturally to them, why must they give women such elaborate and detailed coaching? But as the authors breezily comment to their female audience, "Of course, this is not how you really feel. This is how you pretend to feel until it feels real."

CHAPTER FOUR

FEMININITY

Ms. [Yasmina] Reza, who arrived in New York last week for the opening of "Art," said she had spent so much time listening to male friends talking in Paris that eventually they would forget she was present. "I like the freedom men have in speaking," she said. "Women are not allowed that. We are taught to be polite. It is very funny for a woman to write as a man because you can say things that you would not dare to say as a woman."

—*New York Times* article on
the award-winning playwright Yasmina Reza

The pressure on girls and women to provide recognition to males, while deflecting it from themselves, has large repercussions. Recognition is one of the two most powerful and vitalizing elements required for the pursuit of long-term goals. The withholding of this intangible but avidly sought-after resource—affirmation—is one key type of discrimination that women currently face. Being silenced or ignored, because it is a "sin of omission" rather than one of commission, often remains a baffling and frustrating barrier to women's understanding of how their lives are shaped. It's hard to spot. It's not as obvious as being denied the vote or access to birth control. Women tend to feel foolish asking for more attention for their contributions.

There is another reason why it is difficult for women to acknowledge this pervasive inequality that undermines ambitions: the mandate that females provide recognition to males is a basic requirement of the white, middle-class notion of femininity. Challenging this state of affairs is a high-risk, potentially high-loss venture. At stake is one's sexual identity. Most women believe in all the individual tenets of feminism; what woman doesn't believe in equal pay for equal work, for example? But there is the lurking notion that feminism is an unattractive, desexualizing label. Women who receive recognition equal to that of men—whether it be conversational airtime or institutional recognition, such as increased pay or career promotion—risk violating their assigned sexual role. It is precisely this aspect of feminism, for example, that Camille Paglia, in her lively but incoherent writings about sexuality, zeros in on and condemns. She insists that the "beaming Betty Crockers, hangdog dowdies, and parochial prudes who call themselves feminist want men to be like women. They fear and despise the masculine."

Most of us have only an ill-defined, intuitive sense of what femininity is. We would be hard put to articulate its definition. Many of the meanings we attribute to it are not even conscious. By necessity, however, the definition of femininity is clearly spelled out in psychological studies of gender. The most famous and widely used psychological measure of femininity (and masculinity and androgyny) is an instrument called the revised Bem Sex Role Inventory (BSRI). The BSRI has been used in well over a hundred studies and is considered one of the standard measures in psychology. It is composed of sixty descriptive adjectives on which subjects rate themselves: twenty masculine traits, twenty feminine traits, and twenty neutral items. The traits were originally chosen from two hundred personality characteristics by one hundred male and female undergraduates at Stanford University in the 1970s. The students were asked to rank the desirability of these traits for men and women in American society. Here are the twenty traits chosen to define femininity in the BSRI: *yielding, loyal, cheerful, compassionate, shy, sympathetic, affectionate, sensitive to the needs of others, flatterable, understanding, eager to soothe hurt feelings, softspoken, warm, tender, gullible, childlike, does not use harsh language, loves children, gentle.*

A close analysis of these seemingly harmless adjectives is revealing: the woman they describe is socially recessive, exquisitely responsive to others' feelings, and undemanding about getting her own needs for affirmation met. According to a standard dictionary, to be *cheerful* is to be "pleasant and uncomplaining." *Sympathetic* is defined as "the provision of sympathy to others." To *yield* is to "concede, give up, to surrender, submit, defer." To be *loyal* is to be "steadfast in one's allegiance," and *allegiance,* in turn, is defined as the "duty of a subject." To be loyal, therefore, is to steadfastly perform one's duty toward whomever one owes obedience. It suddenly becomes clear why Hillary Rodham Clinton received her highest popularity ratings when she "stood by her man."

To me, one of the oddest and most telling of the qualities listed is "flatterable." There is something disparaging in the idea of women being flatterable; implicit is the belief that the praise is unwarranted and that pleasure taken in it therefore foolish and deluded. If a woman openly enjoys recognition, it is interpreted as a sign of weakness or vanity. Shyness—that is, fear and anxiety about social attention—is promoted as appropriately feminine.

The BSRI has received its share of criticisms, but the very fact that it has been so widely adopted for psychological research tells us that its definition of femininity can't be too far from that of the general culture. Studies that do not utilize the BSRI tend to use similar criteria. A frequently cited study called "The Effects of Sex and Sex-Role on Achievement Strivings" utilizes the following definition of feminine: "warm, helpful, emotional, gentle, passive." The Personal Attributes Questionnaire (PAQ), a well-known research instrument employed to assess gender-role orientation, uses two scales: the one used for masculine attributes lists active, "instrumental" characteristics, while the "expressive or female-valued scale" lists more emotional, responsive qualities. Studies of mental health professionals, including psychiatrists, psychologists, and social workers, suggest that clinicians use a similar definition of femininity. Comparisons of clinicians' concepts of mental health in women and men demonstrate that "qualities of submissiveness, non-competitiveness, and lack of aggression are central to their ideal of women's but not men's mental health." These qualities, although not identical with those of the BSRI, echo its themes.

As one analyzes the BSRI adjectives, two basic tenets of femininity emerge. The first is that femininity can exist only in the setting of a relationship. A woman's sexual identity is based on qualities that simply can't be expressed in isolation. By definition one can be yielding, affectionate, or sensitive only in relation to someone else; for white, middle-class women, therefore, femininity can't exist in the absence of "significant others." As the author Jane Smiley has written, "Does a woman alone in a dark room feel like a woman? How about a woman doing errands? How about a woman reading a book or climbing mountains?" It's like the famous question: if a tree fell in a forest and no one was there to hear, would it make a sound?

Lack of relationships—particularly but not exclusively romantic, heterosexual relationships—desexes women. There is no such thing as an unattached feminine woman, because it is the very existence and quality of attachments that define femininity. This may help explain women's often desperate attempts to marry—despite the large amount of evidence that once they are in a marriage their work increases and their mental and physical health frequently deteriorates; half will have to suffer through a painful divorce in which they could lose custody of their children. But marriage is a bargain if without it, your sexual identity is forever questioned by yourself and everyone around you.

The second tenet of femininity that emerges from the BSRI adjectives is that a woman must be providing something for the other person in the relationship, be that person a lover, a child, a sick parent, a husband, or even a boss. Giving is the chief activity that defines femininity. The list of services rendered is long, ranging from sex to picking up the dry cleaning to emotional support. As I will show, one of the key provisions that women supply to others is recognition.

Masculinity, by contrast, is defined neither by relationships nor by providing for others. In fact, it is defined by the opposite. You can be masculine in solitary splendor. Bachelorhood has none of the desexualizing connotations of spinsterhood—it's even sexy. The BSRI adjectives that describe masculinity are: *self-reliant, strong personality, forceful, independent, analytical, defends one's beliefs, athletic, assertive, has leadership abilities, willing to take risks, makes decisions easily, self-sufficient, dominant, willing to take a stand, aggressive, acts as a leader, individualistic, competitive, ambitious.* The "other" appears in these adjectives only as someone against whom the man must assert himself. Not only can you be solitary and masculine, but if you are in a relationship that involves overt dependency or being influenced by others (and virtually all relationships do), your sexual identity is at risk.

For men, there are no linguistic equivalents to the terms *spinster* or *old maid* or *maiden aunt* or *dowager* or *matron* or *slut* or even *mistress*. There is also no equivalent to being a *Miss* as opposed to a *Mrs*. The language contains all sorts of words that clarify the status of a woman whether or not she is in a relationship, because that is the key to her identity as a woman—to her femininity.

Although in recent years college women have been shown to identify with more of the "masculine" traits than in the past, they have not dropped any of the "feminine" ones. These young women have, for example, been found to endorse goals such as becoming an authority in one's field, obtaining recognition from colleagues, having administrative responsibilities (power), and being better off financially. But it is unclear what this means in their actual lives. As the author of one study notes, "Soliciting the respondent's expected career goals at only one point in time at such an early period in the individual's life tells us very little about the degree of commitment attached to these career goals."

The question of how to resolve the inevitable conflicts between the two sets of attributes remains central for most women. What happens when a husband wants to move overseas to advance his career even if it disrupts or derails the wife's goals? Should the wife be yielding, loyal, and cheerful—"feminine" traits—or should she be independent and forceful—"masculine" traits? What happens when her partner's meetings last later and later into the night and there's no parent home with the children unless she leaves her workplace early? Should she be "understanding" (feminine) or "willing to take a stand" (masculine)? How does she deal with the tensions that arise if her career advances faster and further than her husband's or if *she* has a career opportunity that requires a move? At present, women have more leeway in forming and pursuing their own goals, but doing so is socially condoned only if they have first satisfied the needs of all their constituents—husbands, children, and elderly parents. If these elements are not in place, their ambitions and their femininity will be called into question.

The impact of white, middle-class notions of femininity is most pronounced in adolescence. It is in adolescence, when sexual identity first becomes an issue, that girls are rapidly socialized to define themselves primarily through interpersonal relationships. These young women experience more disruption of their self-concept than do adolescent males and become more concerned about physical appearance, an aspect of their lives over which they have relatively little control. Relationships, particularly with boys, become defining elements in their identities. John Hill and Mary Ellen Lynch, in their writings on early adolescence, have noted that girls are "more likely than boys to rank popularity as most important when compared to being independent or competent." But "ranking popularity as most important [is] associated with higher self-consciousness and lower stability of self-image."

Clearly it is in adolescence that acquiring "feminine" characteristics becomes an urgent agenda in young women's lives: from this point forward their relational status becomes a primary aspect of their identity. As a teenager, I vividly recall learning this lesson and deciding that if I didn't get married by thirty, I'd persuade a male friend to marry me and get an instant divorce. Being a divorcée seemed infinitely preferable and sexier than being identified as a "spinster." The thought of remaining single conjured up memories of playing Old Maid as a child. To this day I can recall anxiously passing that female face card around, trying to rid myself of the dark, ominous Queen of Spades. Whoever got stuck with it at the end lost the game and was identified as the Old Maid. You can hardly get more explicit than that in defining gender expectations.

Journalistic presentations of prominent women typify our preoccupation with women's relational status. Journalists rush to clarify each woman's relational bona fides. The unspoken question is: has this successful woman had to forgo the relationships that define her sexual identity in order to have a career? A *New York Times* profile of Abby

Joseph Cohen, "the most influential analyst on Wall Street today," opens this way:

> Around 6:30 most weekday mornings, a motherly looking woman in a suit and spectacles catches a commuter bus with her teen-age daughter in Flushing, Queens. As the pair trundle along their 40-minute journey to their destinations in lower Manhattan, an office and a high school, they share the newspaper, do the crossword puzzle and chat about their plans for the day.

So, she's managed to be a real woman. Now we can go on to her career. There's nothing intrinsically wrong with the article stressing Cohen's maternal qualities, although this is certainly not what the article is about. The journalist intuitively realizes that these issues must be addressed first and foremost—otherwise the gender question will nag at the reader until it is resolved. In a profound way, it is assumed that we don't really know who Abby Cohen is, despite her enormous achievements, until we know who she is connected to.

This formula of presenting a successful woman's relational status up front is standard issue. Shelley Lazarus, chief executive of one of the biggest ad agencies on Madison Avenue, is introduced in a *New York Times* profile with the following sentence: "Shelley Lazarus—wife for almost 27 years, mother of 3—has become the most powerful woman in advertising by assuming the job Mr. Ogilvy once had." Contrast this to the passage in which Mr. Ogilvy is introduced: "Decades ago, the legendary adman David Ogilvy sought to raise consciousness at Ogilvy & Mather Worldwide." No stats on the longevity of Ogilvy's marriage or his progeny are included. We don't require them to understand his identity.

But once a woman is in a relationship, her sexual identity is still at risk until she has satisfied the second requirement of femininity outlined in the BSRI and confirmed by large numbers of psychological studies: within her relationship she must assume a caretaking role. Being sensitive to and providing for the needs of others, even at the expense of her own needs, is the emotional core of a woman's femininity. Women who act on their own behalf, rather than that of others, risk being seen as unfeminine.

These qualities can be admirable when the "other" is someone who is weaker or more vulnerable, but it becomes less understandable when the "other" is someone with greater resources. Yet white, middle-class femininity requires that a woman place the emotional needs of a male before her own, whether he be a fellow student, a colleague, a boss, a boyfriend, or a husband. And foremost among the emotional resources she is asked to relinquish to them is recognition. For a woman to openly seek fame or highly regarded professional success is condemned by no less a feminist than Carol Gilligan. In *Making Connections* she describes two types of women: Super Woman and Wise Woman.

> When asked to imagine their lives in the future, Super Women used a lot of superlatives: a famous actress, fabulously wealthy, a corporate president. This is very different from Wise Woman, who talked about the future in terms of the self: self-fulfillment, self-satisfaction, believes in herself. . . . Wise Women . . . are able to envision an ideal of adulthood that makes connectedness to self and others central. It is a vision that supports maturation.

Note her repeated use of the word *self*. These "Wise Women" are supposed to provide for themselves or at best receive affirmation through their interpersonal relationships. Any wishes for recognition in a larger arena—for fame and fortune, God forbid—must be eschewed if one is to be "mature." A healthy woman keeps her wishes for recognition within modest bounds: she must glean whatever affirmation she seeks from interpersonal, purely reciprocal relationships. The mature woman is defined as one who provides recognition for others while limiting her own expressed needs for this highly prized response. If she believes in herself, why should she need any outside approval?

In the "ideal" white, middle-class couple, the deferential position of the woman is expressed in the cultural preference that she be physically smaller and younger than her husband. Exceptions to this rule—

such as Nancy Kissinger, who is taller than her husband, Henry—are much remarked upon. Ideally, a wife should also retain the lean look of a vulnerable, young, adolescent girl and avoid all the bodily changes of full female adulthood. She must be, quite literally, "the little woman." Women's efforts to remain in the low-recognition position relative to their husbands' in order to remain "feminine" put accomplished women—and their husbands—in a bind. Margaret Thatcher's husband, Denis, was the butt of so many jokes that the British humor magazine *Private Eye* devoted a weekly column to him. Women of accomplishment often desperately try to find an even *more* accomplished and renowned man for whom they can play their part as the weaker sex; they have to find the Ted Turner to their Jane Fonda.

Because femininity requires that men receive the lion's share of recognition, women downplay their ambitions and accomplishments. The juncture at which a woman's ambition becomes apparent to her spouse or male peer is frequently a difficult moment of truth, one that may have punitive consequences. A 2002 *New York Times* article described the sorts of reactions that women have learned to expect and fear; the incidents are particularly striking because they took place in relatively liberal academic communities.

The news story was about women being denied tenure on the basis of their personalities. The director of planning and development at the American Association of University Professors was quoted saying, "More and more cases [of denied tenure for women] are coming up on some version of the collegiality issue. We just saw three cases simultaneously that all came down to the same thing. They're all male-dominated departments that hadn't tenured a woman in a long time, or ever, and there's some language about how the woman 'just doesn't fit in.' What comes through is the sense that these are aggressive women who are seen as uppity." The article goes on to note that "some academics say that 'collegiality' evaluations can be a particular obstacle for women who are self-promoting, hard-edged, or otherwise outside the female norm."

One of the cases described was that of Carol Stepien, a biologist who had received national attention for her original professional contributions, coedited a textbook, and been well funded for her research, but was denied tenure. A faculty panel that reviewed the case concluded that the men in the department had not been comfortable with her "demanding and assertive style." A colleague noted, "Because Carol looks rather sweet and compliant, they thought they were hiring the good daughter. But she wasn't the good daughter."

The expectation that deviation from noncompetitive, supportive female behavior will be penalized is equally problematic in the personal and social spheres. One woman I interviewed had started a small magazine when she was in her twenties. To her simultaneous delight and dismay, it became successful. What to do? To this day she second-guesses herself about her ultimate decision:

> I hadn't planned to start a magazine or be successful and make the kind of money I was making. I would have had to work harder and take myself a little more seriously. I had always used a different name than my husband did. Most people at the magazine he worked for didn't know I worked. I would have had to promote myself a little more. I wasn't ready to do it in my life at that point and I saw it as a threat to being a mother. Until that time, I had the perfect situation. I had my secret little life at work.

Reading over the interview, I could certainly understand her worry about having adequate time for her children. But this concern is strangely intertwined with her anxiety about having her success out in the open. She was particularly fearful of her accomplishments becoming known to her husband's colleagues—who in her mind may have been a substitute for her husband himself. If her children were the main issue, why was she alarmed by making more money—certainly something that would not harm them? Why would she feel that it was ideal to have a "secret little life at work"? What was the need for secrecy? At the time of my interview with this college friend of mine, she was in her late forties; her children were going off to college and her marriage had ended. Ten years after abandoning her editorial career, she returned to school to get training in a relatively low-paying, primarily female service profession.

"FEMININE" CAREERS

The mandates of femininity make it clear that certain occupations are more hospitable to women and more socially acceptable. The amount of negative pressure put on a woman's femininity by a given job can be easily calculated. There is little pressure if the job is totally noncompetitive (with men), caretaking, low-recognition, and therefore "feminine." Any "serving" profession will create minimal strain on culturally defined femininity, especially if the person being served is a man or child. There are few articles bemoaning the fact that nurses spend too much time away from their children, despite their often long and stressful schedules of night and day shifts. Social workers, clerical workers, and teachers are virtually never taken to task by the media. In these professions women not only "care" for others, ideally they do it in a way that doesn't compete with males for recognition: they are low paid and receive relatively little prestige.

Working at a solitary, noncompetitive profession, such as writing, places no cultural pressure on femininity, particularly since it can be done from the home. Running a small business in which there is no hierarchy, low levels of remuneration, and minimal prestige is also compatible with a conventional definition of the feminine role.

At the other extreme are professions that include the open pursuit of personal satisfaction, high recognition, and competition with men. (Competing with women—as in professional women's sports—is not a problem.) A business career within a corporation, for example, is hard to frame as a caretaking profession; it involves monetary rewards, competition with males, and public recognition. The business community has been famously hostile to women. Careers in science, engineering, and math, professions that do not directly involve caretaking, have also been inhospitable for women. Law presents a particularly confusing situation for many women. Although in theory the law is a noble calling that protects the rights of the least-powerful members of society, in reality much of the available work is corporate litigation and business deals. And as in the business community, women may encounter fierce competition with men for advancement and high levels of remuneration. Female lawyers often feel uncomfortable, even if they enjoy the intellectual challenge and have no moral or political objection to the work's content. Not surprisingly, numerous articles have bemoaned the high rate at which women abandon the most prestigious law firms despite their many years of training.

"FEMININITY" OUTSIDE THE WHITE MIDDLE CLASS

I have used the terms *white* and *middle-class* in describing the parameters of femininity because femininity is defined differently in the various subcultures of our society. And perhaps surprisingly, some of the alternative definitions appear to be less damaging to girls and women. The most heavily studied constituency, African Americans, has a feminine ideal that overlaps with but is not identical to that of their white counterparts. This is likely the result of the differences in family structures and roles. In the black community a higher percentage of women conceive and rear children outside of marriage. In this social context, predicating women's femininity on the presence and quality of their relationships to men is more problematic. Even when black women are married, the job discrimination against black men more commonly makes them the sole or more highly paid wage earner. Their work is required to provide for their families and is therefore not open to the usual reproach that they are selfishly choosing to work for their own well-being.

Despite the many socioeconomic and cultural factors working against them, black girls tend to have significantly higher self-esteem than their white counterparts. Between the ages of nine and seventeen, they rate themselves higher than do their white, female age-mates on attractiveness, ability to learn, being good at sports, being liked by their teachers, and having many friends. Throughout high school they have higher educational goals and career aspirations than both black males and white females. Black adolescent girls also have "significantly lower dropout rates and higher enrollment rates than black boys." The high self-esteem and aspirations of black girls are particularly notable because, although they initiate more interactions with teachers than do white girls or boys of either race, they receive less reinforcement from teachers than any other group of students.

When black girls enter predominantly white schools they have to adjust to the white, middle-class norms, with problematic results. Black girls who are more assimilated into the "mainstream" white culture, in which femininity is more strictly defined in relational terms, lose their self-confidence. Perhaps because black girls from families with high socioeconomic status are more integrated into the white community, they too have been found to lack the high self-confidence of their poorer black, female cohort.

The independence and high expectations of young black women may help explain why the most powerful woman entrepreneur in America, Oprah Winfrey, and only the second American woman to win a Nobel Prize in literature, Toni Morrison, are both black women. It may also explain their refreshingly independent stance toward men. Even Tina Turner, who had been abused by her former spouse, makes it clear to the public that she has learned her lesson and rethought her relationship to men. In a *USA Today* interview, Winfrey and Turner openly described their position on heterosexual relationships:

TINA: I don't have any desire to marry. Erwin is wonderful. We are perfect just as we are. Why do I need to bring another element in for the sake of tradition? We are as married as we'd be if we had a ceremony. Besides, I want to keep my stuff mine and his stuff his. That's the reality. I need that freedom.

OPRAH: Ditto, absolutely. I really do feel that people want to see a wedding because they want to party and see the pictures. I have a wonderful relationship that works for me.

TINA: Is that your man I saw outside with your dogs? He's very good-looking.

OPRAH: Nooo. That guy is a shmatteh compared to Stedman (Graham). You haven't met him? Oh, you should see him. My guy is really great-looking.

Men are a delightful element in these women's lives but do not define them. By contrast, white women of equal prominence—Madonna and Barbra Streisand, for example—create huge media events to publicize their lavish, traditional weddings, as if to settle once and for all questions about their true femininity. Martha Stewart, perhaps the entrepreneurial equivalent of Oprah, has based her merchandising empire on an image of the tasteful, perfectionist homemaker. It's hard to think of white, heterosexual women of this stature who have made statements openly distancing themselves from traditional male-female relationships based on marriage.

RETALIATIONS AGAINST "UNFEMININE" BEHAVIOR

Given the deferential qualities that define white, middle-class femininity, you might expect that women would be eager to abandon the whole enterprise. Androgyny never looked so good. But there's a catch. If they are unfeminine, if they refuse to relinquish valued emotional resources, they pay a steep price. Whenever women ask for or gain access to resources previously reserved for men—and most particularly sources of social recognition—their sexual identity is publicly attacked. These groundbreaking women are seen (correctly) as having betrayed their feminine mandate to forgo such male privileges. The rage and aggression with which men respond are astonishing but highly predictable. Because ambition involves gaining access to precisely the sources of public affirmation previously reserved for men, such attacks need to be expected and seen for what they are. They are not personal, even though they appear to be. They are efforts to retain time-honored male prerogatives that are under siege. The stakes are not trivial. Men have a lot to lose, and not surprisingly, they often play rough to keep their advantage; they unfailingly attack the successful woman's sexual identity.

On occasion the attacks on ambitious women are actually physical. In the late 1990s an outstanding woman high school coach from New Jersey demanded that female athletes receive parity with the males:

new uniforms, the opportunity to play night games, better pay for coaches. Her house was fire-bombed. She lost her job and had to pursue a year-long legal battle to get it back. More commonly, however, the assault on women is verbal, often in the form of suggestions that the woman is sterile, homosexual, asexual, or, paradoxically, the reverse—promiscuous: something has to be wrong with her sexuality. Professor Lani Guinier of the Harvard Law School, in her study of women law students at the University of Pennsylvania, noted that the women were "ridiculed about their sexuality." One outspoken, married woman law student was attacked by male peers as a "man-hating lesbian"; other female students were referred to as "feminazis."

When a woman assumes a prominent position, her sexuality is attacked, and the attack can be from either extreme: either she is asexual or promiscuous. As a cardiology professor at Johns Hopkins Medical School, Dr. Bernadine Healy—subsequently the first female head of the National Institutes of Health—was singled out for ridicule at the yearly skit of the school's all-male eating club. At the time she was a vulnerable, recently divorced mother of a young child and had protested the skit. It was nonetheless performed. "In the skit she was played by a man dressed in a long blond wig, fishnet stockings, and a coconut-half brassiere and was depicted performing a variety of pornographic acts . . . until at the end she was discovered *in flagrante* with her husband."

Margaret Thatcher was called "The Iron Maiden" despite having a husband and two grown children. Amazingly, at the other extreme she was described—by the prime minister of France, no less—as a seductress with "the eyes of Caligula and the mouth of Marilyn Monroe." One magazine remarked on her "sizzling sexual charm." Barbara McClintock, winner of a Nobel Prize for her work in genetics, was publicly referred to by a colleague as "an old bag." One of the few women to reach the top executive ranks in a British corporation is called "The Ice Maiden" and a "one-time librarian"—an erroneous reference to the start of her career at the London investment bank of S.G. Warburg. When a number of women recently ran for government positions in France, they all agreed on one point, according to an article in *The New York Times:* "They hated the unrelenting ridicule and sexist slurs. Elisabeth Guigou, a former Cabinet minister, said among her 'most objectionable experiences' were the constant 'below-the-waist' jokes, even in parliament. . . . Several provincial candidates complained about slogans written on the walls that linked their names and the word 'whore.' " Kelly Flinn, a graduate from the U.S. Air Force Academy and the first woman to fly the B-52, recalls being ostracized during the last days of her academy experience because she had reported an incident in which someone had written "cunt" on the message board on her door.

In the U.S. media, outright sexual slurs are, for the most part, unacceptable. Women who pursue their ambitions are defeminized in a different, more subtle, and ultimately more frightening way. Their capacity for relationships—the heart of femininity—is called into question. With a mournful tone the media bewails the "fact" that such women will not get married, and if they do get married, they will be too old to have children, and if they do have children, they will be inadequate mothers. Susan Faludi, in her heavily researched book on the American media's response to feminism, *Backlash,* sets out in great detail the grim scenario that ambitious women are told to expect. She cites a typical article from *Newsweek* called "Feminism's Identity Crisis" which quotes

> many experts on women's condition—sociologists, political scientists, psychologists—but none of the many women supposedly suffering from this crisis. The closest the magazine came was two drawings of a mythical feminist victim: a dour executive with cropped hair is pictured first at her desk, grimly pondering an empty family-picture frame, and then at home, clutching a clock and studying the hands—poised at five minutes to midnight.

In 2001 *Newsweek* ran a six-page cover story purportedly on the pressures that parents place on their children to achieve. But the real message was quite different. All but one of the examples of "parents" were, in fact, mothers, and most were working mothers. The hectic schedule of one working mom was set off in a special side-box to emphasize how little time she had with her children. There was no box outlining the father's day. This vignette contains the piece's take-home message:

> "I carve out a slice of my day so I can take him," she says, "but just because I'm there doesn't mean I can switch from working woman back to Mom. There are all these non-working moms looking at me as I get calls on my cell phone." Jack, a first grader, is already showing signs of burnout. Homework that should take no longer than 20 minutes to complete often takes an hour or more to get through. "He doesn't see us much, and this is his time to act out," she says. "We have battles in which he tests us. Maybe this is his way of getting us to fully focus on him." What families risk losing in this insane frenzy, many parenting experts say, is the soul of childhood and the joy of family life.

The problem with this family is not that the kids are overbooked but that the parent, a.k.a. "Mom," works. *Newsweek* found some "experts" to gloomily prognosticate about families with two parents working. But the data suggesting that the children of such families are damaged by it in any way are very limited, and there is some evidence to the contrary, that it has real benefits.

More important, if the quality of family life is actually the main concern—rather than the threat of professional women to male prerogatives—why do men not act to improve it? Men do not rush to do more housework so that their children can have more quality time with their mothers—despite multiple studies showing that women work many more hours than do their husbands. Divorced men with children (a sizable portion of the population) commonly do not even pay the minimal child support that they are court-mandated to provide for their offspring. Nor does the largely male judiciary support adequate provision for children by enforcing these laws. The quality of their children's lives certainly does not appear to be a priority for these men. The House and Senate, overwhelmingly male institutions, have also failed to make children a priority. Our national government has nearly the worst record in the developed world for support of prenatal care, child medical coverage, and provision of early child care. If the true concern about women having careers were the one voiced in *Newsweek,* namely the loss of "the soul of childhood and the joy of family life," why are these issues not addressed and acted upon by men? Why do they not support child-rearing personally and institutionally?

It is interesting to note that several months following this hand-wringing cover story, *Newsweek* reported on an actual study of 2,125 children ages three to six. "Particularly significant was the finding that today's working moms spent about the same amount of time (26.5 hours a week) with their kids as at-home mothers did in 1981 (26 hours)." And it added as an aside that this increased time spent in child care occurred "despite a 50% increase in the number of working mothers and a doubling of the divorce rate for first marriages over the past two decades."

The problem underlying the attack on working women's femininity— their capacity for caretaking relationships—seems to lie elsewhere. It is not only that men must now compete with women for recognition in the professional sphere; they are also called upon to participate in the low-recognition, labor-intensive business of raising children. It's a double whammy for men, but their position is a hard one to defend. All too often the fear of neglected children is used as a cover-up for less-attractive self-interests. But the lack of male support for any child-care provisions other than full-time maternal care belies their actual objectives.

Interestingly, many famous writers have noted that women in later life, after they have raised their children, develop a new resilience and energy. Dorothy Sayers referred to such women as "uncontrollable by any earthly force." Margaret Mead described an age of "heightened vitality" that she called the "Third Age." Isak Dinesen proclaimed, "Women . . . when they are old enough to have done with the business of being a woman, and can let loose their strength, must be the most powerful creatures in the whole world." I have often wondered whether the newfound strength of these women doesn't reflect the fact that their sexual identity is no longer assailable. "Been there, done that," they can say to anyone who questions their capacity for relationships. The classical reproach (always aimed at women and never at men)—that they are promoting themselves at the expense of others who need their care—no longer applies. In a very real sense, it is the first time in their lives when they are free to express, without fear of reprisal, the wide spectrum of feelings and behaviors previously reserved for men.

MARS VERSUS VENUS

> Women are afraid to talk, knowing full well the self-absorption of males and fearing to lose their attention if they dare present their own lives as separate and important. . . . men want to be flattered, soothed, encouraged, helped, and listened to. Not the reverse.
>
> —MARTHA GELLHORN, from a collection of the journalist and writer's letters in *The New Yorker*

The idea that males demand and receive the lion's share of affirmation and support in virtually every relationship that involves females flies in the face of the common wisdom. We are virtually indoctrinated with stereotypes of the "autonomous man" and "relational woman." It is women who are supposed to be invested in and dependent upon relationships and the affirmation they provide. Aren't they the ones who always need to be flattered and attended to? Men's interests, reportedly, lie elsewhere. We are told that they don't require relationships and ongoing recognition, because they are more self-reliant: the standards against which they measure themselves are internalized, allowing them to evaluate and reward themselves. When they've done a good job, they are satisfied and require relatively minimal external acknowledgment.

During my reading of the psychological and sociological literature, I collected a list of the various terms used by authors to describe this much-touted dichotomy in the orientations of men and women:

Autonomous vs. relational
Achievement vs. affiliation
Inner-directed vs. other-directed

Public vs. domestic
Instrumental vs. expressive
Agenic vs. communal
Assertion of self vs. need for others
Impact-oriented vs. process-oriented
Task orientation vs. social orientation

And then there is Mars vs. Venus. Perhaps more than anyone else, John Gray, in his wildly successful *Men Are from Mars, Women Are from Venus* (2.5 million copies sold), brought to the public, in a highly popularized form, a theory that had been widely accepted in the psychological community for decades. Gray repeatedly made two points, one about men and one about women. Men's sense of self, he said, derives from their sense of autonomy and achievement: "Autonomy is a symbol of efficiency, power, and competence. . . . [Men] experience fulfillment primarily through success and accomplishment." These self-sufficient men have little need for relationships that provide recognition of their achievements or encouragement in their endeavors. They derive their sense of self-worth from a task well done.

Women, or Venusians in his parlance, value "love, communication, beauty, and relationships. They spend a lot of time supporting, helping, and nurturing one another. . . . To share their personal feelings is much more important than achieving goals and success. . . . Instead of being goal-oriented, they are more concerned with expressing their goodness, love, and caring." Women, unlike men, want and need to be in relationships. And their greatest desire is to provide, not receive, recognition or support.

The psychological community may scoff at Gray's simplistic book, but he is actually in the mainstream of academic teachings. The theorists who have similar beliefs in this regard are otherwise so diverse that they make strange intellectual bedfellows. Everyone from the sociologist David McClelland in the 1960s to mid-twentieth-century psychoanalysts such as Erik Erikson to the difference feminists Carol Gilligan and Jean Baker Miller have endorsed the belief that women are more "relational" than men, relying more heavily than men on affirmation from those around them. Gilligan is probably the most famous proponent of this theory at present. In *Making Connections* she notes that "in contrast to males, for whom identity development is the outcome of increasing experience of separation and gained autonomy, the female personality develops through attachment to others." Other researchers, too, have proposed that "achievement behavior of both girls and boys is initially directed towards obtaining social approval," but that with development "boys internalize standards of excellence and come to rely on their own satisfaction in meeting these standards rather than reinforcement from others. Girls' achievement efforts remain more dependent on external social rewards."

Yet on close inspection, even Gray's own examples do not support this formulation. What he describes is not female dependence and male independence; it is quite the opposite. If the men he portrays were relatively unaffected by intimate personal interactions, why must Gray give women such intricately detailed instructions on how to respond to their mates in ways that maintain men's fragile sense of manliness and competence? Why are these purportedly emotionally self-sufficient men so unnerved by having to ask directions when lost on a highway?

What Gray is actually demonstrating is how vulnerable men are and how their tenuous sense of identity, paradoxically, requires constant affirmation and support—as is the case with the rest of us. Men's dependence on this service and their anger when it is withheld are at the core of the book: "Women need to learn the art of empowerment [of the man]. . . . Any attempt to change him takes away from the loving trust, acceptance, appreciation, admiration, approval, and encouragement that are his primary needs."

The men described by Gray, far from being paragons of emotional detachment and autonomy, have outsize and persistent needs for affirmation. They require endless reassurance that their actions are correct and "self-reliant." According to Gray, the male's tenuous sense of himself as "independent" is threatened even by the most simple, straightforward, and reasonable requests. Gray cautions women:

> Here are some examples of ways a woman might unknowingly annoy
> a man by offering advice or seemingly harmless criticism. . . . See if you
> can recognize why he might feel controlled.

"You should spend more time with the kids. They miss you. . . ."

"There's a parking spot over there, turn [the car] around. . . ."

"You want to spend time with your friends, what about me? . . ."

"You should give me more [advanced] notice, I can't just drop everything and go to lunch with you. . . ."

"I didn't know where you were. [You should have called. . . .]"

At the end of his list of twenty-three "controlling" suggestions, Gray sums up his advice to women: "To practice gaining acceptance and not giving advice or criticism is a big step."

What Gray is describing is not a qualitative difference in the needs for recognition that men and women bring to a relationship. Rather, it is a difference in the content of the recognition that each avidly seeks from the other. Each elicits recognition from the other for aspects of their identity, and each needs to be aware of the specific attributes that the other wishes to have singled out and affirmed.

The even more crucial point, which Gray drives home repeatedly, is that within white, middle-class culture, men have a right to expect to be affirmed more than women. Contrast his admonition to women to "learn the art of empowerment" and provide "loving trust, acceptance, appreciation, admiration, approval, and encouragement *that are his primary needs* [italics mine]" to his following half-hearted advice to men: allow women a little more time to "ventilate": "By randomly talking about her problems [a woman] becomes less upset." The difference in the quality and quantity of response that Gray advises men and women to provide for each other is stark.

As an interesting aside, the disparity of recognition that men and women can expect to receive in intimate relationships may help explain why "autonomous" men do so poorly outside of them: extensive documentation exists that men fare worse physically, psychologically, and professionally when they are not married. Perhaps surprisingly, men report higher marital satisfaction than women. "Relational" women, on the other hand, have been shown in some studies to be more long-lived and psychologically healthier when they are single—whether or not they have children.

The research literature—as opposed to psychological theories—does not show much support for the notion that adolescent boys and young men have greater autonomy, maturity, or independence of thought than their female equivalents. There is plenty of evidence that young men are more self-confident, have greater conviction that they will achieve their goals, and believe that social affirmation will be provided for their professional accomplishments. But this assessment should not be confused with the notion that they are more self-sufficient and mature. The findings of one meta-analysis of sixty-five developmental studies of males and females from adolescence through college are typical. In every category of maturity and ego strength, including abstract moral reasoning, cognitive complexity, impulse control, and empathy, young women consistently ranked higher than young men.

The construct of the young woman as "overly attached, unindividuated, and without boundaries," "less separate than boys"—to quote from Nancy Chodorow's famous psychoanalytic theory of female development in *The Reproduction of Mothering*—simply has not been substantiated. In fact, scientific evidence points in the opposite direction. In studies that use explicit self-reports, women score higher than men on dependency, but when indirect, nonconscious tests of dependency are utilized, men tend to score higher than women.

Men, far from being autonomous, have been shown to anxiously solicit and receive recognition from whomever is available to provide it—mentors, wives, bosses, colleagues, friends. There are precious few venues at home or at work in which men voluntarily relinquish recognition. On the contrary, as the roles of men and women in our society change, the threat to the hegemony of males with regard to attention may be the most fundamental and bitterly contested area of conflict. William J. Goode, a sociologist at Harvard, notes in an essay on the changing structures of contemporary families that

> [T]he most important change in men's position, as they experience it, is a loss of centrality, a decline in the extent to which they are the center of attention. In our time, other superordinates have also suffered this loss: colonial rulers, monarchs and nobles to name a few.
>
> Boys and men have always taken for granted that what they were doing was more important than what the other sex was doing; the

action was where they were. . . . Men occupied center stage, and women's attention was focused on them. . . .

The center of attention shifts to women more now than in the past. I believe that this shift troubles men far more, and creates more of their resistance, than the women's demand for equal opportunity and pay in employment.

In the past, it was not that men were more self-sufficient than women, it was that they assumed that they would get more than their share of the available attention and affirmation. Men amplify this inequality by diversifying their sources of recognition. By the time a professional man is in midcareer, he has a broad array of individual and institutional structures to provide it. A male lawyer, for example, might have a secretary, young associates, colleagues, professional associations, and clients—and that's just in the work sphere. This is in addition to his college friends, his sports buddies, his current neighborhood social circle, members of his family of origin, and of course, his wife and children.

To add insult to injury, as the eminent sociologist David Reisman pointed out, when men claim credit for their accomplishments, they tend to forget the human infrastructure that made them possible. Once they have achieved their goals, the large cast of supporting (often predominantly female) figures is mentally erased.

However, if by midlife a middle-class woman has not developed ambitions of her own, she *will* develop a greater emotional dependence on her husband than he has on her. Her sources of affirmation will not have grown at the same pace as his and frequently will be all of one type: interpersonal relationships. To say that she is intrinsically more "relational" than he is because she is more invested in her family and friends misses the point. It's like saying that the nineteenth-century Irish were innately more potato-oriented than the English. In reality, the impoverished Irish were as fond of roast beef as their colonial masters. They were obsessed with the potato crop because they had few other sources of sustenance.

Recognition from others, as we will see in the following chapter, is required for the most basic elements of life: identity, learning, work motivation, energy, and self-confidence. Women who depend solely on relationships to provide it are at risk. Their narrow focus makes them much more vulnerable to environmental changes. For such women, a divorce, children who grow up, a move to another community, or friends who no longer share the same values or life situation can be catastrophic. It can devastate what was already a fragile emotional ecology.

CHAPTER FIVE

WHY IS RECOGNITION
SO IMPORTANT FOR AMBITION?

Recognize: To acknowledge by special notice, approval or sanction; to treat as valid, as having existence or as entitled to consideration.

—*Oxford English Dictionary*

For to what purpose is all the toil and bustle of this world? . . . Is it to supply the necessities of nature? The wages of the meanest laborer can supply them. . . . From whence, then, arises that emulation which runs through all the different ranks . . . and what are the advantages which we propose by that great purpose of human life which we call bettering our condition? To be observed, to be attended to, to be taken notice of with sympathy, complacency and approbation, are all the advantages which we can propose to derive from them.

—ADAM SMITH, *The Theory of Moral Sentiments*, 1759

We are not used to thinking of recognition as a fundamental emotional need, particularly in adulthood: it's nice when you get it, but if you don't, it's not the end of the world—life goes on. In fact, we tend to look down on those whose eagerness for recognition is too obvious, too pressing. Such people seem unattractively needy or self-promoting. Although we acknowledge that recognition, in the right circumstances, is gratifying, its impact on the development and pursuit of ambitions, particularly throughout adulthood, has never been systematically investigated.

For white, middle-class women, providing rather than consuming recognition—particularly in the presence of men—is a deeply ingrained behavior. But as tiresome as this role may be at times, it's never been clear what larger consequences result from having to play it, often full-time. It's a crucial question, for if women are expected to relinquish recognition to men, we need to know what, if any, long-term impact this sacrifice has on their own ambitions. What is it exactly that such affirming attention provides? Is it required for ambitions to be formed and skills acquired, or is it just the frosting on the cake, a delicious but nonessential ingredient?

Although clinical psychologists have rarely looked at this question, researchers in many other fields have studied it extensively from a variety of angles. The data from the separate disciplines, however, has never been assembled into a coherent theory. Only when these fragments are pieced together does the full impact of recognition on ambition become clear.

Perhaps the best way to explore the subject is to envision the steps that must occur in the development of an ambition and look at how the provision of recognition shapes each one. As I mentioned previously, the first stage of forming an ambition requires imagining yourself in a role that requires skill and that exists outside the domestic sphere. Creating an ambition is a fundamental part of forming your identity, and once that is done, you must learn the appropriate skills. Perhaps most important, you must have the motivation to pursue your ambition over time and in the face of the inevitable obstacles. Such continued efforts require a belief that the goal is worth attaining and that you personally have the qualities required to attain it. It requires a sense of optimism and capability.

IDENTITY

For what is "identity" but our power to control others' definition of us?

—JOYCE CAROL OATES,
"After Amnesia About Visiting a Prison"

When I look I am seen, so I exist.

—D. W. WINNICOTT, *Playing and Reality*

When I was a young woman, I wanted to be a doctor and eventually
decided that the type of doctor I wished to be was a psychiatrist. Both
of these ambitions formed and continue to form a significant aspect of
my identity. Creating an ambition can best be understood as an inte-
gral part of identity formation; it is the aspect of identity that involves
our work within a community. Such a role inevitably generates a sense
of who we are.

This freedom to "choose" our ambition is, to a large extent, a recent
phenomenon. In traditional societies, social roles were more clearly
defined and opportunities more limited: one's future identity was, to a
far greater extent, spoken for. It was determined by class, gender, birth
order, or the family trade. With the rise of less static and cohesive
social structures came new pressures on identity; it became more fluid
and individually shaped. Members of the middle class had to make
multiple decisions about training and ultimate goals in adolescence
and early adulthood. But how do we form these notions of what we
are capable of and what accomplishment to aim for?

In a rare instance of near unanimity, many psychologists and sociologists, and even some contemporary philosophers, agree that we form
our identity chiefly by interpreting and then appropriating others' responses to us. Erik Erikson, perhaps the most famous psychoanalytic
theorist to study identity, described it in the following way:

Identity formation employs a process of simultaneous reflection and observation, a process . . . by which the individual judges himself in light of what he perceives to be the way which others judge him in comparison to themselves and to a typology significant to them.

A more contemporary psychologist, Diane Bush, defines identity in similar terms:

[Identity] refers to meanings attached to the self by the individual which correspond to the social placement of the individual by others. The creation of identities involves others' reactions to the individual, primarily on the basis of status and role. However, it also includes the individual's appropriations of others' definitions and evaluations of her or him.

This conclusion, that our sense of ourselves is defined by the responses we elicit from others, is not news to the sociology community. The sociological theory of "reflected self-appraisals," articulated by Charles Horton Cooley at the beginning of the twentieth century, posited that, to a large extent, our self-concepts correspond to other people's views of us. Over the years his theory has been refined and elaborated in important ways, but the fundamental observation stands. As the sociologist Morris Rosenberg concluded after reviewing the literature on self-concepts:

The data consistently support the principle of reflected self-appraisal . . . research shows a strong and consistent association between the reflected self and the self-concept that we believe others think of us and our self-concept. If the individual believes others think well of him, then he tends to think well of himself.

Among the various types of evidence confirming or disconfirming a self-hypothesis, probably the most important is interpersonal: others must "legitimate" the individual's role identity if he is to maintain a stable self-concept. We need others, it seems, to define and maintain our sense of ourselves. They apprise us of what they consider our capabilities and characteristics, and we then internalize their assessments, making them our own. In fact, such personal appraisals are so powerful that they can actually override objective evidence. From childhood right up through graduate school, for example, people have been shown to base their assessments of their academic abilities on the perceptions of teachers and parents—even when this assessment is contradicted by hard data such as grades or test scores.

One aspect of the phenomenon of "reflected appraisals" is that recognition by a highly respected person can leave a lifelong imprint. The more a person matters to us, the more important that person's opinion of us is in shaping our self-concept. Many famous people have recalled such fateful moments in their autobiographies—such as the passage quoted earlier from Willa Cather about her defining experience of being encouraged to publish her first newspaper article. But similar incidents occur in many people's lives. A woman artist in her fifties whom I interviewed remembered an odd but powerful experience of this type that set her on her way to becoming a professional artist. When I asked this woman how she had settled on her career, she replied:

> I started drawing horses when I was young. And then in high school I was interested in art. At college I couldn't believe that I could major in something I loved. I remember that I had two famous teachers who influenced me, Anthony Caro and Jules Olitski.
>
> But what I'll never forget is that when I was a freshman a third professor, a painter took me aside and said to me, "You need to know that the life of an artist is very difficult and very lonely." He had only seen a few of my paintings at that point and why he treated me as if I were a potential artist and colleague, I don't know. It was an important moment for me. It meant someone was validating me, was saying, "I see something special in you; I can see that you're an artist." I don't think anyone had ever done that. I'll never forget it.

This memory is particularly striking because the professor's comment was, on the face of it, so discouraging. But despite its gloomy prediction, it contained the respected professor's recognition that the woman was a real artist. And she has remained one to this day.

Such crystallizing moments, when affirmation is received from an esteemed person, are dramatic examples of positive appraisals providing a nidus around which a professional identity can be formed. But it is doubtful that such single episodes alone can create or sustain an identity. Less memorable but more frequent incidents in which recognition is bestowed are required for an identity to evolve over time.

A profile of the actress Dame Judi Dench that appeared in *The New Yorker* gives a sense of the various types and sources of recognition that create and sustain a professional identity. The writer reports that during Dench's childhood, her father served as the official doctor for the Theatre Royal in York. Both parents "took a keen interest in amateur dramatics and, when Dench became an actress, their support verged on the overprotective. They saw their daughter in 'Romeo and Juliet' more than seventy times."

Clearly, the theatrical passions of Dench's parents shaped her childhood ambition to become an actress. But even such avid parental support, in and of itself, cannot sustain a professional identity. If such early backing could leave an indelible influence, we would all unwaveringly pursue the early ambitions our parents cherished for us. Dench, like the artist described earlier, had an experience of recognition from a respected mentor early in her career that helped cement her identity as an actress:

> The turning point in Dench's ambition came during a mime class in her second term [at acting school], when she was required to perform an assignment—called "Recollection"—that she'd completely forgotten to prepare. "I don't remember thinking anything out," she says. "I walked into a garden. I bent down to smell something like rosemary or thyme. . . ." Her teacher, Walter Hudd, gave her, she says, "the most glowing notice I think I've ever had. What is more, he said, 'You looked like a little Renoir doing it.' I thought, Well, I think that I will enjoy what I'm going to do, hopefully get work, go for it."

We may like to believe that once we have gained the inner conviction of our talent and/or competence, we are set for life, that our identity becomes irrevocably internalized and therefore nearly autonomous. But there is little evidence that such self-sufficiency ever occurs. We continue to require and seek evidence that supports our notion of ourselves. Dench notes trenchantly how important her audiences are for her. It's not just the adulation she seeks, but the recognition:

> She claims not to be "good at my own company." Rather, to understand her own identity she needs to be in the attentive gaze of others. . . . Dench is clear on this point. "I need somebody to reflect me back, or to give me their reflection," she says.

With startling honesty, Dench describes her dependence on the audience:

> "I have to hear the audience coming in," she says. "I need to be generated by it—for the jump off. It's like a quickie ignition." Once, an American student asked Dench if the audience made a difference to her; Dench replied, "If it didn't make a difference, I'd be home with me feet up the chimney."

Actors such as Dench are a particularly clear example of an identity supported by recognition. What could be a more straightforward confirmation than applause? But Dench is on to a more universal, if usually more subtle, phenomenon—the continuous redefining and sustaining of our identity by the recognition we receive. As adults we work to elicit recognition to confirm elements of our identity. We try, in Joyce Carol Oates's phrase, to "control others definition of us." Once you start listening for such solicitations, it becomes clear that they are ubiquitous: "Did the boss like my memo?" or "Did our yearly evaluations come in yet?" or "What do you think of my new haircut?" or "Do you think my presentation was effective?"

In every culture, including our own, the economy of recognition is exquisitely defined and regulated; it is the currency of every encounter. We solicit and exchange recognition to sustain our identity in every social context. The philosopher G.W.F. Hegel eloquently described this basic need over a century ago: "Self-consciousness exists in itself and for itself, in that, and by the fact that it exists for another self-consciousness; that is to say it *is* only by being acknowledged or 'recognized.' "

LEARNING

Judi Dench's formative experience of being praised by a mentor occurred at acting school. Acting, like virtually all ambitions, involves learning a skill. Whether the ambition is focused on gourmet cooking, community organizing, or administrative competence, learning is central to its realization. Absorbing a body of information nearly always requires making a conscious effort at mastery, even though some aspects of learning can occur outside our awareness—at times we can absorb information by just observing and copying without being conscious of it. We may watch someone playing tennis on TV and unknowingly adopt the player's ball toss or stance on the court. But there are few areas of mastery where this process alone will suffice; virtually all ambitions require the active, conscious pursuit of relevant knowledge.

As I discussed earlier, scientific evidence indicates that mastery itself is pleasurable. And in keeping with our national obsession with independence, educators tend to focus primarily on this self-motivating aspect of learning. They love to extol the joys of learning for its own sake. Howard Gardner, a professor at the School of Education at Harvard, notes:

> Why are some people motivated to learn, while others are not? . . .
> Researchers now believe that learners are best served when their motivation is intrinsic, when they pursue learning because it is fun or rewarding in itself, rather than because someone has promised them some material benefit.

But he goes on to note that learning has another motivational engine:

> What enhances motivation? Close identification with adults, who may accompany a youngster as he or she broaches a new domain, is also

crucial; youngsters crave the approval of adults whom they love, and these adults can acclimate students to the world of discipline, the dialectic between fun and effort. Certain cultures have long featured a continuous cycle of practice, learning, and public performance.

The cycle that Gardner describes, of learning and then displaying the learning for an appreciative audience, is deeply familiar. We remember it from music lessons that always had an end-of-the-year recital to display our new skills. We recall from it from school, where the children's artwork was put in the halls and students were asked to get up and read their work. The cycle of learning, displaying the new mastery, and then receiving recognition is ubiquitous in educational settings. The recognition received "fuels" the next stage of learning. The early learning theorist Albert Bandura was clear on this point: "Young children imitate accurately when they have incentives to do so, but their imitations deteriorate rapidly if others do not care how they behave."

Research has confirmed that in the overwhelming majority of cases, the acquisition of expertise requires recognition, either as an immediate response or as an expectation for the future. A rare longitudinal study by the renowned psychologist Jerome Kagan looked specifically at this issue. He and his coauthor, Howard Moss, examined the relationship between "the tendency to strive for a mastery of selected skills (achievement behavior) and social recognition through acquisition of specific goals or behaviors." They followed a cohort from childhood through adulthood, and at the end of this massive project concluded:

> The data presented reveal a high, positive correlation between ratings of these two behavioral variables. This interdependence suggests that it may be impossible to measure the "desire to improve a skill" independent of the individual's "desire for social recognition."

Subsequent to the study by Kagan and Moss, other investigations have substantiated their findings; in fact, contemporary learning theories acknowledge the primary, motivating role of recognition. The Columbia University psychologist Carol Dweck and her associates, in their studies of motivation in relation to achievement, have again found an interdependence between the learning process and recognition. She has discovered three major factors that come into play in any sustained effort to achieve: (1) the goal to increase competence [to learn the skill]; (2) the goal to obtain favorable judgment of one's competence [to obtain recognition]; and (3) the goal to avoid unfavorable judgment of one's competence. Capability alone, she points out, is insufficient to produce the vigor and persistence required to learn a skill.

Interestingly, recognition does not have to be verbal. In fact, some of the most powerful affirmations of our efforts are nonverbal: hand-clapping at a recital, a gesture, or a smile. Such responses elicit in us a primitive but profound motivation to continue the approved behaviors. As Charles Darwin noted in one of the earliest studies of the emotions:

> The movements of expression in the face and body, whatever their origin may have been, are in themselves of much importance in our welfare. They serve as the first means of communication between the mother and her infant: she smiles approval, and thus encourages her child on the right path or frowns disapproval.

Darwin's observation of a mother teaching an infant behavior through positive and negative responses foreshadows Dweck's observation of older children who shape their behavior to "obtain favorable judgment and avoid unfavorable judgment."

One of the earliest and most famous studies demonstrating the effect of recognition on learning was carried out by Robert Rosenthal, an eminent sociologist at the University of California, Los Angeles. Rosenthal randomly assigned children in a public school to one of two sets of classes. In half of the classes the teachers were told that they had gifted children or "spurters"; in the others the teachers were told that they had "average" children. By the end of the year, the "spurters" had dramatically improved their scores on IQ tests; the "average" children had scarcely improved at all. Perhaps even more interesting were the teachers' interviews at year's end:

The children from whom intellectual growth was expected were described as having a better chance of being successful in later life and as being happier, more curious, and more interesting than the other children. There was also a tendency for the designated children to be seen as more appealing, better adjusted and more affectionate, and as less in need of social approval. In short, the children for whom intellectual growth was expected became more alive and autonomous intellectually, or at least were so perceived by their teachers.

After looking at several possible factors that might have influenced this outcome, the authors concluded:

> The explanation we are seeking lies in a subtler feature of the interaction of the teacher and her pupils. Her tone of voice, facial expressions, touch and posture may be the means by which—probably quite unwittingly—she communicates. . . . Such communication might help the child by changing his conception of himself, his anticipation of his own behavior, his motivation or his cognitive skills.

One of the most brilliant aspects of this experiment was that the teachers' recognition of the children's talents was sincere; they were not making a conscious effort to praise the children—they truly believed in their own positive appraisals of the "spurters" and conveyed them to the children. Someone who convincingly affirms one's efforts and predicts future admirable accomplishments creates a self-fulfilling prophecy. By year's end the "spurters'" IQs had shot up while those of the controls had not. The recognition received by the "spurters" had intensified their efforts at mastery.

MOTIVATION TO PURSUE AMBITIONS IN ADULTHOOD

> To feel that we are taken no notice of, necessarily damps the most agreeable hope, and disappoints the most ardent desire of human nature.
>
> —ADAM SMITH, *The Theory of Moral Sentiments*

Why make art? Because there's a child's voice in every artist saying: "I am here. I am somebody. I made this. Won't you look" ...
What is it about people that, since the dawn of time, we've
wanted to mark our presence so that other people will see us?
                    —CHUCK CLOSE, interview in *The New York Times*

In keeping with our cultural preference for adult autonomy, researchers in achievement behavior have tried mightily to divorce accomplishment from the pursuit of recognition. The psychologist David
McClelland, perhaps the preeminent early researcher of motivation, is
a typical case. His work used male undergraduates and looked at their
responses to Thematic Apperception Tests (TATs), cards showing ambiguous scenes about which his subjects were invited to create stories.
McClelland's work, in the 1970s and 1980s, asserted that achievement
motivation can exist wholly independent of the motivation to receive
recognition:

> The goal . . . is to feel powerful and influencing others is only one of
> the many ways of feeling powerful. When a man collects trophies or
> prestige possessions, why must we assume that he must do so to
> impress other people? Why not accept the simple fact that sometimes
> he enjoys being surrounded by his possessions and feeling the power
> they convey to him, even when others are not around?

But to say that trophies, in and of themselves, convey power begs
the question: powerful to whom or over whom? one might ask. Power
exists nearly exclusively in relation to other people. Trophies, to use
McClelland's example, are the tangible symbol of prior competitive
relationships: one has been recognized for a performance superior to
that of others.

McClelland's own research belied his theory. Joseph Verhoff, another
important motivational researcher, inadvertently exposed these contradictions in McClelland's work. Verhoff approvingly paraphrased
McClelland's definition of the achievement-motivated person as one
for whom "the social world makes itself felt only in the original learn-

ing of or adaptation to norms of excellence." Presumably, after this initial learning phase we rely primarily on self-evaluations. According to Verhoff, settings in which no external recognition is provided "still motivate an achievement-oriented person." Later in the same essay on McClelland, however, Verhoff noted:

> An interesting result is that men who have high achievement motives are more likely to be in jobs that are supervised than in jobs that permit them to be autonomous. On the face of it, this seemed like a surprising result. With deeper reflection, one can suggest that men whose achievement orientations are high enjoy being in jobs that give them feedback about their performance. McClelland long ago saw feedback for performance as critical to maintaining an achievement orientation in the work setting.

Achievement and ongoing recognition seem to be inextricably joined even in McClelland's own research findings.

In truth, no evidence supports the notion of the autonomous individual willing to pursue an ambition for its own sake, in the absence of ongoing affirmation or hope of future recognition. Even the treasured cultural cliché of the lone genius doesn't bear up to scrutiny. Read the biography of any such hero of "Mythic Individualism," to use the sociologist Robert Bellah's phrase, and you will find a social structure that provides affirmation. It may be a single passionate advocate, or a small appreciative community, or a massive public, but it is present. In fact, it's often instructive to look at the innovative and often painstaking ways that such sources of recognition are assembled. For women, in particular, there is often a virtually desperate ingenuity in their creation of such structures.

Emily Dickinson was perhaps as isolated an individual of her stature as ever existed. Barely published in her lifetime, removed from the larger world in her family home in Amherst, a social recluse, Dickinson nonetheless assiduously collected a series of mentors to whom she referred as her tutors, preceptors, or masters. Despite her eccentric and modest mien, she was a woman of large ambition who discussed with family members the possibility that she might one day be a great poet. She was keenly aware that she could not do this alone.

Her earliest mentor, Ben Newton, was the first person outside her family to recognize her talent and, even more important, to see her as a poet. She met him in her teens when he was a law student in her father's office, and they shared a love of poetry. Little is known about the extent of their literary communication, but his belief in her had a lifelong impact. After his early death, Dickinson recalled him as a crucial supporter: "My dying Tutor told me that he would like to live till I had been a poet."

Thomas Wentworth Higginson, a well-known writer of his day, was arguably Dickinson's most important and long-lasting "preceptor." It is fascinating to see how this painfully shy but determined young woman seized upon a total stranger and fashioned him into her literary mentor—almost against his will. She had read an article of his in an 1862 issue of *The Atlantic Monthly* called "Letter to a Young Contributor" and was encouraged enough by his attitude toward young writers to send him some of her poems. They corresponded briefly, but then Higginson apparently urged her to find a friend to help her with her poems. Dickinson, undeterred, wrote him back a masterly letter— seemingly meek but in fact rather firm. She wouldn't take no for an answer:

> Would you have time to be the "friend" you should think I need? I have a little shape—it would not crowd your Desk—nor make much of a Racket as the Mouse. . . . The "hand you stretched to me in the Dark," I put mine in.

The letter concluded, "But will you be my Preceptor, Mr. Higginson?"

Higginson did reluctantly become *the* major literary support in her life. Dickinson was acutely aware of how desperately she needed his presence as a person to whom and for whom she could write. In her inimitable way she described, in one letter, the impact of his praise of a poem she had sent to him: "Your letter gave no drunkenness, because I tasted Rum before. . . . I have had few pleasures so deep as your opin-

ion, and if I tried to thank you, my tears would block my tongue."
Dickinson later told Higginson that he had saved her life.

In my own field of psychiatry Sigmund Freud is often held up as an
example of a genius who persevered despite rejection by his professional community that lasted many years. And to a large extent this
story is true. How did he survive and continue to create new works?
Early in his career he found an eminent mentor, Josef Breuer, with
whom he worked. But as his theories diverged further and further from
those of Breuer, their difference precipitated a personal and professional break. Freud, whose theories were not well accepted by the academic community, worked assiduously to find colleagues to recognize
his contributions.

For many years during this period of relative isolation, Freud depended heavily on an intense friendship with an eccentric Berlin physician named Wilhelm Fliess. Freud was deeply dependent on Fliess's
approval and encouragement and wrote voluminously to Fleiss, con-
fiding his ideas. As Freud himself said, Fliess's praise of him was "nectar and ambrosia." As one reads Freud's letters and writings to Fliess,
the massive affirmation he needs in order to remain productive is
starkly evident. To some extent Freud internalized Fliess's affirmation
and noted that he was "a friend whose sympathy I remember with
satisfaction whenever I feel isolated in my opinions." But memories
would take Freud only part of the way—the immediate presence of his
enthusiastic colleague was a more powerful motivator. In a typical letter he wrote:

> In general I miss you badly. Am I really the same person who was over-
> flowing with ideas and projects as long as you were within reach?
> When I sit down at my desk in the evening, I often don't know what I
> should work on.

Over time Freud, by sheer dint of will, created an admiring, appreciative
group of supporters. But whenever he lost any member of this group,
such as Carl Jung, he became despondent and deeply discouraged.

Not until 1909 did Freud finally receive acceptance by the academic
community. He was given an honorary degree at Clark University in

Massachusetts and presented a series of talks on psychoanalysis. Ernest Jones, in his early biography of Freud, noted that Freud was visibly moved as he delivered the first sentence of his speech: "This is the first official recognition of our endeavors."

RECOGNITION AND PRODUCTIVITY

The psychological community has long been invested in the notion that early experience shapes individuals' subsequent motivations. (McClelland actually did a large study on the impact of a person's toilet training on his adult earning capacity.) Clinical psychologists in particular have been loath to acknowledge our continuing dependence on affirmation. But there is one field—a much more pragmatic and less theoretically hidebound one—on which the powerful effect of recognition on motivation has not been lost. In our capitalist system practical information often trumps ideology, and the business world has learned to do its own research into motivation and productivity. The field is called occupational behavior, or OB for short. OB research focuses specifically on work behaviors. Its mandate is unusually clear and outcome oriented: maximize productivity. Productivity is an end point that may not be inspiring, but in terms of pure science it is concrete and measurable.

As I began to look into this research literature, an undeniable trend emerged. During the course of the twentieth century occupational behaviorists moved from theories like those of Frederick Taylor, who saw people as economically motivated and rational in their efforts to optimize their gains, to theories in which complex social factors— especially recognition—play a huge and often determining role.

The Hawthorne experiments in the 1920s, one of the most surprising and influential series of psychological studies ever done, overthrew the accepted contemporary theories. These famous experiments, originally designed to determine what kind of working conditions maximized productivity, were carried out at the Western Electric Company's Hawthorne Works in Chicago. Variables for the study included physical parameters such as number of hours worked, number of rest periods, and lighting. A group of women factory workers was asked to perform their jobs in a specially designed environment. At certain intervals the experimental variables were changed: lighting would be increased or decreased, noise level would be reduced or heightened. All this occurred under the close scrutiny of the researchers.

To the chagrin of the investigators, *every* change in work conditions, for better or for worse, increased output. Factors totally unrelated to physical work conditions played the determining role in motivating these workers. Much speculation, experimentation, and criticism of the original study ensued, but certain conclusions eventually came to be widely accepted. Morale had been extremely high in this cohort of women workers; according to a popular OB text, the women "perceived themselves as special and important to management because they were singled out for this research role." The powerful effect of interest and responsiveness from management and researchers was entirely unexpected. It had an enormous impact on subsequent research and became known as the Hawthorne Effect. As Robert Rosenthal summarized the research:

> It soon became evident that the significant thing was not whether the worker had more or less light, but merely that she was the subject of attention. Any changes that involved her, and even actions that she only thought were changes, were likely to improve her performance.

Rosenthal might have added that it was not just attention but real interest in their opinions and productivity that the women experienced. It has been shown that negative attention—punishment or disapproval, for example—does not have the same effect.

Since this set of experiments was conducted, nearly all OB theories embrace recognition as a powerful motivator in the workplace. An article in the *Harvard Business Review* that reviewed the data from twelve important studies of motivation put achievement and recognition in first and second place, respectively, as motivators. Financial remuneration came in a distant eleventh. Rosabeth Moss Kanter, a professor at Harvard Business School, in her groundbreaking book *Men and Women of the Corporation,* quotes a senior executive casually remarking, "Money is not a motivator, anyway. It's just a way for the company to cut its losses by insuring that people do their job at all. The reward we really control is the ability to promote."

Businesses have learned this lesson well. They quickly picked up on the fact that recognition (which is relatively cheap to provide) works as or more effectively than costly incentives involving perks or monetary rewards. When Jack Welch, the ex-CEO of General Electric who is credited with making GE the most valued corporation in the world, was asked on public television to describe "the values, the concepts that have guided [him]," he replied without hesitation:

> That every person counts, that you've got to work your tail off to involve everyone in the game, use all kinds of techniques—management awards, celebrations, parties, fun. Create an atmosphere where everybody counts, and they know they count. . . . We celebrate the ideas. We publish them. We put them on line. We tell people.

This is not a new insight. Most corporations understand the huge motivational power of recognition and have institutionalized it. They have employee recognition programs, service awards, clear promotion incentives, and even employee appreciation days. Valued employees are written up in the company newsletters and sent on expensive vacations. One time several years ago I tried to order flowers for a sick friend, only to be told by multiple florists that I would have to wait twenty-four hours. It was Secretaries' Day, and there wasn't a rose or daisy to be found in Manhattan.

MOOD AND RECOGNITION

> The looking glass vision is of supreme importance because it charges the vitality: it stimulates the nervous system.
> —VIRGINIA WOOLF, *A Room of One's Own*

The emotions are mechanisms that set the brain's highest goals. Once triggered by a propitious moment, an emotion triggers

the cascade of subgoals and sub-subgoals that we call thinking
and acting.

    —STEVEN PINKER, *How the Mind Works*

Mood isn't usually mentioned in discussions of ambition, yet the qualities required for pursuing an ambition are intimately linked to mood.
At the least, normal levels of energy, concentration, optimism, social
confidence, as well as assertiveness and a sense of capability are all required to pursue an ambition. Depression characteristically produces
the opposite qualities, making it virtually impossible to realize an
ambition; typical symptoms of depression include fatigue, disturbed
concentration, harsh self-criticism, introversion, pessimism, and low
self-esteem. In the past such affective qualities were thought of as long-
term phenomena, extending over weeks or even a lifetime. We believed
that the brain chemistry was "set" either genetically or by early repetitive experiences. And to some extent we were correct; moods can
unquestionably be chronic or cyclic over extended periods of time, and
these patterns do have genetic and environmental determinants.

    But over the last several decades a new phenomenon has come to be
appreciated. The levels of neurotransmitters that regulate mood are
exquisitely sensitive to social feedback, and their fluctuations can produce transient but powerful mood changes. Such transmitters can soar
or plummet minute by minute in response to events in the environment, particularly interpersonal events. Levels of serotonin, adrenaline,
dopamine, cortisol, oxytocin, vasopressin, and testosterone, to name a
few, fluctuate dramatically in response to social context.

    Blood levels of testosterone, for example, plunge when men are
placed in low-status positions, such as recruits in a boot camp, but
they go up in competitive situations and in dangerous environments.
Testosterone decreases when men are in happy marriages. Oxytocin
and vasopressin, hormones produced in the brain that effect feelings of
empathy and attachment, are stimulated by face-to-face social interactions. Such encounters, unless they are threatening, can reduce the
levels of other hormones that act on the brain, such as cortisol, epi-

nephrine, and norepinephrine. Many of our day-to-day experiences confirm these findings. We're all familiar with phrases that express such brief, reactive emotional states: being "pumped up," "turned on," "keyed up." An encounter can either "bum us out" or make us feel so good that we're "psyched." One evening when I had just begun to research this subject, I heard a particularly vivid description of the phenomenon of mood elevation in response to positive social feedback. I was watching MTV with my daughter, and a rock star was being interviewed about performing for crowds of fans. "It's the most amazing rush you can imagine," he said. "I've taken a lot of drugs, but none can compare with this. It's an unbelievable high." I suspect that the sensation the rock star was describing resulted from an outpouring of mood-enhancing neurotransmitters. In fact, it would be hard to come up with an alternative explanation.

Of the multitude of neurotransmitters now recognized, serotonin appears to be the one most exquisitely responsive to social affirmation. Serotonin is a neurotransmitter that, as Peter Kramer pointed out in his influential *Listening to Prozac*, "enhances security, courage, assertiveness, self-worth, calm, flexibility, resilience." In experiments with primates in which the social milieu can be easily manipulated, a monkey's brain level of serotonin can be quickly elevated or depressed by placing it in different animal groupings. Prior to achieving dominance, a male monkey's serotonin level will be unexceptional. If the monkey then receives submissive behavior from surrounding monkeys, the blood serotonin level will dramatically rise. Taking a dominant male away from subordinate males and housing him with several females will cause the levels of his brain serotonin to fall.

The admittedly preliminary information available suggests that similar reactions to social responses occur in humans. It is probable that in humans, too, social affirmation translates into the production of mood-elevating neurotransmitters; again, the most likely candidate for such a neurotransmitter is serotonin. Studies of college students living in fraternities show that those who were elected officers of the organization or were deemed "team leaders" by their peers had higher serotonin levels—findings similar to those in their simian relatives. Low status appears to engender low serotonin levels. Robert Wright, a writer and well-known proponent of evolutionary psychology, summarized the new findings about the reactive nature of this neurotransmitter: "Self-esteem (read serotonin) keeps rising as long as one encounters social success, and each step in this elevation inclines one to raise one's sights a little higher."

Evidence that social affirmation raises the level of neurotransmitters that enhance mood also comes from research in clinical psychology. Certain types of interactions between patient and therapist are as effective as medication in the treatment of mild to moderate depression. The most heavily documented results involve a process called interpersonal therapy (IPT). IPT is a down-to-earth intervention in which the therapist sympathetically focuses with the patient on one of four possible problematic areas in the patient's life. The therapy lasts for a limited number of sessions. Not only does this process improve mood, it produces observable changes in the brain. Single-photon emission computed tomography (SPECT) scans of the brain show that following IPT, several areas of the brain become more metabolically active—presumably by producing more neurotransmitters, which in turn increase neuronal activity. The changes are similar to those seen after the use of an antidepressant.

Although proponents of IPT would like to attribute its positive effects on mood to the specific technique involved, little evidence supports this assumption. To the dismay of the therapeutic community, outcome studies show that the technique used in therapy, whether it is psychoanalytic, cognitive-behavioral, IPT, or any other type, appears to be largely irrelevant. As Donald Klein, an eminent contemporary psychiatric researcher, has concluded after reviewing therapeutic outcome studies:

> When you go through the psychotherapy literature, the standard thing that you find when you compare two psychotherapies is that there isn't any difference. It's hard to find differences between psychotherapies. If they have entirely different frameworks of reference and theory, why are they getting the same sort of results unless it's the com-

mon feature of psychotherapy that's responsible for whatever benefits they're getting?

In other words, some recurring element in the intense relationship established in all psychotherapies accounts for its effectiveness. Klein, quoting Jerome Frank, dubs it the "antidemoralization factor." As best we can tell at present, this factor is based on the therapist's developing a detailed understanding of the patient that feels accurate and affirming— in other words, recognition. Patient-therapist rapport has been singled out both in patient reports and in objective outcome measures as having the single largest impact on positive therapeutic results. Clearly such an "antidemoralization" factor would have a large impact on the pursuit of any goal.

One day I was discussing some of these findings with a well-known researcher in the field of depression when he burst out laughing and told me the following story. During a recent antidepressant trial he had collaborated with numerous psychiatrists, among them a colleague whom we both knew and disliked. The psychiatrist, George, is a rather self-important man whose thin veneer of bonhomie poorly disguises his underlying coldness. When the researcher was reviewing his data from the study, he found that the antidepressant had clearly been more effective than the placebo. But then, out of curiosity, he decided to break out the data to look at each individual therapist's record of patient response. He discovered that none of George's patients had gotten better, while all of his own patients had shown a positive response. His research team began to joke about patients who got "Georged"— that is, whose antidepressant response was nearly negated by the presence of this unpleasant man. The researcher concluded that combining an antidepressant with an interaction with a responsive, attentive doctor maximized the antidepressant effect. On the other hand, a patient seen by someone who was clearly indifferent got "Georged." The quality of the relationship was a powerful mood-altering factor, even in combination with medication.

The interactions between a therapist and a patient, like virtually all social encounters, cause changes in brain chemistry. In some cases such alterations are small and transient; in others they are more significant. Responses to social interactions are now known to occur at the deepest biological level, namely gene activation. Social feedback constantly reconfigures the expression of our DNA. As Erik Kandel, the Nobel Prize–winning neurophysiologist, has stated:

> Learning, including learning that results in dysfunctional behavior, produces alterations in gene expression. Thus all of "nurture" is ultimately expressed as "nature." . . . The regulation of gene expression by social factors makes all bodily functions, including all functions of the brain, susceptible to social influences. These social influences will be biologically incorporated in the altered expressions of specific genes in specific nerve cells of specific areas of the brain.

In other words, our social encounters transform us at the most basic biological level.

If, as the evidence suggests, recognition increases the production of energizing, focusing, confidence-enhancing neurotransmitters, many apparently disparate findings fall into place. It explains why recognition promotes learning. It explains the finding of the OB researchers that recognition increases productivity. We sustain effort on projects that maximize present or future affirmation.

If recognition directly enhances mood, it also explains why people are willing to pursue high-recognition careers such as acting or dancing with very little financial reward. In fact, it sometimes seems that the entire waiter and waitress population of New York City consists of such would-be performers. You could almost create a mathematical equation to express this phenomenon. It would be an inverse ratio: the higher the direct recognition a type of work provides, the lower the pay demanded by people in the field (unless they are among the super-famous). Writers, dancers, musicians, poets, artists, journalists, and actors are not, by and large, at the top of the wage scale. It's hard to picture accountants or doctors or lawyers pursuing their jobs while waiting tables. People in more traditional careers usually receive less direct and less public recognition. In recompense, they receive a greater portion of the indirect, impersonal, and generic form of recognition provided by society—namely money.

We can now begin to imagine the impact of being placed in a low-recognition position in society. In terms of the economy of recognition, the rich get richer while the poor get poorer. Those who have received recognition can sustain the effort required to pursue their interests successfully; this in turn leads to more recognition and increases their feelings of self-worth and capability. Furthermore, they are motivated by the realistic expectation, based on prior experience, that future efforts will indeed produce additional recognition. As in the Rosenthal experiment with schoolchildren, if you are perceived as talented and bright and motivated, you actually become more talented and bright and motivated.

Even if we reserve judgment on the preliminary evidence that recognition enhances the production of specific neurotransmitters, the general impact of recognition is firmly established. Sociologists, learning theorists, clinical psychologists, research psychologists, and the business community all independently acknowledge that recognition is key to learning, motivation, productivity, and sense of identity. Without it there can be no goals set and no sustained effort at a task. In the family, at work, at school, and in therapy, recognition is formative and enlivening. It is the motivational engine that allows one to develop the mastery required to pursue an ambition. Ambitions are at first the product and then, later, the source of this profoundly animating and defining response.

DEVELOPING RELIABLE SOURCES OF AFFIRMATION

The acceptance by these audiences may have done something for me in another way. It may be that they made me feel that I need not be cautious with such things as Lieder, and it is possible that I sang with a freedom I had not had before. I know I felt this acceptance provided the basis for daring to pour out reserves of feeling I had not called upon.

—MARIAN ANDERSON, *My Lord, What a Morning*

Finding structures that provide recognition based on talent, skill, or hard work—rather than on appearance, sexual availability, or subservience—is a major goal of ambitions. The stability and quality of such structures are important determinants of the satisfaction a given life provides.

If we use this vantage point to examine women's choices, a certain logic begins to emerge. The situations of Alice and Katherine, the two women lawyers I described in the introduction, are more easily understood. Both women enjoyed and had a talent for legal work, and both were in stable, long-term relationships. Yet Alice was so discouraged that she was thinking of quitting her job without any other goal, while Katherine was enlarging her ambitions; she was considering starting a new type of law-media company. In terms of the social structures each had available to provide recognition, their lives were in fact profoundly different. Alice, despite her excellent legal work, was seen chiefly as a confidante by her boss, as an inadequate mate by her fiancé, and as a threatening competitor (and potential target of sexual slurs) by her colleagues. It's hardly a surprise that her legal ambitions withered. She had no intact sphere of affirmation in any area of her life. She was running on empty.

Katherine, on the other hand, was reliably receiving recognition in a multiplicity of such areas. She had found a type of legal expertise in which her work was admired and sought after by her colleagues. Her husband, a lawyer who longed to be an entrepreneur, was enthusiastically pushing her to go out on her own—with him as a business partner. She had been elected to the steering committee of the communications arm of a national professional organization. Her work was providing her with recognition from multiple sources and even new social structures within which she was valued. The reason seems obvious in retrospect, but it was not obvious to either lawyer at the time: the focus of our discussions was their choice of the legal profession per se as the determining factor in their lives.

I do not mean to minimize the impact that the legal profession can have on women's access to well-earned recognition. There is ample documentation that the legal profession makes itself inhospitable to women. But we can learn from the two women lawyers a way to assess in advance the likely outcomes of our choices. If women are to thrive, we must identify, critically assess, and purposefully develop situations that can provide sustaining affirmation—spheres of recognition. If we have no opportunities for appropriate support, we have to acknowledge this and find other venues. The situation is not only a dead end but one that will engender painful and unnecessary self-doubt.

Women who work in the home, no less than those with professions, require appreciation of their skills. A woman can be in a stable, extended family and function as a respected, productive member of her local school, zoning board, church, or political party. She may be recognized for a multitude of contributions and talents by her husband, family, and community members. Another homemaker will have recently moved to the suburbs, have a husband who travels extensively for work, and have two preschool tots who absorb every minute of her day. It comes as no surprise that in our country, where most families move approximately every five years, the demographic group most vulnerable to depression is housewives with small children.

Our lives in contemporary society nearly always contain a multiplicity of dissimilar social contexts in which we are appreciated for different qualities or accomplishments. When I go to my son's school, I am correctly seen as a mom with a certain set of concerns about school programs, summer camps, or chaperones at school dances. At work I am seen as a psychiatrist. To my editor, I am a writer. At home I function as a wife and mother. In many lives such a multiplicity of roles may be necessary, since all the traditional sources of recognition in our society—marriage, family, job, geographical community—are highly unstable. A marriage can end in divorce, a job can be terminated by downsizing, a community can be lost by job relocation, grown children can move far away.

In our highly fluid society, a multiplicity of social structures can help buffer the uncertainty. But this is not the only successful model. If a single source of recognition has great depth and dependability, diverse roles may be unneeded. During my medical training I met a single sixty-year-old geneticist who spent twelve hours a day in her large lab and functioned there as a kind of materfamilias. She not only headed up the highly regarded research laboratory but also had a weekly brunch and musicale at her house for students, colleagues, and neighbors. This woman intensely enjoyed her life and had no need for a variety of social roles.

Because sociologists have failed to factor in the impact of recognition, their debate about the effects of multiple roles on women's lives has been protracted and ultimately unproductive. Some back the "role accumulation" theory, which posits that having many roles provides "privileges, resources, and enhancement of self-concept." "Role conflict" theorists, by contrast, believe that having multiple roles leads to conflicting demands and debilitating stress. Both theories are undoubtedly true in specific circumstances. But by ignoring the availability of recognition provided by various roles, the investigators have missed the unifying principle. A woman can have many gratifying roles and thrive (like Katherine) or have multiple roles and be miserable (like Alice). Or she can have a single, unconflicted role and find life boring and miserable—like the housewives described by Betty Friedan in *The Feminine Mystique* who suffered from "the problem that has no name." Or she can have a single, deeply gratifying role, as the geneticist did.

Women who do not formulate life plans that are supported by appreciative communities pay a steep price. They often fail to understand why, in the absence of such affirmation, they feel unmotivated and demoralized. They blame it on their lack of discipline or character or talent. But if sources of recognition are unavailable or inadequate or outside a woman's control, the chances are dim that she will thrive in her chosen enterprise.

CHAPTER SIX

UNEQUAL REWARDS

Nor am I Robinson Crusoe alone on my island . . . some, perhaps all, of my ideas about myself, in particular my sense of my own moral and social identity, are intelligible only in terms of the social network in which I am . . . an element. The lack of freedom about which men or groups complain amounts, as often as not, to the lack of proper recognition.

—ISAIAH BERLIN, "Two Concepts of Liberty"

We define ourselves and our capabilities by the recognition that we receive from others. Recognition motivates us to learn and to work harder; it energizes and concentrates our efforts. Without it, our ambitions fade. Yet there is ample documentation that girls get less recognition than boys and that women get less recognition than men—even when the behaviors, words, math solutions, papers, grades, paintings, books, performances, scientific data, business accomplishments, or even phone messages left by females are identical to those of male peers. A deep and pervasive cultural prejudice leads to the reflex bestowing of recognition on males and a largely unconscious withholding of recognition from females in all but the sexual sphere—where it is complementary to male needs.

Most women learn to expect and even assent to this unequal distribution of recognition. In fact, it is so pervasive and ingrained that it comes to feel "normal" even for women who are aware of the problem. One scientist, however, had an opportunity to see this disparity from a fresh vantage point, unburdened by past socialization as a female. Dr. Jonathan Roughgarden, one of the world's most important theoretical

ecologists, decided in 1998 to have a sex-change operation and become Dr. Joan Roughgarden. As Jonathan he had felt himself to be
transsexual, but his colleagues had perceived him as the "quintessentially macho academic: aggressive, abrasive, and competitive," according to an interview in *The New York Times*. Jonathan was extremely
influential and highly respected in his field. Joan, however, discovered
that, unbeknownst to her, her professional status also underwent a sex
change: she insists that she is in many ways entirely unchanged, yet she
acknowledges that life as a woman is quite different.

> "At first I was amused," Dr. Roughgarden said, describing how she is
> now much more frequently interrupted, ignored, and condescended to
> by men, particularly those who did not know her as Jonathan. "I
> thought, if women are discriminated against, then I'm darn well going
> to be discriminated against the same way. Well, the thrill of that's
> worn off, I can tell you."

Dr. Roughgarden's experience is an unusually vivid example of a
widespread phenomenon. The inequality of recognition allotted to
males compared to females of equal accomplishment has been massively documented, and the findings are consistent. I will give only a
short tour of the research on different age groups; it provides a rather
bleak, if straightforward tale.

In preschool, between ages three and five, the differential in positive
attention received by boys and girls is already pronounced. In a typical
study of fifteen coed preschool classrooms, investigators found that
"all 15 of the teachers gave more attention to boys. . . . They got both
more physical and verbal rewards. Boys also received more direction
from the teachers and were twice as likely as the girls to get individual
instruction on how to do things." As one researcher summarized the
data: "Nursery school classroom teachers are much less likely to react
to a girl's behavior, whether appropriate or not, than a boy's. The girls'
actions have considerably less effect on their environment, at least in
terms of adult reactions."

In grammar school, where one might assume that the girls' higher
verbal skills would serve them well, girls continue to receive fewer

positive responses from teachers. One three-year project looked at more than a hundred fourth-, sixth-, and eighth-grade classrooms in four states and the District of Columbia. The teachers and students were male and female, black and white, from urban, rural, and suburban communities. The conclusion: "Teachers praise boys more than girls, give boys more academic help and are more likely to accept boys' comments during classroom discussions. . . . Teachers behave differently, depending on whether boys or girls call out answers during discussions. When boys call out comments without raising their hands, teachers accept their answers. However, when girls call out, teachers reprimand their 'inappropriate behavior. . . .' Boys receive more teacher attention, as well as more precise and dynamic feedback."

In a telling follow-up to this study, the investigators showed videotapes of the teachers' classroom discussions to teachers and administrators at the participating schools and asked them to estimate who was talking more, the girls or the boys. "The teachers overwhelmingly said that the girls were, but in reality, the boys in the film were out-talking the girls at a ratio of three to one. Even educators who were active in feminist issues were unable to spot the sex bias until they counted and coded who was talking and who was just watching."

Not only do teachers give more attention to the boys in their classes, they actively withhold positive feedback from girls who achieve academically—again, undoubtedly without any consciousness of what they are doing. In a study of fifth and sixth graders, "the teachers switched from positive ratings of task-oriented girls in the fall to negative ratings in the spring on such dimensions as how much they liked the student. Apparently such behavior by girls resulted in a withdrawal of reinforcement by the teachers. Social work among bright girls, by contrast, was associated with positive ratings by the teachers suggesting that teachers reinforce achievement orientations if they were evidenced in a social context, but reacted negatively to female task orientation that did not have a social component. This pattern did not occur for boys." A different study found that high-achievement boys (as judged by teachers) and low-achievement girls received the most attention from teachers, with high-achieving girls receiving the least attention.

A more detailed investigation of coed classrooms singled out and quantified four types of teacher response: praise, acceptance, remediation, or criticism. The findings were unambiguous: "Boys received more of all four, but the difference favoring boys was greatest in the more useful and directive reactions of praise, criticism and remediation." Another group of researchers reported that "teachers initiate 10% more communications with boys in the classroom. . . . Teachers ask boys more complex, abstract, and open-ended questions, which provide better opportunities for active learning. Teachers are more likely to give detailed instructions to boys and more likely to take over and finish the task for girls."

In high school the pattern of encouraging active learning in boys, but not in girls, becomes more pronounced, particularly in math and the sciences. As has frequently been noted, girls and boys enter high school with similar math achievement, but by senior year boys outperform girls in every math category. A typical study of a high school math class, this one reported in the *Harvard Education Letter,* concluded that "although the girls studying geometry took more initiative in class, teachers directed most of their questions and comments to boys and more often encouraged boys to persist when they answered incorrectly." In another study of teacher responses to students in high school math classes, researchers found that girls received only 30 percent of encouraging comments but 84 percent of discouraging comments.

Let's say that an eager young woman, undeterred by her prior discouraging academic experiences, now proceeds to college. What is her experience likely to be? In the late 1980s a women's college, in the process of becoming coed, set up a Teaching and Learning Project that videotaped and analyzed classes in order to "make sure that the quality of the women's education would not be affected." Let me quote the abstract summarizing the paper:

> Do men get more for their money than women when they invest four years and tens of thousands of dollars in a college education? Close examination of videotapes of classroom interactions reveals that they generally do. For example, men are more likely than women to get the attention of faculty members. . . . Should a teacher choose a first vol-

unteer to answer a question (as often happens), that student will most likely be male. Moreover, the videotapes disclose that men talk at greater length, interrupt others more, and are less subject to interruptions themselves. Men also adopt a challenging, sometimes abrasive style, which may elicit responses from other men but silences most women. Tacit collaboration of faculty members permits men to dominate class discussions disproportionately to their numbers. Additionally, men's contributions appear to be taken more seriously than women's.

Further along in the paper, more descriptive material is given: in one class, "one of the males contributed 12 times the per capita allotment of class time or three times more than the dominant female." In another class the males talked approximately two minutes apiece, while the women spoke for only forty-four seconds. In one woman professor's class, "[W]hen the students were giving oral presentations, all of the women stayed at their seats, but each of the men got up, walked to the front of the room, used the board, used the map, and moved me [the professor] out of the way." But aggressive, entitled male peers are only part of the problem. Multiple studies show that men faculty tend to "affirm students of their own sex more than students of the other sex, and often perceive women students primarily as sexual beings who are less capable and less serious than men students."

And so on to graduate school, where "there is evidence that women students receive lower rewards and receive less encouragement. As graduate students, they are more likely to be teaching assistants rather than research assistants, as compared to men, and receive on the average, less financial support."

When women leave graduate school and enter the job market "they are hired in lower-level jobs and are paid less than their male peers. . . . Male job applicants tend to be selected more frequently than equally qualified females for managerial, scientific and semi-skilled positions. . . . The same pattern of results has been found among the supposedly more enlightened population of college and university chairpersons."

Multiple studies have looked at the effect of gender on evaluations in the work environment. Here is a summary from one typical investigation:

> Two groups of people were asked to evaluate particular items, such as articles, paintings, resumes, and the like. The names attached to the items given each group of evaluators were clearly either male or female, but reversed for each group—that is, what one group believed was originated by a man, the other believed was originated by a woman. Regardless of the items, when they were ascribed to a man, they were rated higher than when they were ascribed to a woman. In all of these studies, women evaluators were as likely as men to downgrade those items ascribed to women.

Finally, a study gives a vivid sense of what it feels like to be at the receiving end of this gendered recognition system. The men and women researchers took turns assuming leader and nonleader roles with subjects performing a problem-solving task. The researchers found that no matter which role the woman took,

> [T]he trained females received a greater number of negative facial reactions than positive ones. The trained males, by contrast, always received more positive ones. . . . When women [were] assertive and acted as leaders the negative reactions outnumbered the positive ones; women end up with a net loss. . . . The naive participants [the subjects] paid less attention to the women than the men; for example, they made fewer facial reactions to the women per minute of talking time.

The studies could hardly be clearer: the entire texture of women's lives is permeated with small events of nonrecognition. My favorite is one that shows that men lose interest in a taped phone message if it is spoken in a woman's rather than a man's voice. As one woman executive said to me, "I often feel at work like I'm behind a scrim. I'm in the room, but in a slightly faded out, removed kind of way."

The recognition differential is ubiquitous, even in my own liberal, gender-conscious profession. I was surprised to find it in a letter from a female psychiatrist printed in *The Psychiatric News*, a journal sent to psychiatrists by their professional organization, the American Psychiatric Association. The journal issue referred to in the letter is one that I had read with no conscious awareness of the problem described. Here is the letter:

> The 3 July issue provides an interesting illustration of how the APA [American Psychiatric Association] portrays women. In the entire 48-page issue, the only picture of a woman psychiatrist (page 12) occurs with her 7-month-old baby, both of whom had attended the meeting. Group pictures of non-psychiatrist women show women as wife, mother, APA staff member, musician, judge, spectator, demonstrator, and mother to quintuplets conceived through IVF....
>
> There are no pictures of individual women while there are 12 of men (and a total of 32 pictures of identifiable men). Women are better represented in the large advertisement pictures, where six adult women and two girls extol the benefits of Prozac, Luvox, Zoloft, or Effexor for depression and obsessive-compulsive disorder (pages 9, 14, 23–25, 33) so the child can "get mommy back."

The example may seem mundane, but one can only wonder at the long-term impact of these images—or lack of images.

CHAPTER SEVEN

PSEUDO-RECOGNITION:
HISTORICAL AND CONTEMPORARY

Women's longings for mastery and affirmation have always persisted—not surprisingly, since they constitute fundamental human needs. Right up through the nineteenth century, women pushed to the limits the few areas of expertise that were open to them. Domestic chores such as quilt-making, cooking, letter-writing, gardening, needlework, and weaving were elevated to art forms. Skills that were deemed inappropriate for men were seized upon: midwifery, an area that was considered for many centuries to be solely a woman's concern, was developed into a medical specialty. Religious orders for women were founded and administrated by women. But such venues for expertise outside the home were few and far between. As a result, women devised strategies, at once impressive and heartbreaking, to feel that their lives and accomplishments were recognized. Women adopted whole literary genres to provide themselves with an imagined "other" who would attend to and appreciate their experiences.

Many of these genres have survived right up to the present and continue to serve their original function. Journals, for example, were (and still are) a staple in women's lives. The personification of the diary, Dear Diary, as a sympathetic listener has been a commonplace for girls and women but is virtually unheard-of among their male peers. The diary provided an unthreatening stand-in for the unavailable listener. We have little access to the wishful, idealized "relationships" that girls and women have had with their journals—except in a few unusual cases, they remain private. These written communications, which include important events, ideas, and aspirations, are dead-ended; they commonly go completely unseen by any eyes other than those of the writer. When, through unusual circumstances, such diaries do emerge into the public sphere, their contents often demonstrate astonishing powers of literary skill and observation. The diary of Anne Frank is a case in point—and undoubtedly it would have gone unpublished if she had survived the war.

Even in this overtly private format, however, it's been difficult for women to suppress their wish for worldly recognition. Often when a diary does eventually make its way into the public sphere, the writer's intense desire for it to be read or even published is embarrassingly transparent; the vehicle is freighted with longings for attention. A wonderful example of the ambivalent privacy of women's journals from a prior era is the diary of Alice James, the talented, hypochondriac sister of Henry and William James. The author of a book on Alice James notes with puzzlement, "It is one of the more striking facts about those ostensibly private pages [her diary] that many of them had first been recorded by the hands of others—dictated by the invalid." And again: "Despite her apparent wish for secrecy, Alice had asked for the manuscript to be typewritten before her death." And: " 'Though she never said so,' Karen Loring [her companion] reported, 'I understood that she would like to have it published.' " The desire for readership was clearly present but decorously denied.

Why Alice James had to resort to imagined, posthumous sources of recognition while her brothers won international acclaim for their contributions becomes clear if one reads some of the half-teasing letters written to her by her brother Henry. Despite their humorous tone they contain, like most humor, more than a small element of truth. It's all too clear who got the attention and affirmation in this family:

> I don't see how when I get home I can do any thing else than sit with my arm round thy waist appealing to thee for confirmation of everything I say, for approbation of everything I do, and admiration for everything I am, and never, never, for a moment being disappointed.

On a less august level, in our own time the "crisis" evoked when an adolescent girl's diary is "left out by mistake" and read by family members is a virtual commonplace. Typically howls of betrayal come from the adolescent, despite the overwhelming evidence that the journal was left open or in a place where it would inevitably be found. A typical version of this scenario, with a young woman, was recently published in *Elle* magazine:

> I've kept journals since I was in elementary school. They are intensely private, and I've never allowed anyone to read them. It drove X. [her boyfriend] crazy. . . . One day when I was out shopping for eye shadow, he read a few, like an adolescent reading a bodice-ripper, scanning until he got to the sexy parts. And then he threw those events in my face. From then on, I kept my old journals hidden in Food Emporium bags in the back of my closet.

Why, one might ask, were these "intensely private" diaries not in the back of the closet to begin with? Clearly, the author had made sure that her boyfriend was aware of and tantalized by their existence: "It drove X. crazy."

Diaries are just one of the many genres women created to provide themselves with phantom listeners—or listeners whose actual presence is hoped for but not required. Historically, letter-writing provided women with another socially tolerated venue for expressing themselves. In this format women again needed only imagine the recipient's response; they did not need the corporeal presence of a listener or reader. Women, for many centuries, wrote letters in astonishing numbers and at astonishing length. Marie de Sévigné's correspondence to her daughter alone averaged some twenty-five hundred folio pages a year! And because letter-writing was ostensibly restricted to the personal sphere, it was above reproach. But the letters were clearly, to their author, more than a private conversation with her daughter. They constituted a literary document, and I suspect that Marie de Sévigné would have been gratified but hardly surprised to discover that her letters were published posthumously.

In rare instances women managed to move these skills into the public sphere during their lifetimes—as in, for example, *Evelina,* the early epistolary novel by Fanny Burney. Lady Mary Wortley Montague, who lived in the late seventeenth and early eighteenth centuries, wrote her first novella as a letter. And in fact her entire literary reputation rests on her letters. (Her journal was burned by her family after her death.) Lady Mary, when she returned to England for the last time in her life, asked the Reverend Snowden to keep her letters from abroad for publication, presumably posthumously. Her family, horrified by the prospect, paid five hundred pounds to get the letters returned, but to their chagrin, they discovered that copies had been made. They were later published to great acclaim: the literary giant Samuel Johnson himself praised the letters, and Edward Gibbon said of them, "What fire, what ease, what knowledge of Europe and Asia."

One could hypothesize that in the 1600s writing itself became one of the first public occupations for women, precisely because it can be a solitary "dialogue." An actual reader need not exist. When, in the seventeenth century, the poet Katherine Philips had a volume of her work published, she protested to a friend that the poems had been written for herself alone and published without her knowledge:

> The injury done me by that printer and publisher surpasses all the troubles that to my remembrance I ever had . . . who never writ a line in my life with the intention to have it printed. . . . I have always had an incorrigible vanity of rhyming, but intended the effects of that humour only for my own amusement in a retired life.

Less literate women found alternative expressive venues that required no human response whatsoever. For many, prayer has served the function of providing an imagined listener. Throughout history prayer has been a largely female enterprise. (If you don't believe me, go into any church or cathedral in off hours and see who is sitting in front of the altar and in the chapels.) Like diaries, these are solitary "conversations" in which no one else is required to participate—at least no one of flesh and blood. They provide another medium for the ghostly dialogues that women have turned to as a substitute for the real thing.

I have even wondered whether, in more recent times, psychotherapy has come to serve this age-old function for women. Not infrequently women patients come to me for psychiatric care reporting that they have been in therapy for much of their lives, but many of them are not particularly in need of treatment. On the contrary, they are often very highly functioning people who feel that therapy helps them "process" their experiences. At first I was totally baffled by what appeared to be a self-indulgent and extravagant use of treatment. Eventually I came to see that what they were seeking was something quite necessary and fundamental, even if the therapeutic setting was inappropriate. They are willing to go to great lengths to have a thoughtful and sympathetic person listen to them, affirm them, and reflect on their lives. After all, how many opportunities outside of therapy do women have to focus exclusively on their own lives with another person's full attention? This theory would help explain the puzzling fact that twice as many women as men seek treatment.

One could even see the psychotherapeutic dialogue as an advance over prayer, since there's a real (if often silent) other person in the room. On the other hand, women still do not presume that such attention is simply their due: they must, quite literally, pay for the privilege. Furthermore, psychotherapy is purposely constructed to be outside the usual rules of social discourse. Undoubtedly it's this very suspension of normal etiquette that permits women to be expansive and expressive in the therapeutic setting. And because they are in the "patient" role, they need not worry about being perceived as dominating the interaction: the therapist is, by definition, the authority.

Many women, however, left without any meaningful sources of recognition, simply try to provide it for themselves, not even pretending that there is an appreciative "other." Since women function largely as providers of attention and affirmation, they often need solitude to do it: when anyone else is around, they are instantly drafted back into the subordinate listener role. Women's habit of "retreating" in order to appreciate their own experiences is the opposite of men's. Men's bids for recognition occur primarily in social contexts, either at home, at work, or at play.

Seeking respite from the emotional demands of others is a recurrent theme in women's writing. If they can't get their needs met by others, they can try valiantly to find the physical and emotional space to nourish themselves. And this requires time alone. In *Journal of Solitude,* May Sarton starts with a description of her need for isolation:

> Begin here. It is raining. I look out on the maple, where a few leaves have turned yellow, and listen to Punch, the parrot, talking to himself and to the rain ticking gently against the window. I am here alone for the first time in weeks, to take up my "real" life again at last. That is what is strange—that friends, even passionate love, are not my real life unless there is time alone in which to explore and to discover what is happening or has happened. Without the interruptions, nourishing and maddening, this life would become arid. Yet I taste it fully only when I am alone here and "the house and I resume old conversations."

One can celebrate such solitary "conversations," as Sarton does, but I would suggest that there is often a slightly sad quality to them. The very images of the rain and the autumnal leaves conjure a kind of melancholy. It's not just that Sarton needs to get away to concentrate and write; it's that she needs to be alone to establish that dialogue about her experiences that we all require. Sarton, like many women, tries to provide this conversation for herself. But there is a cost to such pseudo-dialogues (in this case with a house); like Punch the parrot, she is talking to herself. Dialogues without listeners are, in reality, monologues.

SEXUAL ATTENTION AS A SUBSTITUTE FOR AMBITION

For women, recognition has always been in short supply. But attention, recognition's less precious alloy, is another story. Unlike recognition, which reflects an individual's particular contributions, attention can be produced by attributes or events over which a person has no control. It may not be as meaningful or long lasting as recognition, but receiving it is far better than being ignored.

Attention is readily available to women, at least during their youth, when they are deemed sexuality attractive and sexually available. The drawback of sexual attractiveness as a primary source of self-worth is its inherent instability. From adolescence to young adulthood and then on to maturity and old age, the issue of how to obtain and sustain sexual attention keeps shifting and becomes more problematic. The sexy young woman admired by her suitors all too soon becomes the desexualized mother. The talented professional mentee, doted on by her flirtatious mentor, becomes the not-so-loved peer and competitor, bad-mouthed as tough or cutthroat or aggressive. The attractive middle-aged woman suddenly becomes "a woman of a certain age."

In an autobiographical essay, the writer Kennedy Fraser described one such transition vividly:

> A man of my own age, with whom I was talking at a party, withdrew his attention from me to look hungrily at a pretty young woman many years my junior. As a young woman I had relied on the attention of older men and depended on their approval. I saw very clearly at that instant when the man's gaze shifted that one kind of power had passed from me. The time had come to develop other resources.

Historically and right up through the present, women's sexuality has provided them with their chief socially sanctioned opportunity for affirmation. Courtship remains the stage in a woman's life when she can draw attention to herself without fear of painful social reprisals. She is, after all, not competing with men, but presenting herself as a potential source of male pleasure.

Nearly all the attention paid to women in the media focuses on their sexual availability. The overwhelming majority of females in literature, in cinema, and in representational art are in the courtship stage of their lives, and nearly all plots with female protagonists center on potential sexual liaisons. A 1996 study of the media found that women in films, on TV, and in magazines "are more likely to be shown preoccupied with romance and personal appearance than they are having jobs or going to school." In the movies, for example, 60 percent of men but only 35 percent of women were shown working. As many actresses have bitterly noted, women perceived as not romantically available are deemed unworthy of attention. They disappear from view. All the common plot lines—buddy stories, picaresque adventures, tests of character, life crises, coming-of-age stories—are commonly reserved for males. In fact, although women make up the majority of the population, the vast majority of characters on TV and in movies are male.

One might expect that, as women have gained access to more public roles in our society, the nearly exclusive attention given to women during courtship would lessen. But this has scarcely occurred. Dr. Jane Brown, a professor of journalism and mass communication at the University of North Carolina, Chapel Hill, has noted: "We are where we have always been. We are finding the same preoccupations among girls, with being attractive enough to lure a male. Women are seen primarily as sex objects."

In fact, instead of reducing this problem, one could make an argument that the reverse has occurred. Instead of expanding the roles in which women can receive recognition, new efforts have been made to valorize their moment of sexual availability. Women are now depicted as more aggressive participants in romantic liaisons. *Sex and the City,* one of the most popular programs on TV, tries to put this new spin on the old romance formula by describing sexual relationships with greater candor and, purportedly, from the woman's perspective. It focuses on women's quests for sexual experience and a mate, but as in the past, aspects of the women's lives apart from their mating dance are mere window dressing.

WEDDINGS

For women, courtship remains the most unconflicted venue in which they can openly seek attention. The intensity with which they work to maximize this brief moment in the sun can reach tragicomic proportions. Weddings are a case in point. They represent the apotheosis of the courtship phase and as such have enormous meaning to women. For many it is the single day in their lives when they can enjoy the undivided admiration of their community. It is the one event in which they receive affirmation with no built-in conflicts and losses. And women play it for all it's worth.

Although we live in a society in which weddings no longer denote the beginning of sexual intimacy or cohabitation with a partner and where half the marriages end in divorce, weddings have ballooned over the last decades into a megaindustry. A 2001 issue of *Bride's* magazine set a Guinness world record as the largest consumer magazine ever published: it weighed in at 4.9 pounds and had more than twelve hundred pages. Its closest competitor, *Modern Bride*, was not far behind. The *average* cost of a wedding that year was $20,000—nearly two-thirds of the post-tax income of the median American family. Paradoxically, the expansion of the wedding industry into an even more ritualized event run by wedding planners may be the result of the greater financial resources now available to working women.

The media's awareness of women's near-obsession with weddings has led to a vast proliferation of wedding-related themes and products. *The New York Times* reports:

> It's been proven that weddings sell . . . there are dozens of movies in development with "wedding" or "bride" in the title. Even fashion seems to be surrendering its former snobbism about weddings: *Vogue* came out with its first bridal issue in June [1998] . . . designers are sending out enormous made-for-television bridal dresses. There are weddings during the soap-opera sweeps, and weddings, or almost weddings, in pilot series of every television show from the new "Will & Grace" to "Friends" to "Suddenly Susan" to "E.R." And weddings, or weddings canceled by cold feet, in the last television shows of the season.

Significantly, the wedding phenomenon is almost entirely driven by women. It is women who plan and micromanage these hugely expensive events. There are no magazines named *Modern Groom* or special shops for grooms and best men. A roundup review of wedding books noted:

> The weird thing about wedding books is that they rarely mention the groom. Colin Cowie's *Weddings,* a book written by a man who

designs weddings for a living, gives the bridegroom barely a nod; a few pages are sufficient to cover proper attire and the boutonniere.

Why should this one day be so overwhelmingly important to women—and so much less so for their male partners? I suspect that the answer is straightforward. A groom knows that many future opportunities for attention and recognition lie before him. He's at the beginning, not the peak, of his trajectory toward social affirmation. He's happy to show up and be lionized at the wedding fete, but for him it's not as singular an opportunity. His fiancée, on the other hand, will likely never again experience this level of attention.

RECOGNITION BY PROXY

What happens after the relatively brief phase of courtship? By what strategies have women in the domestic sphere been able to get some "living wage" of affirmation?

One time-honored strategy for married women has been to try to glean recognition indirectly, as a by-product of providing it for others. They have settled for a kind of "trickle-down" economy of recognition, to use the old Republican "supply-side" jargon. Their unspoken plan has been to provide emotional largesse for others and hope that the dependence and appreciation they foster will supply their own emotional needs for attention and appreciation.

In past generations, as well as my own, many women expressed ambitions by proxy. They vicariously enjoyed their husbands' professional accomplishments, feeling themselves to be part of a successful "team." Such a woman participated in business functions, traveled to meetings, entertained her husband's colleagues, and absorbed whatever reflected glory came her way. But the illusion of shared recognition was shattered in the 1960s and 1970s as the divorce rate climbed and more and more women were left financially and socially stranded. The plot of the popular movie *First Wives* hinges on the rage that older, divorced women feel toward the young female companions their husbands leave them for. One of the many articles spawned by the movie noted, "When the marriage ends, so does the visibility, power, and anything else usually provided for first wives. Very few maintain the status and prestige that goes along with being Mrs. Somebody." The article contained a sidebar about wives of the rich and famous entitled, "Still on the Throne: First Wives Not Divorced—Yet."

Women have been left with the stark realization that society does not, in fact, view their marital contribution—social or financial—to their husbands' career as significant. I remember discovering this fact when my own father, a college president, died. My mother had been a major figure in the academic community, entertaining, decorating, and participating in the public affairs of the college town. But soon after my father's death, she discovered that she had minimal status on her own. She had to struggle to maintain even a foothold on the fringes of the community, that is, until years later, when she married a prominent professor at another academic institution.

I see this same phenomenon frequently in the lives of friends as well as patients: a married woman without a career who loses her husband often finds herself socially stranded. She lacks the relationships of the workplace and no longer fits into the couple-based social life to which she is accustomed. She becomes isolated and begins to feel like a social pariah.

CELEBRITIES

Women's strategies for gaining affirmation—either as gratitude for service in a supportive role or as a by-product of ambition by proxy— remain risky. One tried-and-true backup plan for many women when all else fails is sheer fantasy. They identify with celebrities and glean vicarious pleasure from the attentions received by these hugely famous women. Magazines and TV shows about movie stars, royalty, and other celebrities are staples in the lives of a large number of women.

The only common denominator of those who are idolized is the amount of attention they receive: Rosie O'Donnell and Gwyneth Paltrow and Jennifer Lopez and Laura Bush don't have much in common except their fame. Women with impressive accomplishments who are not constantly in the spotlight barely interest most women: articles on Nadine Gordimer, a Nobel Prize–winning author, or Rosa Parks do not sell women's magazines the way articles on Jackie O and Queen Elizabeth do. It's the very fact that certain women receive vast amounts of attention that makes them exciting for other women to dream about.

Soap operas represent yet another venue for fantasies of attention; they are popular daily fare for a nearly exclusively female audience. The plot lines inevitably center on amorous (and illicit) male attention received by their heroines. For many women, it is a televised re-creation of their golden years of courtship, when their sexuality could command social notice. The women who assiduously follow "the soaps" seem like the Madame Bovarys of our time, longing for a romantic escape from a largely invisible existence.

CHAPTER EIGHT

PARENTS, MENTORS, INSTITUTIONS, AND PEERS

PARENTS

Many girls and women, particularly over the last several decades, have not had to choose a substitute for recognition. Rather, they have had opportunities to learn a broad number of skills and to use those skills in an ever-growing number of professional and nonprofessional communities. A disturbing number of talented young women, however, drop by the wayside at each stage of this journey and abandon the development of their interests and goals. Researchers have looked for the cause of this phenomenon, and inevitably, much of their work has focused on the timing and sources of the recognition that females receive.

Psychoanalytic theories that stress the impact of early childhood on all subsequent development are deeply ingrained in our culture, and in this country have generated an astonishing preoccupation with parenting. Vast amounts of instructional material about child care are published and avidly read, despite the fact that almost none of the books are based on research or outcome studies. Americans, in particular, have a virtually religious belief in the indelible impact of early familial experiences.

In keeping with this tradition, most developmental theorists have assumed that the foundations of ambition—specific goals and a feeling of capability—are instilled in children by their parents. It hardly comes as a surprise, therefore, that during the 1960s, 1970s, and 1980s, when the subject of women's ambitions became a major focus of academic interest, the first area that researchers explored was parental influence. Multiple studies looked at the impact of parents on their daughters' ambitions.

The results were less than overwhelming: research did not reveal a powerful relationship between any particular parental attribute and women's achievements in adulthood. Relationships were found in the various studies, but they were weak and inconsistent. Researchers in the 1960s, for example, concluded that "girls revealed a significant association between their aspirations and their perception of dissatisfaction with the father-daughter relationship. . . . For such women successful professional achievement would compensate for their personal inadequacy and help them gain parental acceptance." Poor father-daughter relationships were thought to spur women to accomplishment. A study of successful women executives around the same time came to the opposite conclusion. The vast majority of these women described having had "extremely close relationships with their fathers and had been involved in an unusually wide range of traditionally masculine activities in the company of their fathers." Investigators interpreted this research as indicating that "if the father approves of achievement, this male encouragement may enable a female to integrate high achievement with her concept of femininity."

The data on maternal influences were no less confusing. A longitudinal study, which included a large number of women physicians, found no connection between mother-daughter relationships and the daughters' later career choices. Similarly, a study of women's goals between the ages of twenty-seven and thirty-seven concluded that "the behavior and perceived orientation of the mothers of these women [were] not powerful predictors of their daughters' behavior and orientation." On the other hand, Jerome Kagan's studies of women's ambitions found that "adult achievement in females was positively correlated to early maternal hostility." Even research on the influence of parental occupations on daughters' ambitions was a wash. One researcher observed that "no relationship has been found between career commitment or salience among college women and [their] father's occupation, [their] father's education or [their] mother's education." A later study, however, found that women with working mothers tended to be more career-oriented than those with mothers who did not work.

The findings were not what the researchers had predicted; no clear pattern of parental influence emerged. A review article entitled "The Impact of Family and School on Adolescent Girls' Aspirations and Expectations" flatly stated that "parental encouragement had no significant impact on attainment values for girls." Another large study of career choices in gifted women reached the same conclusion; it found no discernible relationship "between the lifestyle chosen by women and the amount of influence their mothers and fathers had upon their life accomplishments."

Before we try to make sense of these unexpected findings, it is important to note that recent scientific literature has not supported the assumption on which these studies were based: that parenting (in the absence of true neglect) has a consistent and even preeminent role in forming adults' sense of capability or their goals. Unusual childhood deprivation or trauma can have a lifelong deleterious impact, and an unusually intense parent-child relationship can have a significant influence, positive or negative. But in the absence of such extremes, the effects of parenting appear to have been vastly overestimated. Eleanor Maccoby, a distinguished sociologist and former Stanford University professor, reviewed the developmental research on the long-term impact of parenting on adult behavior and concluded:

> In most cases, the [statistical] relationships that have appeared are not large . . . the implications are either that parental behaviors have no effect, or the only effective aspects of parenting must vary greatly from one child to another within the same family.

A more recent exhaustive review of the scientific literature by Judith Rich Harris published in her prize-winning book *The Nurture Assumption* arrived at much the same radical finding:

> Study after study [showed] that pairs of people who grew up in the same home were not noticeably more alike in personality than pairs

who grew up in two different homes. And yet the results didn't fit the entirely genetic predictions either, because genetic relatives weren't alike enough—the correlations were too low. Something other than genes was exerting an effect on the subjects' personalities, but it didn't seem to fit the home in which they were reared.

Research on the development of ambition in girls and women is in line with these new psychological findings; the impact of parents on their offspring's adult aspirations has been overestimated. Kathleen Gerson concluded from her extensive study of women's life choices over time, "Taken alone, early childhood experiences poorly predict and do not explain adult behavior or orientation." Changes from domestic to career orientation or vice versa were more common than not, she noted, and "remarkable change was more common than stability."

In place of the prior received wisdom about parenting, a new theory has emerged: that children are shaped and motivated by the recognition they receive from *any* respected person in their social milieu. In the absence of such recognition, motivation flags. A woman in her forties whom I interviewed described such an experience:

When I was a child, I wanted to dance either in the ballet or in the musical theater. That's where I was bound, and I worked very hard dancing and going to classes. I loved to perform and I loved my teacher. I worked for myself and I worked for him; it was great.

Then we moved away from that town, and the dance school I went to in the new town left me cold. To be thrust into a new arena at another ballet school where I was no one special was quite upsetting. I missed my teacher, and eventually I stopped dancing.

The ballerina's parents encouraged her to continue dancing and enrolled her in a new school, but in the absence of her much-loved ballet teacher and with little encouragement from her new instructor, her ambition rapidly faded.

MENTORS

The point is not that parents are totally unimportant, it's that they are only two out of many significant people in a child's development, and parental influence usually attenuates as a child reaches puberty and early adulthood. One study that looked at mothers' and daughters' ambitions discovered that "although the influence of mothers and daughters was bi-directional, direct influence on the daughter's choice of careers came more from teachers, coaches, peers, and siblings." Mentors, individuals in comparatively high-level positions who take a particular interest in someone more junior, often become crucial. No wonder the research is so contradictory: there are many influential people in a person's life, and they are influential at different times and in different ways.

Eleanor Roosevelt's life is a virtual case study of early parental neglect followed by a "rescue" by a mentor and admiring peers in late adolescence. During her childhood Roosevelt's alcoholic father was largely absent, and her mother appeared to be incapable of loving her. As Roosevelt's biographer Blanche Wiesen Cook has described this mother-daughter relationship, "Eleanor craved her mother's approval and sought comfort in her company. But she was continually disappointed."

Roosevelt was painfully aware of the deprivation she suffered, later writing that during her early adolescence "I admired some of [the family's] friends who were professional singers. I felt that one could give a great deal of pleasure and, yes, receive attention and admiration! Attention and admiration were the things throughout my childhood which I wanted, because I was made to feel so conscious of the fact that nothing about me would attract attention or would bring me admiration."

Then at age fifteen Roosevelt was sent to a British boarding school, where the charismatic and erudite headmistress, Marie Souvestre, took an instant liking to her. She admired Roosevelt's intelligence and kindness and took her into her inner circle, singling her out for praise. The young Eleanor Roosevelt began to flourish. Among the students, she became a much-loved leader; her academic interests blossomed, and she even became something of an athlete, citing her acceptance into the field hockey team as one of the most pleasurable moments of her life.

When Eleanor Roosevelt left the school in her late teens, she was still somewhat shy and awkward, but in large measure she had been transformed into a young woman with a powerful sense of her capabilities and a developing sense of her ambitions. She was keenly aware of the source of these changes. For the rest of her life she kept a picture of Marie Souvestre on her desk and always carried her teacher's letters with her. It was as if they were talismans that reminded her who she was and who she could become.

Roosevelt's story illustrates how ambitions and the motivation to achieve them can change irrespective of parental influence. There can be a single "primary" mentor, such as Marie Souvestre, but as we will see, the greater the number and availability of supporters, the greater the likelihood that an ambition will be realized. One single early supporter is usually insufficient. Eleanor Roosevelt had many periods of intense confusion, paralysis, and self-doubt later in her life, despite the early influence of her mentor. Not until she was finally able to form a close-knit group of admiring friends and colleagues did she truly hit her stride and unapologetically espouse the social causes she believed in.

Of the various sources of recognition that continuously reshape and energize ambition, mentors such as Marie Souvestre are perhaps the most studied. The impact of such support has been shown to have a large practical component: mentors will often provide teaching, special career opportunities, and social access to powerful colleagues for their mentees. But research has shown that the relational aspect of mentoring is at least equally powerful; mentors have been found to provide crucial "emotional support, such as . . . reassurance of self-worth, listening, concern, and appraisal support, such as feedback and confirmation." The immediate positive impact of such relationships on work satisfaction, motivation, and advancement has been repeatedly documented.

The impact of mentoring on men's careers has been abundantly documented. Daniel Levinson, for example, in *The Seasons of a Man's Life*, based on interviews with forty men, describes this effect: "The mentor relationship is one of the most complex, and developmentally important, a man can have in early adulthood. . . . The mentor fosters the young adult's development by believing in him, sharing his youthful Dream and giving it his blessing, helping to define the newly emerging self in the newly discovered world."

Mentoring for men and women is crucial for the evolution of ambitions. And the converse is equally true; the absence of mentoring—even when it was formerly present—rapidly deflates ambitions. Elaine Seymour and Nancy Hewitt, in *Talking About Leaving,* describe their research on college women who abandon their majors in math and the sciences. Girls with scientific ambitions frequently received individualized attention and encouragement from elementary and high school teachers, they reported. A typical student is quoted as saying, "I think two reasons why I kept going in physics is because I had brilliant physics and chemistry teachers in high school—just excellent. That really kept me going. We had much more interaction and participation in class time, even in larger classes."

In college, however, mentoring was often absent for these women. This lack of encouragement, the study showed, was the single most important factor in causing women to abandon science and math.

> Preserving the self-confidence which young women bring into college depends on periodic reinforcement by teachers . . . the abrupt withdrawal of familiar sources of praise, encouragement and reassurance by faculty . . . is, in our view, the most common reason for the loss of self-confidence that makes women particularly vulnerable to switching [out of the sciences].

No individual qualities predicted which women would leave their majors. The "switchers" and "nonswitchers," the authors note, did not differ in terms of their "performance, attitude, or behavior to any degree sufficient to explain why one group left, and the other group stayed. Rather, we found a similar array of abilities, motivations and study-related behaviors distributed across the entire sample." External factors, rather than preexisting personal characteristics, were ultimately decisive in determining which women pursued their goals and which abandoned them.

The fact that the women in the study needed "periodic reinforcement" from their teachers may suggest that they required more personal encouragement than their "autonomous" male peers. There is little evidence to support such a conclusion. Another study of male and female undergraduates in the sciences discovered that, while appearing to work autonomously, "the male students receive informal 'mentoring' from male advisors who reflect them and see themselves reflected in these students." It has also been noted that the men, more than the women, can confidently look forward to recognition for their accomplishments when they join the professional world. In other words, the men, while appearing to be "independent," are able to receive recognition from a variety of sources unavailable to women.

The playwright Eve Ensler, whom I interviewed for this book, told a dramatic story of the evolution of her own ambition. It demonstrates vividly how ambitions wax and wane in response to the availability of encouraging mentors. Ensler originally came from a family with an abusive father:

> He called me stupid every day of my life and I really bought into that. Eventually I started behaving stupidly as you will do if someone says [you are]. Then these two teachers, Mr. Feig and Mr. Rothschild, got together and decided that I wasn't stupid. It was my senior year in high school and they put me in this advanced placement class. . . . Someone saw something in me for the first time in my life. It totally transformed my idea of myself.
>
> I remember thinking, "I can't be in the AP history class." I remember sitting with them the night before the AP exams. And they sat with me and said, "Oh, of course you'll pass this exam, you're brilliant." And in fact I did. It was so profound. Even though it didn't catch up with me until later, it planted the possibility in me that I might not be a stupid person.

This sounds like the beginning of a Hollywood script. The young genius is suddenly discovered and goes on to a new life—rather like the math prodigy played by Matt Damon in the movie *Good Will Hunting*. But real life is not so simple. Ensler, after high school, became an alcoholic; not until she sought help and, in essence, restarted her life did she begin to write. She wrote a few plays, including one for her adopted son, but as she recalls it was "readings, readings, readings—that play never got done."

Ensler had an ambition, but it was unclear if or how it would develop. She taught school, developing a method for instructing children how to read using plays for texts. She became more politically active. Her life could have gone in any of several directions. Around that time Ensler's son attended a workshop taught by the actress Joanne Woodward, and he brought to class a play that Ensler had written. Woodward read it and was enthusiastic. As Ensler recalled:

> [Joanne Woodward's] kindness absolutely changed my life. She was one of the first people who ever saw the artist in me, who I could become. Because of that she demanded, without being the least bit demanding, that I rise to it. When someone really special sees you, you can't fuck around. And then I wrote *The Depot*, which was about nuclear disarmament. I wrote it for Joanne Woodward, and she ended up directing it. And then my career really began.

In Ensler's life, as in many lives where ambitions are realized, one can trace an archipelago of supporting figures stretching out over time—islands of recognition that serve as stepping-stones toward the desired goal. The effect of each mentor is inspiring and mobilizing, but when the mentors are no longer available, their impact lessens and new sources of affirmation must be established.

Although individual mentors are an important support system for ambitions, they represent only one of many possible social configurations that provide essential recognition. There is a spectrum of sources that ranges from interpersonal relationships at one end all the way to institutional and cultural support on the other, with many gradations in between. Monica Higgins, a Harvard Business School professor, carried out a longitudinal study that compared the impact of individual mentors with "constellations" of supporting figures—and found that the latter are at least as, if not more, important in career development: "While the quality of one's primary developer affects short-term career outcomes, it is the composition and quality of an individual's entire constellation of developmental relationships that account for long-run protégé career outcomes."

What might such a constellation look like? How can we envision such a multiplicity of individuals providing support? In truth, once you start looking for examples, you realize that they are ubiquitous. Few achievements exist that are not built on a broad social scaffolding. The acknowledgments section of almost any book is generally a group portrait of the people whose encouragement allowed the author's project to come to fruition. Here are some quotes from the acknowledgments in two academic books that I read in preparation for the preceding chapter. The first is from a book by a psychologist, Daniel Schacter:

> I have had much help along the way. Herb Crovitz ignited my interest in memory, and Endel Tulving nurtured it during my years in graduate school and ever since. I have been fortunate to work closely with many fine psychologists and neuroscientists during the past two decades. . . . The members of the memory working group . . . have helped me to think through issues addressed in this book during numerous discussions. . . . [My wife's] love and support throughout this project have helped me more than she can imagine. I am especially grateful to colleagues and students who provided perceptive comments on various drafts of the entire manuscript.

Schacter goes on for several pages, acknowledging more than seventy people who mentored, contributed to, and supported his work in myriad ways. Such acknowledgments are standard. They lay out the massive, multifaceted, and continuing recognition that a successful career entails. This academic author is hardly alone, working away in his cell in the ivory tower. He has assembled an extensive group of

individuals who appreciate his contributions and encourage him to
pursue his work.

In case you think this assemblage is unusual, I will quote from the
acknowledgments in the book I happened to have read next, this one
by a neuroscientist, Joseph LeDoux:

> I also wanted to thank Mike Gazzaniga, my Ph.D. advisor, for show-
> ing me how to have fun while being a scientist, and for teaching
> me how to think about the mind. He encouraged me to write a book
> on emotions years before I actually got around to it. I'm also grate-
> ful to Don Reis who took me into his lab as a postdoc, taught me
> neurobiology, and provided me with the resources I needed.

LeDoux goes on to mention more than forty individuals. Like Schacter—
and like virtually anyone who successfully pursues an ambition—he
created a large gallery of individuals who affirmed his work in myriad
ways, both emotional and practical.

Relationships with colleagues are needed to give individuals the
opportunities to further their aims in the workplace. For women today,
even though most of the formal barriers to training and career opportunities have been removed, forging these friendships has remained
a major problem. This phenomenon has been identified as a leading
cause of women becoming demoralized and leaving their jobs. Professional isolation powerfully erodes the confidence and energy required
to move any project forward. The very fact that it is a negative problem, an absence, makes it all the more elusive and problematic.

No doubt conscious and unconscious discrimination contributes to
women's relative paucity of professional relationships. A study of law
school students in the 1990s discovered that the female students received
less attention from the faculty in class and less one-to-one follow-up
after class. The professors were more likely to mentor male students.
Not surprisingly, despite the fact that the male and female students had
identical law school entry credentials, by the end of the first year the men
were three times more likely than the women to be at the top of their
class. At graduation the women had fewer competitive academic credentials than their male peers.

Similarly, studies have shown that women graduate students in the sciences are excluded from career-promoting collegial relationships. In one Ivy League university in the 1990s, two hundred young scientists, male and female, were interviewed. "Compared to men," the researchers found, "women on average experienced less collaboration as an equal or senior partner. More women than men said that their post-doctoral advisors ignored them or that their advisors treated them as subordinates." Perhaps equally damaging was the paucity of professional friendships with peers. The authors surmised that the women scientists ultimately remained "on the margins in regard to the more informal aspects of social interactions, but these aspects may be crucial elements in the search for career success."

Even when discriminatory factors are not at play, women have much more difficulty than men developing relationships with people who have the power to advance their work. Actively pursuing advantageous connections runs counter to the classic ideal of femininity. Women in virtually every profession express their distaste for cultivating such relationships, labeling it as "pushy." When I asked a woman artist I interviewed whether she promoted her work, she replied:

It would mean spending more time in New York City, going to more art functions and schmoozing with the right people. I just have not been able to do that. . . . It's like you're being deceitful because you have an ulterior motive—to get your work recognized. There's a double motive. It's not just being there to talk with them, but to make sure they know who you are and therefore take an interest in your work.

Not surprisingly, this woman, at the time I interviewed her, had lost the New York gallery that had previously sponsored her shows. A woman writer told a similar story:

I know people whose biggest talent is self-promotion, and they get very far ingratiating themselves with people, making calls, going to the parties, being political. I have this outdated notion that the quality of your work will get you all the rewards that you fantasize about.

A study of women academics quotes similar disparaging comments about their male colleagues' efforts to forge work relationships: such encounters were "chatty self-promotion," "bull sessions." One subject reported that "men stood in the hallways and found the great men and went over and shook their hands or asked them to have a drink with them. . . . They took themselves terribly seriously and they said any kind of thing that came to their head. I call it 'professor talk' and I found it a waste of my time."

The idea that merit alone is sufficient is one that women have long cherished. It gives them a rationale for avoiding the "unfeminine" chore of soliciting support. Unfortunately, there is ample data that high-caliber work, in and of itself, is unlikely to produce appropriate recognition for accomplishments.

While relationships within the work sphere are crucial for the realization of ambitions, they are only one part of the story. No less important is the recognition provided by institutions. This affirmation can come in myriad forms: an acceptance to a college, a promotion, a grant, an appointment to a prestigious committee, an award. Such institutional endorsements can be life-transforming. They are also a staple in most successful endeavors. One of the authors whose book acknowledgments were quoted above named nine institutions that supported his work—not including the institution where he was currently a professor.

Women in virtually all fields receive fewer such institutional rewards. Even in the field of writing, a profession that historically has been very open to women, disproportionately few women receive the prestigious awards. A study of women professors at MIT found that they routinely received less institutional support in every category that was investigated. A book-length study of women in academia by the Committee for the Equality of Women at Harvard concludes:

> While in the past, some have suggested that it is marriage and children that interfere with women's progress, we find that this is not the case. Neither marriage nor having children predict women's lower salaries

or publication rate. Instead we believe that women's success in the academy is often stymied by the fact that women's work commitment to education and serving are not what is valued and rewarded in higher education.

The lack of institutional support for women often occurs in ways that seem trivial—less secretarial support, a smaller office, no funding for a much-needed computer upgrade. Often women professionals are loaded down with committee assignments and other tasks that are time-consuming but provide little opportunity for advancement. Focusing on such small events feels petty, and most women try to get the work done in spite of the handicaps. Yet such gestures reflect how the work community views one's contributions. Does it recognize the efforts as exciting and worthy of support—or as unremarkable?

Cumulatively, such events permeate the texture of daily life and have an undeniable impact on morale. The deficits in institutional recognition—so clearly delineated in the research literature—are insidious. Since women are used to receiving less response to their efforts, such slights often go unnoticed. And when they are noticed, women must decide whether acting on their own behalf does them more harm than good. They may fear that asking for appropriate institutional support will jeopardize important work relationships. It is often a lose-lose situation.

One of the many positive developments in the last few decades has been the creation of professional women's organizations to investigate the institutional treatment of women. These organizations also provide opportunities for creating informal networks with colleagues. Catalyst, a women's organization in the business community, funds and publishes research on the institutional treatment of business-women. National professional organizations such as the American Bar Association have established special committees to investigate discriminatory practices against women.

The progress has been real if uneven. Women have achieved near-parity in many fields at the lower reaches of the professions, but they continue to remain hugely underrepresented at the top. When institutional recognition is largely based on objective criteria, such as test scores or grades, women often achieve equal advancement. When opportunities for institutional advancement are based on subjective criteria and personal connections at work, women incrementally fall behind their male peers.

SOCIAL APPROBATION

Mentors and institutions provide the direct feedback that nourishes ambitions within the work community. But much of our lives go on elsewhere, and broader social affirmation necessarily plays a huge role in shaping and sustaining our goals. We are constantly surrounded by people with opinions about what we do. A neurosurgeon once told me that every time he announced his profession, it elicited an admiring gasp. He also confessed that it was precisely this type of universal admiration that had led him to choose his surgical subspecialty in the first place.

The responses from others that we experience on a daily basis tell us which activities and skills evoke social approval, and we are much more likely to pursue those endeavors. An elderly woman I interviewed told me that in the 1950s, after marrying and having two children, she received so much disapproval for her business career from family, friends, and neighbors that she quit and opened a small dress boutique in her attic. Five years later her husband suddenly died of a heart attack, and she and the children were left without financial support. Now, with the blessing of the previously critical social circle, she felt free to reactivate her ambitions and return to work. She became one of the earliest brokers for mutual funds and thrived in her career.

At any historical moment a culture, shaped by economic and political realities, dictates which ambitions are socially admired. Those who pursue culturally approved ambitions receive recognition for their accomplishments; those outside this purview receive little. The speed with which ambitions are reworked to fit changing social norms and therefore maximize social affirmation is nothing short of remarkable.

The radically changing nature of women's ambitions in the United States over the last half-century is a case in point. Sue Whistler and

Susan Eklund investigated the ambitions of women in three consecutive family generations. The social attitudes of their historical period emerged as the most important factor influencing these women's goals. The ambitions of the women across each generation were more similar than were the ambitions of the various generations of women within a given family. The influence of contemporary culture easily overwhelms that of the home environment.

In certain periods women's ambitions can be transformed virtually overnight in response to social pressures. Certainly the careers that many women embraced with the country's blessings during World War II were a radical departure from those that were culturally acceptable a year prior to the war and several years after.

In my own college experience, the social expectations for women's ambitions turned on a dime—and young women's ambitions quickly fell in line with the new social mandate. In 1968 the seniors in my (all "girls") dorm were planning their trousseaux and jokingly talking about going on for their MRS degrees. By the time I graduated four years later, "girls" had become "women," the dorms were coed, and there was a general assumption that we would have ambitious plans for the future. Women's applications to professional schools went up exponentially.

THE FLUIDITY OF AMBITION IN RESPONSE TO AFFIRMATION

Recognition in all its forms—admiration from peers, mentoring, institutional rewards, societal approval—creates our ambitions and modulates our efforts to fulfill them. As profoundly social beings, we work constantly throughout life to maximize affirmation. In some ways this is a disturbing realization; we would like to believe that by adulthood our goals are formed and we are largely self-motivated. The available research, however, does not support this view. Ambitions can be transformed throughout life. They can be redirected at different stages of life and can flourish after years of neglect. They are remarkably fluid. Like seeds that lie dormant, ambitions can suddenly grow and flower— but only if they receive the nutrients that they require.

Perhaps the most heavily publicized such change is the one that occurs in adolescent girls. Numerous research reports and books have described how girls, as they go to junior high and then on to high school, focus on a narrower range of careers than do their male peers. Ambitions in many fields deteriorate; new values emerge that prioritize sexual attractiveness and popularity. Over recent decades, as awareness of this shift has spread, it has become something of a cause célèbre. There have been multiple school initiatives to reverse the process, and some, particularly at girls' schools, have met with success—suggesting how responsive ambitions are to social cues.

College ambitions appear to be as malleable as those developed in high school. In 1988 the Illinois Valedictorian Project followed the college careers of eighty high school seniors of high ability. The investigators reported "a significant loss by [college] sophomore year of previously high self-esteem among women, and a lowering of career ambitions despite high performance levels. Over the same period the self-esteem and career aspirations of their male peers rose."

At what point, then, does an ambition become "fixed"? The short answer appears to be: never. To an astonishing extent, the evidence suggests, opportunities for mastery and recognition continually reshape our ambitions and modulate the effort we expend on them. Powerful mentors, opportunities for learning new skills, promotions, admiring peers who provide collegial support, institutional recognition, and broad cultural trends all continuously mold ambitions.

Examining exactly how and when people reformulate their ambitions to maximize recognition can be illuminating. If you look for people's strategies for obtaining this resource, it often clarifies the career decisions that have shaped their lives. It explains why certain ambitions work out and others do not, why one person chooses to focus on a job or career and another chooses to devote more effort to the interpersonal sphere. It explains the pathways typically taken within a given work situation.

A rare longitudinal study, by Sharon Rae Jenkins, followed the ambitions of sixty-four working women for fourteen years. Jenkins found that, as a group, their motivation to achieve *increased* over the time period. She then divided the women into two groups—those whose careers had ultimately provided the possibility of advancement and those whose careers had not provided opportunities for "status mobility." What she discovered was that only the women in the first group showed an increase in their motivation. In other words, actual events—the possibilities of career promotions—intensified the women's ambitions.

The flux of ambitions in response to recognition, even at midcareer, is also apparent in Margaret Hennig and Anne Jardim's study of women managers, *The Managerial Woman.* The women interviewed identified "a critical make or break factor [for their careers], the good boss." And when each woman was asked to describe what a good boss provided, the answers couldn't have been more effusive; he was "her supporter, her encourager, her teacher, and her strength in the company." When the boss retired or moved to a different job, the woman manager usually became less career-oriented, switching her interest to the personal sphere in an effort to glean recognition from other sources. Hennig quotes a woman manager who, after the departure of her boss, suddenly became involved with her appearance, changing her hairdo and wardrobe. The woman explained that "everyone seemed to look at me in a new way and so I did at myself, and I liked the way it felt to be looked at in that way."

In Rosabeth Moss Kanter's *Men and Women of the Corporation,* the author describes what happens to managers (male and female) when career opportunities for advancement are blocked. Their self-esteem drops, they lower their aspirations, and they become critical of those who are more successful.

Perhaps most interesting is Kanter's finding that when managers no longer have career advancement, they reorganize their lives in order to find new sources of recognition: "When they are blocked from organizational recognition, people substitute a variety of forms of 'social recognition,' finding ways to look good in the eyes of at least some other people." Kanter notes that such professionals often turn their energies to relationships with subordinates and with other "blocked" colleagues. One chapter contains a poignant diagram:

TYPES OF DEAD ENDS AND THEIR CONSEQUENCES

Source of Opportunity Blockage	Amount of Disaffection	Common Alternatives for Recognition
Low-ceiling occupation	low	peers
Individual "failure" in high-ceiling occupation	high	outsiders
Wrong route to high-ceiling occupation (lack of background for further progress)	moderate	subordinates or less advantaged

Kanter's finding that people who are unable to advance in their jobs substitute other forms of recognition has been corroborated by the research finding that lower-class and lower-middle-class men seek much more of their sense of identity and satisfaction in their family life than do upwardly mobile middle-class executives.

Arlie Hochschild's much-heralded and wonderfully researched *The Time Bind* looks at this issue from a somewhat different angle. Hochschild examines the lives of workers in a large, liberal-minded company that provides part-time options for parents and other workers with family responsibilities. The central question she addresses in the book is "Why don't working parents, and others too, take the opportunity available to them to reduce their hours at work?" Why are they not taking advantage of options that could provide time for family and leisure pursuits? Interestingly, Hochschild never fully answers the question to her own satisfaction. Near the end of the book she muses that any group that wanted to organize workers to reduce work hours "would have to explore the question of why working parents have yet to protest collectively the cramped quarters of the temporal 'housing' [the lack of time outside of work and in the home] in which they live."

Hochschild believes that workers' lives are increasingly emotionally impoverished because of their reduced leisure and family time: "In essence, [the employees] denied the needs of family members, as they themselves became emotional ascetics. They made do with less time, less attention, less fun, less relaxation, less understanding, and less support at home than they once imagined possible. They emotionally downsized life."

But the research in the book itself tells a different story. The workers Hochschild interviews do not feel emotionally shortchanged. Their needs have not been downsized; their sources of fulfillment have simply been shifted from the home to the workplace. It is in the workplace that they receive substantial social and professional recognition—much more than they receive at home. Hochschild describes a typical woman who anticipated returning home, on a normal workday, to find "an urgency of demands and the unarbitrated quarrels." In contrast, when arriving at her job as a shift supervisor, "I get there at 2:30 P.M., and people are there waiting. We sit. We talk. We joke." The workers Hochschild interviews identify the workplace as their most dependable and gratifying source of affirmation. It is Hochschild, not the employees, who worries about the employees' emotional health.

In these employees' lives, as in the lives of the executives studied by Kanter, Hennig, and Jardim, the fundamental need for reliable sources of recognition determines the direction of ambitions and the intensity with which they are pursued.

PART THREE

WOMEN AND MASTERY

CHAPTER NINE

DEVELOPING SKILLS

The thoughts and feelings that I have now I can remember since I was six years old. A profession, a trade, a necessary occupation, something to fill and employ all my faculties, I have always felt essential to me, I have always longed for. . . . Everything has been tried, foreign travel, kind friends, everything. My God! What is to become of me?

—FLORENCE NIGHTINGALE, in her diary as a young woman, quoted in *Eminent Victorians* by Lytton Strachey

Nightingale's description of mastery is as accurate as it is poignant: "something to fill and employ all my faculties." Her yearning to utilize her talents is, in fact, a universal one, as psychological theories and research both confirm. We see the drive toward the learning and practice of skills continually: people enjoy their expertise at work, whether it is teaching preschool, deal-making, or designing landscapes. Perhaps even more striking is how large a role mastery plays in people's "leisure" activities. In their free time they chose to play bridge, chess, tennis, soccer, or baseball; they learn gourmet cooking or carpentry. They learn to identify mushrooms or stars or antiques. Every bookstore is stacked with "how-to" books and books on arcane subjects that can be mastered. At a small bookstore I recently saw an imposing tome that catalogued and pictured every type of lichen. Out of curiosity I asked the clerk if anyone had ever purchased it. "It's selling briskly," she replied to my astonishment. Learning and exercising skills, honing them to a high level, is one of the great pleasures that life provides.

The level to which a skill is developed has a strong, if not direct, correlation to the enjoyment it produces. This is not to say that neophytes do not have fun trying out novel activities; and pleasure may be derived from performing tasks at a simple or routine level—cooking a regular dinner can be relaxing and fun. But there is no doubt that a qualitatively different level of enjoyment occurs when a certain level of mastery is attained. Yo-Yo Ma's experience playing the cello is profoundly different from my daughter's during her cello lessons. Oliver Sacks's passionate search for obscure ferns in Mexico, as described in his recent *Oaxaca Journal,* is permeated by his intense delight in deeply pursuing this interest. On a more mundane level, as a psychiatrist and doctor, I take pleasure in discovering and using new information to help patients. Immersion in a subject and an earned sense of competence bring their own profound rewards.

Attaining such skills requires having several conditions present. One must have access to information and training, time to pursue the interest, feedback from others with similar interests, and of course, recognition for accomplishments. In the past, women, excluded from the public sphere, lacked all of these components.

Women's current situation is radically different. Opportunities for training, from grammar school right up through graduate and professional schools, are now readily available to girls and young women. Women also have access to entry-level positions in most fields; a few women have even gained access to the upper reaches of most professions. Unfortunately, subtle, incremental, but ultimately powerful conditions remain that militate against women's attaining mastery in most fields.

MOTIVATION FOR MASTERY IN WOMEN

"Well, did anything interesting happen today?" [my father] would begin. And even before the daily question was completed I had eagerly launched into my narrative. . . . It never crossed my mind to wonder if, at the close of a day's work, he might find my lengthy account [of the Dodgers baseball game] the least bit tedious. For there was mastery as well as pleasure in our nightly ritual. Through my knowledge, I commanded my father's undivided attention, the sign of his love. It would instill in me an early awareness of the power of narrative, which would introduce a lifetime of storytelling, fuelled by a naïve confidence that others would find me as entertaining as my father did.

—DORIS KEARNS GOODWIN, *Wait Till Next Year: A Memoir*

During her childhood Doris Kearns Goodwin, the noted presidential biographer and historian, learned to link her mastery of narrative with her father's attention. It was an association that she would later enlarge to create a writing career; her professional life was "fuelled" by the conviction that she had the ability to craft narratives that would engage an audience.

Goodwin's description of her dramatic renditions of baseball games succinctly captures the elements that motivate mastery. They at first appear to be deceptively simple: the motivation to learn a skill or for that matter to pursue any goal, including an ambition, can be roughly calculated on the basis of two factors. The energy and persistence with which an enterprise is engaged depends on how valued the expected rewards are and how certain the person is that he or she will be able to attain the desired goal. For Goodwin, the expected rewards were highly valued: the pleasure of recounting an exciting game and her father's attention and love. The goals seemed achievable. She was convinced by his enthusiasm for her blow-by-blow accounts of Dodgers games that she could master storytelling. This conviction spurred her to further develop her narrative skills.

Goodwin's calculations are typical of ones we constantly make. We estimate (consciously or unconsciously) the potential rewards of a given project and our likelihood of attaining them. That specific goal can then be compared with others. For each potential opportunity we evaluate the desirability of the outcome (factoring in the possible losses it could entail) and our chances of achieving it. Are we capable of mastering the skills involved, and is the reward worth the effort?

The social learning theorist Albert Bandura succinctly summarized the first part of this motivational paradigm, the assessment of potential rewards:

> Past experiences create certain expectations that certain actions will bring valued benefits, that others will have not appreciable benefits, and that still others will avert future trouble. By representing foreseeable outcomes symbolically, people can convert future consequences into current motivators of behavior.

As discussed in previous chapters, the reward factor of this calculation is problematic for women. Although they may find mastery per se as satisfying as do their male peers, the social rewards that women can expect to reap for their skills are relatively diminished. The personal and societal recognition provided for their accomplishments is quantitatively poorer, qualitatively more ambivalent, and perhaps most discouraging, less predictable. High-achieving schoolgirls, for example, far from reaping social rewards, are the least popular group in coed schools—and high-achieving boys constitute the most popular group. Girls with good academic records are more likely to be rated as "unfeminine" by their peers. To make matters even more confusing, not only are girls evaluated less favorably than males when they perform well, they are evaluated *more* favorably than males when they perform poorly!

If you are a successful woman professional, not only might you have a paucity of positive feedback, but the responses you get may well be spiked with negative innuendo about sexual identity or based on totally uncontrollable factors such as sexual attractiveness. For grown women, mastery can carry with it the threat of intense guilt and anxiety— worry that one is not an adequate wife or mother.

A SENSE OF CAPABILITY

Unfortunately, the mixed response to women's achievements is only the first variable in the motivational equation. The second element is equally problematic: to attempt to master a skill, and particularly one that requires prolonged effort, you must believe that you are likely to succeed. And here again we see the long-term impact of the relatively low recognition that girls and young women receive. Despite the fact that girls' and women's achievements, particularly in the academic sphere, frequently outstrip those of their male peers, they routinely underestimate their abilities. As we shall see, this miscalculation commonly leads women of accomplishment to view themselves as frauds. How otherwise could such an unexceptional person have achieved so much? Clearly someone must have been tricked along the way!

Boys and men, by contrast, have repeatedly been shown to have an inaccurately high estimation of their capabilities; this exaggeration is particularly pronounced if a task is labeled as "masculine." The impact of these findings on the selection and pursuit of an ambition is obvious: if you don't think the chances are great that you will reach a career goal, you won't attempt to reach it—even if the rewards are highly desirable.

Efforts to understand the characteristic male and female distortions regarding capability have produced a large body of research literature centered on two closely related concepts. The more global psychological theory is that of locus of control (LOC). This behavioral paradigm, which has been around for many decades, posits that everyone develops an internal model to predict whether their actions will produce the results they desire. Some individuals are confident that they have the power to determine the outcomes for many aspects of their lives; these people are said to have an "internal locus of control." They attribute their successes to stable factors such as innate ability, while attributing their failures to modifiable factors such as effort or transient factors like bad luck. Not surprisingly, people with an internal LOC come to tasks with energy, determination, and optimism. Such generalized feelings of competence and control have been shown to enhance people's physical as well as mental health.

On the other hand, individuals who feel that uncontrollable external factors determine whether they will succeed at their endeavors are said to have an "external locus of control." They do not expect that their work will reliably produce a desired result. When such people achieve success, they attribute it to an unstable or external factor such as luck. When they fail, they attribute the failure to an inalterable factor such as lack of ability.

Beliefs about one's effectiveness in the world, one's LOC, can function as post hoc explanations for virtually all outcomes, positive or negative. Such belief systems inevitably become self-reinforcing and self-fulfilling. If you believe a failure of yours is due to lack of ability, you're likely to feel discouraged, ditch the enterprise, and experience a sense of helplessness. Because of a low sense of capability, people with an external LOC have reduced resiliency after a setback; they will give up on a project more easily and feel worse about themselves. On the other hand, if you think that your failure is due only to poor effort, you'll try harder the next time and have a better chance of succeeding. It has been shown, for example, that students who think they are smart work harder.

Numerous studies have suggested that girls and women are more likely to have an external LOC and boys and men an internal one: males are more likely to take full credit for their successes and discount failures as due to lack of effort. When confronted with a new task, males frequently expect to perform at a level that is not justified by their past efforts, while females predict that their performance will be below that suggested by their actual experience.

Females chalk their successes up to luck and attribute their failures to lack of ability. Throughout their school years, for example, girls more frequently than boys assume personal responsibility for failure to accomplish a goal. When a girl or woman encounters difficulty in performing a task—even if she is doing as well as her male peers—her efforts will deteriorate more rapidly, because she attributes her failure to lack of aptitude and so feels helpless about improving her performance. A review of research in this area concluded that girls "are more likely to condemn their abilities when they encounter difficulties and to show decreased expectations of success than do boys, across a wide variety of domains."

A closer look at the data, however, suggests that the LOC story in males and females may not be as straightforward as was previously thought. Newer evidence suggests that girls' and women's inaccurate sense of their capabilities is often specific to certain types of work and settings. This discovery has been codified in the more limited concept of "self-efficacy," which refers to a belief about one's ability to perform a particular task in a particular situation. The notion of self-efficacy emphasizes that a person's sense of capability in one context is not necessarily generalized to other areas. A young woman may have low self-efficacy for a college mathematics course and high self-efficacy for one in anthropology. Doris Kearns Goodwin may believe that she is a world-class historian but hopeless in economics.

The situations that elicit girls' and women's feeling of ineffectiveness tend to be ones in which gender issues are in play—girls in a coed math class or softball game, for instance. In the same way that women relinquish recognition to males, they also experience and express a lowered sense of competence when males are present. In tasks that women perform with a male partner as opposed to a female partner, they are more likely to attribute their failures to lack of ability. Similarly, in a group of women and men with equivalent skills in both math and English, when given a "masculine" task, women predict that they will be less competent than their male peers.

The encouraging news in this otherwise rather disheartening scenario is that although girls and women often reflexively assume that their failures are due to lack of ability, this belief may be less deeply ingrained than was previously thought. Several studies have suggested that defeatist patterns of attribution can be reversed rather rapidly. When girls are told that completion of a task depends on the effort they expend, they can change their expectations and express as much confidence as boys. Even Albert Bandura, the originator of the idea of "effectance," developed therapies designed to reverse people's feeling of helplessness in anxiety-producing situations.

Specific information about skills can also reverse preconceptions about capability. In one revealing study, when mixed-sex groups were assigned a task, the men automatically perceived themselves as more competent than the women—and the women shared this view. The men proceeded to show more "active task behavior," giving opinions and information, while the women engaged in more "positive social behaviors," agreeing with speakers, acting friendly, and speaking less than the men. But when all the group members were given the false information that specific males or females within the groups had greater aptitude, no sex-stereotyped behaviors were noted. The belief that the males had greater competence disappeared.

The lack of "self-efficacy" in girls and women, at times, simply reflects the "information" they are currently receiving. A girl who believes that she is incompetent in math may be relaying what she is being told rather than expressing a permanent sense of incompetence. Parents, evidence shows, attribute their daughters' math skills to hard work rather than to capability. Parents also note giftedness for math in girls later than in boys—if at all—and tend to be surprised when their daughters' math talents are pointed out to them. Teachers commonly attribute girls' success in math to effort and boys' to talent. Why wouldn't a girl assume that these assessments were true, until she received contrary information?

Finally, girls' and women's low expectations of being able to reach specific goals often reflect reality. Young girls planning careers in male-dominated fields have been shown to (correctly) expect to experience discrimination. They believe that many of the factors that will determine their success are external—and they are right.

FEMININITY AND CAPABILITY

The research on LOC and "self-efficacy" has provided important insights into women's reduced sense of capability when they are faced with certain tasks. But strong evidence is lacking that these concepts alone are successful in predicting the long-term trajectory of women's accomplishments. What has emerged as a potentially more useful measure is "gender role identification." Measuring an individual's endorsement of traditional "masculine" and/or "feminine" traits tells us a surprising amount about their goals, their sense of capability, their self-confidence, and their future level of achievement.

This finding should come as no surprise. Assumptions about capability are embedded in gender roles. The characteristics required to take on and complete a project are virtually identical to those used by the BSRI (Bem Sex Role Inventory) to describe masculinity: self-reliance, independence, analytic ability, assertiveness, willingness to take risks, leadership qualities. Some authors have dubbed these qualities "the competency cluster." As might be expected, a sense of capability is more strongly correlated with endorsement of "masculine" qualities than with the person's actual male or female gender.

"Femininity," by contrast, is all about supporting others' needs and endeavors. It is about nurturing and caretaking. Because these roles are predicated on meeting someone else's agenda or requirements, much of the control is *in fact* external. Motherhood, the prototype for women's "feminine" role, is a case in point. Any mother who has raised a child can tell you that it is not an endeavor in which one can be "independent, analytic and assertive." It's hard to pursue a plan even from minute to minute, because children's needs are so intense, time sensitive, and time consuming. Women writers have captured the astonishing lack of control one feels as a parent. Rachel Cusk, in *A Life's Work,* gives us a sample of the experience:

> Months after [my daughter's] birth I still found myself affronted and incredulous, as if at some foreign and despicable justice, by the fact that I could no longer sleep in or watch a film or spend a Saturday morning reading, that I couldn't stroll unfettered in the warmth of a summer's evening.

In a book of essays about contemporary women's lives, one author describes "a typical night":

> Owen, who is six, tosses a bouquet of flowers—a gift from Gabrielle's garden—onto the grass as we get out of the car. Three-year-old Hugo sees the moon. I mention that the sun is out, too; he runs from one end of the front walk to the other, trying to find it, getting closer to the street with each lap.
>
> Owen says he wants the milk shake *now.* . . . I walk back to pick up the flowers, the wet towel (swimming lessons). . . . Back into the house with flowers, towel, bags. As I put my keys in the bowl next to

the front door (small attempt at order), I knock over a framed picture beside it. The glass in the frame shatters.

Hugo calls, insistent, for me to come back outside.

Parenting has its deep pleasures and satisfactions, but it also undeniably has chaotic and reactive qualities. And many of the supportive roles that women assume entail this same loss of autonomy and control. If a woman works to socially advance her husband's career, but he turns out to be incompetent (or divorces her), she will have a minimal impact on the final outcome. If she devotes her life to her children but ultimately disapproves of their life choices, there is little she can do. If a woman takes on a useful but relatively powerless volunteer position within an institution, she may find herself alienated as its leadership or organizational goals change. "Femininity," with its emphasis on purely supportive activities, has an external LOC built into its mandates.

"Masculinity" and "femininity," it turns out, aren't just different values or styles; nor are they only about who receives recognition or status. They describe profoundly different levels of initiative, competence, and control in an individual's life. Perhaps not surprisingly, "masculine" characteristics have been found to correlate in women, as well as in men, with a sense of well-being. Women (and men) are healthiest, mentally and physically, in situations in which they express the "masculine" traits of independence and agency, and in which they have some control over their environment. One study involving thirteen thousand women found that those working outside the home had less heart disease, lower cholesterol, lower blood pressure, and less anxiety and depression than homemakers—despite the added stress of increased roles and commitments. The more committed the women were to their jobs, the healthier they were.

In women, identification with "masculine" traits, with or without additional "feminine" ones, is a more powerful predictor of career success than parental expectations or maternal employment status. Young women with nontraditional sex-role identifications have higher educational objectives and are more likely to value their own achievements at least as highly as those of their husbands. Those women who identify with "masculine" attributes are less hindered by failure than women who identify predominantly with "feminine" ones, and their performance tends to be more enhanced by success.

Not surprisingly, women who choose traditionally male careers have a relatively high masculine role identification, but interestingly, this finding is true irrespective of how many "feminine" attributes they endorse in addition to the "masculine" ones. In other words, a woman can endorse at least as many "feminine" traits as a stereotyped, purely "feminine" peer, but it is the addition of "masculine"—instrumental—traits that is the crucial factor. The combination of the two sets of attributes can be highly effective. When I was practicing medicine years ago, the head of my division was a woman who was so soft-spoken and gentle that some of my colleagues jokingly nicknamed her "Bambi." She was one of the most attentive physicians I've ever met, as well as being an enormously effective woman. Currently she is head of my former colleagues' department.

Importantly, women who described themselves as having more of the "masculine" attributes did not differ from those with more purely "feminine" profiles in terms of marital status or number of children. Their increased sense of effectiveness and capability apparently did not produce any negative social consequences.

In contrast, women who chiefly endorse traditional "feminine" traits are less empowered by success and become more discouraged by failure. They tend to take setbacks to heart. As a group, they are more prone to depression than are women with less stereotyped gender roles. In fact, homemaking, the most purely "feminine" of work choices, is a predictive factor for major depressive disorders—ranking alongside unemployment and shift work.

"FEMININE" TRAITS AND SUBORDINATE ROLES

You would never know . . . that men, individually and collectively, are signal beneficiaries of female nurturance, much less than this goes far to explain why society encourages nurturance

in women. No, it is always children who women are described as
fostering and sacrificing for.

—KATHA POLLITT, *Reasonable Creatures*

Society has never barred women from breadwinning roles, but
only from economical roles that are profitable and respect-
able. . . . Men do not bar women from taking part in politics, but
only hamper their efforts to participate in power.

—JEANE KIRKPATRICK, *Political Woman*

It has been suggested that the supportive attributes that characterize traditional "femininity" are not actually specific to the female
gender role. Numerous writers and researchers have pointed out that
many of the "empathic," caretaking, supportive qualities identified with
women, are, in fact, ones that characterize all subordinate groups.
Individuals in subordinate roles are typically more deferential and self-
effacing than those of higher status. They are more sensitive to the feelings of their "superiors" than high-status people are to theirs, and they
are more conscious of the impression they are making on those who
hold greater power. As one researcher noted, individuals in subordinate roles "need to be aware of the feelings, thoughts, and responses of
their superiors to respond to their superiors' needs and acquire their
favor." Jean Baker Miller, an eminent psychiatrist who writes about
the psychology of women, notes that subordinates of all kinds typically "become highly attuned to the dominants, able to predict their
reactions of pleasure and displeasure. Here, I think, is where the long
story of 'feminine intuition' and 'feminine wile' begins. . . . If a large
part of your fate depends on accommodating and pleasing the dominants, you concentrate on them."

Those who dominate, by contrast, make little effort to understand
their subordinates. As Jessica Benjamin explains in *The Bonds of Love*,
the refusal to understand or appreciate the other is precisely what characterizes domination. The dominant person's needs, wishes, or visions
are imposed on the other. The subordinate's viewpoint receives less
acknowledgment and has less impact.

In any interaction, the style and level of an individual's participation depends on his or her status. In situations where there is a professional hierarchy, the individuals at the top take a more active role than those beneath them. Work with military pilots and their crews, for example, found: "Pilots influence decisions more than navigators, navigators more than gunners; and this is true even when the pilot's opinion is objectively incorrect." Observations and suggestions from lower-status crew members are frequently ignored—at times with deadly consequences.

In the absence of this type of professional hierarchy, characteristics such as race, age, and sex are used as markers of status and therefore set levels of participation and power. Women are, of course, in just such a "lower external status" position with regard to men, and they demonstrate all of the expected "supportive" characteristics when placed in mixed-sex work groups. They are more deferential, agree more with the men's ideas, hold lower expectations about their own capabilities, are less proactive about tasks, and express more emotion than their male colleagues. Deborah Tannen, the linguist and popular writer, has pointed out that much of the verbal style that girls learn is really about communicating that they are assuming the "one-down" position.

Girls and women convey their subordinate status with gestures as well as words: they frequently avert their eyes while speaking, particularly with males or anyone in a position of authority. As a result of their empathic and supportive stance, they tend to be "nicer" than their male counterparts. As the old nursery rhyme goes, "Sugar and spice and everything nice is what little girls are made of." But as the writer Malcolm Gladwell has noted, "niceness" often serves to maintain the status quo:

> It [is] the practice of niceness that [helps] keep other values, such as fairness, at bay. Fairness sometimes requires that surfaces be disturbed, that patterns of cordiality be broken, and that people rudely or abruptly be removed from their place. Niceness is the enemy of fairness.

One key element of "niceness" is smiling at others during social interactions—a response that is more common in girls and women than in their male counterparts. Women have also been found to commonly display "inappropriate smiling," for example, while asking a question or making a serious point. Smiling conveys a reassuring message of accommodation to others; it is the facial equivalent of speaking softly and tentatively in order to appear pliant. Animal ethnography has raised the startling possibility that frequent smiling may actually serve as a stereotyped gesture of subordination. Studies of rhesus monkeys found that when nondominant monkeys worry about an attack by a dominant animal, they convey their nonthreatening, subordinate status by lowering their bodies to appear shorter and smiling—an expression known as the "fear grin."

Because indiscriminate "niceness" signals compliance, it can undercut an individual's effectiveness in promoting his or her beliefs or ideas. As one researcher pithily noted, "Likeability's relationship to actual influence [is] slight." Yet in women being "nice" can become so habitual that they are unable to communicate disagreement or anger even when it's clearly appropriate. When issues arise that are worth fighting for, women often become paralyzed, unable to tolerate the disapproval that their opinion might generate. When women do manage to achieve power, they frequently exaggerate their "niceness" to disarm male colleagues who might find them threatening. Pat Schroeder, the former congresswoman from Colorado, reportedly draws a smiley face in the capital *P* when she writes her signature.

Karen Horney, in *Feminine Psychology,* described what she saw as the healthy opposite of indiscriminate female "niceness." She coined the term "adequate aggressiveness" to capture this important quality:

> By this I mean the capacities for work, including the following attributes: taking initiative; making efforts; carrying things through to completion; attaining success; insisting on one's rights; defending oneself when attacked; forming and expressing autonomous views; recognizing one's goals and being able to plan one's life according to them.

Horney outlined the consequences that occur when "adequate aggressiveness" is lacking:

[O]ne usually finds widespread inhibitions on this score, which in their entirety account for the feeling of insecurity, or even helplessness in the life struggle, and explain the subsequent dependency on other people, and a predisposition to look to them for support or help.

Like individuals from other low-status groups, women must often resort to indirect methods to influence those with higher status; when women are more forceful and direct, it has been found that their suggestions are often disregarded. Women in mixed male-female groups have greater influence on decision-making when their contributions are couched in self-deprecatory terms. In order to have an impact in such groups, they must present themselves as devoted to the group interests, with no wish for personal gain.

"Femininity" has this darker dimension: an unstated but profoundly important agenda promoting the subordination of women's needs to those of men. Because of the linkage of subordination and female sexuality, positions of authority strike terror in the hearts of even the most dedicated feminists. According to a *New York* magazine item, when Gloria Steinem read the proofs of an upcoming biography of herself, she was unhappy with the portrait and asked for alterations in the text:

> Among Steinem's requested changes: When [the biographer] wrote that her air of "authority" attracted her peers in high school, the suddenly power-shy Steinem wanted that changed to "mystery."

Mystery, with its seductive, hidden essence, felt much more comfortable (and sexy) to Steinem than being an authority—even one that her peers were attracted to.

For many women, authority has become insidiously mixed up with dominance—that most "unfeminine" of concepts. Dominance, as noted previously, is defined by the failure of a person in power to acknowledge and respond to the wishes and needs of those with less power. The very word makes women queasy—unless perhaps they have a penchant for whips, stilettos, and leather.

But hierarchy in no way implies dominance; it simply denotes stratification of roles in terms of expertise, resources, and power. Hierarchies exist in families between parents and children, in schools between teachers and students, in employment between mentors and mentees. There is nothing particularly sinister or debilitating about these arrangements. I worked for several years in a research lab with an extensive hierarchy of positions. For the most part, the coworkers liked each other and worked effectively together. We were supported by grants obtained by the scientist who headed the lab, and we felt that those above us were reasonably responsive to our needs. There was hierarchy but not dominance, and we all benefited.

The real issue for women is not dominance; it is their fear of being desexualized for stepping out of the supportive feminine role and into that of an authority. And those in positions of authority have power. At its core the traditional white, middle-class definition of "femininity" is not simply about being sensitive and caring. It requires that women "voluntarily" relinquish scarce resources: time for their careers, time for recreation, financial remuneration, power, and social recognition. When push comes to shove (as it often does in the workplace or at home), it is these coveted commodities that are at stake.

As an article on gender roles in O, *The Oprah Magazine* from 2002 noted:

> We want our girls to be strong, self-reliant, and healthy individuals—though not so much so that they don't get invited to the prom, yet we all suspect, even if we don't want to, that for girls, strong, smart, and healthy isn't always the most reliable predictor of prom-ability.

"Prom-ability" remains the issue. Failure to achieve it is the constant threat faced by girls and women who attain the sense of independence and authority that mastery so often brings. A paper called "The Politics of Power" delivered at the Women in Management conference by Patti Mancini, a vice president of the Rockwell International Corporation, gave her audience straightforward advice: "Don't start a debate with a man on an important issue if there are other men present in the room. Men don't like to see other men's egos hurt by women."

Girls and women fear that they will be rejected or attacked by men if they do not assume the one-down position: less smart, less capable, less self-confident, less prominent. And they have good reason to worry. Males, understandably, resent encroachments on their traditional areas of hegemony: feeling superior to women has long been a key male prerogative. Having the lion's share of social resources, including exclusive access to many types of skills, has been a male entitlement.

When women step out of traditional roles by taking initiative and assuming leadership, they engender hostility in men. Those women who achieve authority and power correctly expect that men will retaliate by treating them as unattractive, if not downright sexually deviant. They become targets for sexually humiliating words, gestures, or acts. The reality is that as women's rights have expanded, men have incurred huge losses. They have lost their exclusive right to attend colleges and professional schools, their privileged legal status, their monopoly on political power, and perhaps most bitterly, their huge advantage in gaining employment and promotions. Men's anger at these losses is expressed, virtually without exception, by attacking women's sexuality as too available (slut) or too unavailable (spinster or lesbian).

A 2003 cover story from a national newsweekly is paradigmatic. Ostensibly about the lack of sexual intimacy among married couples, its clear subtext is that women who work risk their marriages and their sex lives. "No Sex, Please, We're Married" banners the front cover. Here's the first sentence of the story: "For Maggie Weinreich, sex had always been a joy. . . . But teaching yoga, raising two kids and starting up a business—not to mention cooking, cleaning and renovating the house—left her exhausted. . . . When Roger wanted to have sex, she would say she was too beat." Read on to page two: "Have you heard of DINS? . . . It stands for dual income, no sex." Clearly it's those pesky two-career marriages that are the problem.

If any woman is masochistic enough to continue reading the piece, on page six of the article she'll finally get to the heart of the matter: "Men are mad too. 'The big loser between job, kids, and the dogs is me,' says Alex, a 35-year-old financial executive from Manhattan. 'I need more sex, but that's not the whole story. I want more time alone with my wife and I want more attention.' " Or getting down to the nitty-gritty: "When women have those kinds of choices [divorcing their husbands and earning more than their husbands], marital 'duties' become options and the debate over how much, or how little, sex to have is fundamentally altered." Excuse me, "marital 'duties' "? Furthermore, if one of the marital partners is "unhappy," the authors euphemistically opine, they're likely to get divorced; those working women better watch out!

What we're actually hearing is a lot of grousing from men who resent sharing power and resources with their wives in a more equitable fashion. Buried in the article is a single paragraph of actual data that completely contradicts the thesis of the story:

> The statistical evidence would seem to show that everything is fine. Married couples *say* they have sex 68.5 times a year, or slightly more than once a week, according to a 2002 study by the highly respected National Opinion Research Center at the University of Chicago. . . . At least according to what people tell researchers, DINS is an urban myth: working women appear to have sex just as often as their stay-at-home counterparts.

The targeting of women's sexuality by men has occurred at every historical juncture at which women claimed rights previously reserved for men. A typical attack is cited by Barbara Ehrenreich and Deirdre English in *For Her Own Good*. These authors quote G. Stanley Hall, an eminent psychologist of the late nineteenth and early twentieth centuries, who reviewed thirty years of medical arguments against female education and concluded that women's colleges were fine for "those who do not marry":

> These [educational] institutions may perhaps become training stations of a new-old type, the agamic or agenic [i.e., sterile] woman,

be she aunt, maid—old or young—nun, school-teacher, or bachelor woman.

In retrospect, the idea that education destroys a woman's sexuality sounds absurd. But attacks on women's sexuality predictably continue with each new challenge to men's control over areas of mastery. Such attacks range from subtle disapproval to demeaning insult to physical assault. In 2003 it became public knowledge that the recent addition of women soldiers to the Air Force Academy had led to an epidemic of rapes of female cadets by their male peers. These crimes went unpunished by the appropriate (male) authorities. A column in *Newsweek* noted:

> Those who have always been hostile to female soldiers say that this is inevitable, given the atmosphere of esprit with which women interfere, given the machismo that is essential for trained fighting forces.
>
> The truth is quite different. Sexual trauma has reached epidemic proportions for women in the military—with numbers twice as high as in the civilian population, according to a Department of Defense study—because it can. The offense is not adequately investigated or punished.

The article goes on to observe that like many male-female issues where sexuality is the ostensible issue, what is actually at stake is status and power. Unpunished sexual assaults at training academies is only one of several ways that the military has discouraged women from entering the officer level of the profession. The United States Air Force, for example, requires that upper-level officers have combat experience, but women soldiers are not allowed to join combat units.

The conflict between women seeking equal status and men protecting their advantaged position has no easy solutions. There are real potential losses for each side. Women who take a traditional subordinate position may gain male favor but lose personal opportunities, social power, and economic autonomy in a culture that provides them with minimal financial protection. Those women who decide to pursue ambitions are threatened with damage to their relationships and are ridi-

culed or harassed when they are pioneers in previously male-dominated
fields. Men are also in a bind. If they accept women into positions
of authority, they double their competition at work and lose a full-time
caretaker and support system at home. Not a happy prospect.

Perhaps surprisingly, when women finally do gain access to previously male privileges, societal norms adjust relatively rapidly. While
women of each new generation are threatened with social rejection if
they deviate from traditional roles, as the gains become institutionalized, they are quickly integrated into the social fabric. We no longer
think of women who wish to vote as bluestockings. Women who graduate from college are not believed to be sterile. Women who want jobs
are not assumed to be heading for spinsterhood. But the emotional cost
to the women on the front lines, who initiate these changes, should not
be underestimated. The price has been and continues to be steep. We
remain in the midst of a profound shifting of women's roles—with all
the inevitable contradictions, resentments, losses, and gains.

As contemporary women evaluate their goals, they must decide how
much of the stress and discomfort that currently comes with ambition
they are willing to tolerate. I have vivid memories of being among
the first large wave of women medical students and doctors. My first
interviewer for medical school, a surgeon, asked antagonistically how
I could possibly care for my children. In medical school many of the
physicians who taught us were openly hostile to women students. I
recall a lecture on endometriosis entitled "The Working Woman's Disease." The lecturer repeatedly stressed the high rates of sterility in
women who postponed childbearing for a career. There were almost
no women professors. The hospital didn't even have uniforms that fit
us—for a while we all looked like little girls dressed up in Daddy's
clothes. When my cohort of women moved on to our residencies and
fellowships in our early thirties, there were no established policies
about pregnancy leave, no options for part-time work, no available
child care. I gave birth to one of my children after finishing my patient
rounds at nine o'clock at night. Luckily the delivery room was only
across the street! Would I do this training again? I'm not sure. I love

being a doctor, but at that historical moment becoming a woman physician was a brutal, confusing, and often demoralizing process.

Twenty years later many of the problems my colleagues and I faced during our training have been addressed. Women are a widely accepted part of the medical community. But in this field as in many others, the most intense social pressures around femininity are now shifted to a later phase of women's lives—when they have families. Women who pursue careers must cope with jobs structured to accommodate the life cycles of men with wives who don't have full-time careers. It's a situation that still creates agonizing choices. As at each prior time when women gained new opportunities, the early stages of change are exhilarating but also painful.

CHAPTER TEN

COMBINING FEMININITY
AND MASTERY

W e tend to think of the issues facing the present cohort of women as contemporary ones, and the compromises that we devise as innovative. But women's efforts to integrate mastery with traditional femininity have a very long history. Huge social changes in women's lives began to occur in the early 1800s and accelerated in the following decades. During this period, as other disenfranchised groups within the United States won increasing rights, women's status in society slowly grew to be a national issue. Working-class men gained the right to vote near the beginning of the nineteenth century, and African American men obtained voting privileges when the Fifteenth Amendment was passed in 1870. The extension of civil participation to these previously socially marginalized groups brought the issue of denying equal status to women into stark relief.

From the 1840s through the 1860s women's property acts were passed by individual states, for the first time allowing married women to have control of their inheritance. Prior to these laws women's status with regard to property had been similar to that of children. Women's organizations demanding equal legal standing and suffrage for women gained momentum throughout the nineteenth century. By the late 1800s many institutions of higher learning for women had been founded: Vassar College in 1861, Wellesley College in 1870, Smith College in 1871, Radcliffe College in 1879, Barnard College in 1889. Women also gained admission to some state universities. By the early twentieth century, women were receiving undergraduate educations in ever-increasing numbers, and a few women even attended professional schools. Finally, in 1920 the women suffragettes won the right to vote.

Decade by decade legal, political, educational, and medical barriers to the advancement of women were removed, in significant part due to the work of women activists. Additional pressures for change were applied by financial, corporate, and political institutions that expected to reap pragmatic gains from advances in women's status. Labor shortages, for example, led businesses to view women as a new and potentially lucrative segment of the workforce. Certain debt structures were more advantageous to banks if women had rights to property they inherited. As the sociologist Robert Max Jackson has pointed out, often the ultimate impact of these incremental changes went largely unappreciated by the very institutions that had implemented them.

Women's role as central, contributing members of agrarian households diminished. Much of the population relocated to urban areas. Furthermore, many of the products that women had contributed to their families' economies—cloth, soap, clothing, preserved foods—could now be more cheaply produced in factories. Numerous domestic skills became obsolete.

Scientific advances began to provide women with more control over their reproductive life. Anesthesia became available for childbirth; maternal and infant mortality rates fell due to public health measures. As more children survived their early years (and were no longer needed for labor on family farms), the birth rate plummeted. From early in the nineteenth century on into the twentieth, each successive generation of women gave birth to fewer children. By the 1930s women were bearing only one-third the number of children that their female ancestors had borne a century earlier. An interesting consequence of this reduced family size was that many more families did not have sons: a couple with five children statistically has approximately a 3 percent chance of having no sons, while a family with two children has a 25 percent chance. One can only imagine how this affected parental, and particularly paternal, attitudes toward the daughters who would be their only heirs. Presumably securing property rights and other legal protections for daughters became a higher priority.

In the twentieth century, medical and public heath advances extended women's life spans far beyond the childbearing and child-rearing years. Between 1900 and 1995 women's life expectancy increased from forty-nine to eighty years—a difference of thirty-one years. Safe, easy birth control methods were discovered and made widely available. Abortion became legal with the Supreme Court's 1973 ruling in *Roe v. Wade.*

The structure of women's lives was radically transformed by these broad social and medical developments. Virtually every aspect and stage of their life cycle had to be reconfigured. Men, during this same period, were frequently shifted from one type of labor to another, commonly experiencing a severe sense of dislocation with each transition. But unlike women, their position in the family and community was relatively stable. They held authority in most institutions and were expected to work outside the home to support their families. For women, the opposite was true: virtually every aspect of their social roles was open for reevaluation and restructuring to an extent that was without historical precedent.

DOMESTIC ARRANGEMENTS

During these decades of social change, as the tasks of motherhood lessened and the pressures to join the workforce increased, women struggled to resolve the contradictions between mastery and the feminine role. Despite the massive shifts in women's lives, the ideal of femininity had remained surprisingly intact. The widening gap between women's participation in civic life and notions of "refined" womanly behavior was increasingly problematic. In response to this conundrum, women devised a variety of "solutions"—some more successful than others.

Many of the earliest pioneers, in their effort to lay claim to the privileged masculine qualities of agency and initiative, simply adopted male characteristics wholesale. Some of these women dressed as males; others used male names or took on male roles. As Phyllis Rose noted in *Writing of Women,* George Sand and George Eliot assumed male noms de plume, while Jean Rhys (née Ella Gwendolyn Rees) chose her first husband's name as her pen name. Willa Cather used the name William Cather through high school and college, while Colette, née Sidonie-Gabrielle Colette, chose for her writing name her patronymic, which is also a woman's name—merging the masculine and feminine. Gertrude Stein essentially assumed a conventional male role in her lesbian relationship with her "wife," Alice B. Toklas.

Other early women of achievement chose the reverse approach. Rather than assuming elements of male identity, they limited the demands placed on them by traditional femininity. They minimized role conflicts by removing themselves from customary caretaker roles: before the mid-twentieth century, most women of accomplishment did not even try to combine the traditional female roles of wife and mother with their vocations. Among women writers—one of the professions most hospitable to women—prior to the mid-twentieth century, a hugely disproportionate number were single or childless: Jane Austen, George Eliot, Charlotte Brontë, Emily Brontë, Edith Wharton, Emily Dickinson, Willa Cather, Gertrude Stein, Virginia Woolf, and Katherine Mansfield, to name but a few.

Women with groundbreaking careers in social services, such as Florence Nightingale and Jane Addams, also tended to be unmarried and/or childless. Nightingale, who was born into high society, had many suitors and at one point was sorely tempted to marry a young man courting her. But she had the self-knowledge and understanding of the contemporary limits imposed by marriage to refuse his offer. As she wrote in her diary:

> I have an intellectual nature which requires satisfaction, and that would find it in him. I have a passionate nature which requires satisfaction, and that would find it in him. I have a moral, an active nature which requires satisfaction, and that would not find it in his life.

Jane Addams, another young woman from a prosperous family, artfully dodged parental efforts to get her "married off" by extending her grand tour of Europe, a trip that was de rigueur for young women of her time and class, by an extra two years. After returning home, she again set out for Europe—away from familial pressures. During these years of young womanhood Addams suffered long bouts of illness, some physical but others more likely of psychological origin. These ailments, as well as her travels, permitted her to withdraw from many of the social events designed to encourage courtship and marriage.

Right up until the last quarter of the twentieth century, a disproportionate number of accomplished women remained single, including such famous scientists as Barbara McClintock, a recipient of the Nobel Prize; Lise Meitner, one of the founders of nuclear fission research; and Rosalind Franklin, a pioneer X-ray crystallographer who many believe should have shared the Nobel Prize for the discovery of DNA with James Watson and Francis Crick.

The few women who managed to have successful careers as well as being wives or mothers did so only by devising highly unconventional support systems. Accomplished women in heterosexual relationships frequently chose unconventional men for husbands or companions. These men were not simply supportive of the women's careers, they were intensely invested in them, devoting extensive time to reading, editing, or otherwise promoting their work. George Eliot's out-of-wedlock partner, George Henry Lewes, deeply admired her writing and encouraged her to begin writing fiction. Leonard Woolf nursed Virginia Woolf through her periods of psychotic depression, agreed not to have children, and set up the Hogarth Press as a kind of occupational therapy for her. In each of these dyads, the woman was creative and productive within a relationship that in many ways reversed traditional male-female roles. Or perhaps it is more accurate to say that both husband and wife assumed broader, more androgynous gender roles.

In the few cases in which a woman of accomplishment had both husband and children, the relationship was, if anything, even more culturally anomalous. Pierre Curie, the husband and collaborator of Marie Curie, actually abandoned his own scientific projects to collaborate on her study of radiation. He devoted himself to this enterprise until the end of his life, and their joint efforts famously won them the Nobel Prize. (Less well known is the fact that after his death she went on to win a second Nobel on her own—and their daughter also won a Nobel.)

There are, of course, exceptions to all generalizations. Not every accomplished woman before the mid-twentieth century was unmarried, childless, or in a relationship with a highly supportive man. But an examination of the few exceptions is illuminating. By and large these women were able to pursue their goals only by fashioning original support systems that relieved them of sole caretaking responsibilities for their families and/or provided support for their work.

The life of Elizabeth Cady Stanton, a founder of the women's rights movement, at first glance seems to defy all predictions. She married a man who, despite his radical past, settled into the staid bourgeois role of the paterfamilias, and she gave birth to no fewer than seven children. But Stanton's apparently traditional life was, on second glance, highly innovative. For a significant part of her adulthood she was in a relationship with Susan B. Anthony that easily rivaled the intensity of her marriage. It was probably an intimate friendship, although some biographers have suggested that it had sexual undercurrents: she and the unmarried Anthony formed, for many years, a productive and highly complementary pair.

Anthony lived with Stanton during Stanton's years in New York and frequently helped out with the domestic chores; reportedly she even supervised the weaning of one of Stanton's children! Stanton was well aware that without this devoted colleague, she might have had to abandon her cause: "I might, in time, like too many women, have become wholly absorbed in a narrow family selfishness." The unmarried Anthony had the freedom and mobility to carry out many of the political strategies that Stanton and she devised. As Stanton described the collaboration, "I forged the thunderbolts and she fired them." Elizabeth Cady Stanton, even with her famously high energy, could not have managed the roles of mother, wife, and political activist without the unstinting commitment of her friend.

By the early to mid-twentieth century, a new option became available to women who had difficulty combining the traits of "feminine" and "masculine" roles. For the first time, women who chose a traditional marriage—only to discover that the demands it placed on them were too confining—had the option of divorce. And many women of accomplishment decided to take it.

Margaret Bourke-White, the famous photographer, described how, after a first, unsuccessful marriage, she remarried—against her better judgment—only to separate again:

> We had talked this over so often. I did not want to marry again. It was
> not that I was against marriage, despite my initial unhappy experience.
> But I had carved out a different kind of life now. . . . The very secret of
> life for me, I believed, was to maintain in the midst of rushing events
> an inner tranquility. . . . This was something I could not have if I was
> torn apart for fear of hurting someone every time an assignment
> [involving travel] came up. . . . I wanted no conflict of loyalties—that
> would be too painful.

After her divorce, Bourke-White commented, "I was relieved when it was all over and glad we parted with mutual affection and respect which still endures. Now I could put my personal problems behind me."

Margaret Mead, reflecting back, like Bourke-White, on an unsuccessful marriage that ended in divorce, recalled:

> He was too demanding and jealous of my attention; he begrudged
> even the attention I gave to a piece of mending. I had always felt that
> my father demanded too much of my mother and took her away from
> us to satisfy his own immediate and capricious requests to do some-
> thing or find something for him. I did not want a marriage that re-
> peated this pattern.

Only after she had achieved fame for *Coming of Age in Samoa* did Mead marry again, this time to a colleague and collaborator. It was in this third marriage, after her career was well established, that she had given birth to her daughter.

Eva Hesse, the innovative sculptor, spent much of her artistic life known chiefly as the wife of the successful painter Tom Doyle. Hesse developed her influential, signature style only in the 1960s, as their marriage fell apart and finally ended. Describing the marriage, Hesse reported: "Resentments enter most precisely if I need to be cooking, washing, or doing dishes while he sits King of the Roost reading." Doyle's rebuttal is equally telling: "Hearing that quoted all the time really pisses me off. It's like I never did anything. I did as much as I could." As much as he could? According to whom, one might ask. But whether Doyle encouraged Hesse's work sufficiently or not, Hesse was publicly perceived and perhaps personally experienced herself chiefly as his wife until she left him.

In *Einstein's Wife: Work and Marriage in the Lives of Five Great Twentieth-Century Women,* Andrea Gabor describes a rather grimmer "solution" to the conflicts women experience in combining their own ambitions with the demands of the feminine role. Two of the five women she studied—an artist, Lee Krasner, and a renowned architect and city planner, Denise Scott Brown—were able to develop their careers in large part because their spouses died:

> Like Lee Krasner, Denise Scott Brown had been suddenly, violently—albeit unwillingly—liberated from her marriage. And as with Krasner, that liberation allowed her to accomplish a body of work that she may well never have mastered at the side of a husband whose needs often came close to overwhelming her own. Robert [Brown]'s death initiated a period of mourning and a five-year bout of intense work and study in which grief clarified Denise's intellectual interests and helped lay a foundation for her career as an architect and urban planner.

Prior to Robert Brown's death in a car accident, he had been resentful and depressed by his wife's academic successes, which surpassed his own. Denise Scott Brown, aware of these escalating marital tensions, had agreed with her academic adviser that she needed to assume a professional position "behind her husband." When Denise Scott Brown later remarried, again to an architect, her work again took the backseat to his. Brown agreed to have her husband become the first author on a collaborative book based on her early work. For over a decade after she joined their architectural firm, its title did not include her name.

If there is a message from these earlier women of accomplishment, it is that at least up until the last half century, the traditional feminine marital role was largely incompatible with the pursuit of personal ambitions. Those few women who were able to combine marriage or family with a public role did so only by devising radically innova-

tive domestic arrangements. For the most part these enormously productive women were single, divorced, gay, childless, or within socially
anomalous relationships that provided highly unusual amounts of support for their work. There was no easy solution for combining a traditional feminine role with mastery within the domestic sphere.

THE PUBLIC ARENA

As women slowly began to move into the public sphere during the last
two centuries, they strove mightily to redefine previously male professions in a manner that placed them within the purview of the traditional, self-effacing, supportive feminine role. The writing of family
letters and diaries was expanded into more formal literary produc-
tions. Women extended their domestic chores by becoming spinners
(hence the word *spinster*), seamstresses, and milliners. They went from
positions as nannies or governesses for individual families to employment as schoolteachers.

The caretaking role within the home was incrementally enlarged
and redefined to encompass caring for the needy within the community. Middle-class women correctly perceived that they would be less
vulnerable to attacks of being "unwomanly" if they were active in
"selfless" and unremunerated work. With this in mind, women of the
nineteenth and twentieth centuries created and staffed organizations
designed to aid the least privileged members of society. They were
active in the abolitionist movement and underground railway, the Sal-
vation Army, the nursing profession, and settlement houses. Harriet
Beecher Stowe's politically explosive *Uncle Tom's Cabin* publicized the
cruel exploitation of slaves.

During the nineteenth century many women began to work in jobs
at the very bottom of the employment ladder—in textile mills or as
seamstresses in private shops or factories. These brutal positions fit in
well with the mandates of femininity: they were clearly low-level positions with little in the way of social or financial rewards. Furthermore,
these women were engaged in providing basic subsistence for their
families. Women were allowed to move into the labor market if they

did not challenge the fundamental aspects of the traditional gender divide.

Later, in the first half of the twentieth century, secretarial jobs were introduced that reiterated the traditional male-female marital dynamic: women did the low-level daily tasks required to support the professional needs of a male boss who received greater pay, power, and status. The new "modern sector" of the economy produced a host of other service jobs for women as retail clerks, telephone operators, waitresses, boardinghouse keepers, and laundresses. Each of these venues allowed a woman to master new skills and participate in the larger community while remaining within the dictates of the subordinate feminine role. Interestingly, despite the fact that a steadily increasing number of women were joining the job market, occupational segregation by sex was nearly total: there were separate "women's jobs" and "men's jobs." This division persisted unchanged through much of the twentieth century.

In the rare instances when a woman's role clearly exceeded the accepted feminine mandates, this fact was often artfully hidden behind a public image of humility and self-sacrifice. Florence Nightingale is a wonderful exemplar of this tactic. She was one of the powerhouses of the Victorian era, a pioneer in expanding women's role in the community—and spinning it as simple nurturing of those in need. Lytton Strachey, at the beginning of his 1918 biographical essay on Nightingale, noted:

> Everyone knows the popular conception of Florence Nightingale. The saintly, self-sacrificing woman, the delicate maiden of high degree who threw aside the pleasures of a life of ease to succour the afflicted, the Lady with the Lamp, gliding through the horrors of the hospital at Scutari, and consecrating with the radiance of her goodness the dying soldier's couch—the vision is familiar to all.

Strachey tried to rectify this "feminized" portrait of Nightingale by documenting her massive role in devising and implementing new public health measures in England. She was a hugely effective administrator. She organized the government's medical services for its military, helped found the field of biostatistics, and even designed hospitals and clinics. (The hospital where I did my medical training in the late twentieth century was based on her architectural plan.)

But Nightingale was aware that as a woman she could not afford to be seen as deriving enjoyment or power from her accomplishments. Self-sacrifice was the order of the day. In addition to her many other talents, Nightingale was a brilliant career strategist. She maintained her huge influence on government policy, at a certain remove. Returning to London after the war, she lived out her life as a reclusive, delicate, mysterious presence, a disembodied angel of mercy, while keeping her contacts and influence in high places and managing to send out for publication an endless stream of books, reports, and pamphlets. It was something of a stealth operation—she rarely appeared in public—but it was so successful that her name still evokes little more than the image of a devoted nurse, selflessly ministering to wounded soldiers on the battlefield. Nightingale managed to found one of the first professional occupations open to and socially accepted for women by carefully positioning it as womanly. It is, after all, a field whose very name derives from female lactation, and what could be more feminine than that?

OUTLAWS: WOMEN WHO EMBRACED DEVIANCE

Not all the women who pioneered active roles in the public sphere tried to integrate traditional femininity with the "masculine" attributes required for mastery. Some of these women had no wish to quietly and artfully blend their innovations into the preexisting social fabric. Instead, they chose to openly defy the cultural norms and take the consequences. In fact, they used their opposition to conventional beliefs as the basis for their identity, taking their "deviance" as a source of pride. Rather than expecting or needing broad social acceptance, such women saw themselves as daring innovators, spokesmen for beliefs that they held to be morally and socially correct. They fully expected and accepted that their challenges to the status quo would evoke resistance in the form of social rejection.

But who, one must ask, did these women use as models for their

new rebellious role? Historically up to this point, there had been pitifully few examples of women with dynamic, productive public lives:
the female saints, a few queens, a handful of authors, and some biblical
or mythological figures. There have been many theories about the ori-
gins of women's increasing demands for a broader social role. But
undoubtedly the abolitionist movement provided an important social
context, moving human rights to the center of public debates and promoting political activism of all kinds.

As a part of this vast national debate during the nineteenth century,
an extraordinary literary development was instrumental in shaping a
new narrative of women's lives. Jill Ker Conway observes in her collection of women's autobiographies, *Written by Herself,* that when the
stories of women slaves, such as Harriet Ann Jacobs, began to be published, they provided a new type of protagonist: the brave, independent woman:

> These [slave] narratives escape the bourgeois convention that a
> woman's story ends in marriage, because slavery allowed a woman no
> family. . . . Slave narratives are heroic stories of survival, accounts of
> endurance and of inextinguishable identity which transcend the usual
> Western quest for romance. This gives them their formidable power
> and explains their dynamizing impact on white women abolitionists.

The stories of such self-reliant women helped provide a template for
white, middle-class women to imagine their own lives as distinct from
those of men. These memoirs provided an alternative to the previously
accepted structure of a female life: the romantic story of courtship,
marriage, and family service. For those white women whose personal
experiences had already convinced them that they had little to gain
from customary feminine roles, here was a radical new concept of a
woman's life. Furthermore, a growing number of black women, some
of them former slaves, actively and publicly supported women's rights.
The former slave Sojourner Truth as well as free blacks such as Harriet
Forten Purvis and Margaretta Forten toured and spoke out at public
gatherings on the issue of suffrage.

As white, middle-class women began taking on active political roles, the stakes were high. The more radical their departure from cultural norms and the earlier it occurred historically, the more severe the consequences. As Susan B. Anthony wrote:

> Those who are really earnest [in their efforts to bring about reform] are willing to be anything or nothing in the world's estimation, and publicly and privately, in season and out, avow their sympathies with the despised ideas and their advocates, and bear the consequences.

There can be no question about the almost unimaginable amounts of courage that such a stance required. During her lifetime Anthony faced hostile crowds, was hung in effigy, and suffered threats on her life. Margaret Sanger, the founder of the birth control movement, was indicted for publishing information about contraception and had to flee the country, leaving her three children behind. She later returned to serve a jail term for her activities.

How were these women able to sustain their morale and convictions in the face of such massive social criticism? It should not detract from our admiration of them to observe that such rebellious stances rarely occur in isolation. There must be a strong personal support system: a powerful mentor, an involved family, or a local group that embraces their anomalous social or political choice. Women who chose a "deviant" role often flourished within an unconventional artistic community, a politically radical family, a political party, or a religious organization that admired and encouraged their work.

Frequently these women innovators were raised in families that forcefully encouraged unconventional beliefs and actions. Women within such supportive contexts could both predict society's outrage at their radical ideals and interpret the inevitable attacks, painful as they might be, as badges of honor. Opposition could be interpreted as validating their identity as a moral crusader.

Susan B. Anthony was raised in a family that was active in the antislavery movement. Abolitionists met weekly at her house when she was growing up, including Frederick Douglass and William Lloyd Garrison. Two of her brothers grew up to be antislave activists in

Kansas. Three of her sisters were arrested with her on one of her suf-frage speaking tours. Political activism was a major part of the family's religious beliefs, values, and traditions. It permitted Anthony to sur-vive, and even at times relish, the fights to which her beliefs gave rise. Her actions were often dramatically adversarial, garnering attention for the cause and for herself. She famously refused to pay the streetcar fare when the police took her into custody, refused to pay bail after her arrest, and refused to pay her court-mandated fine.

Many other early women reformers came from similar backgrounds. Jane Addams was raised in a family with a tradition of political activism in the service of moral causes. Her parents were also raised in the Quaker abolitionist reform movement. Anna Howard Shaw, a pioneer woman preacher, advocate of temperance, and early suffra-gette, was raised in a large Scottish family of serious Unitarians. Their reform-based religious sect met with harsh repression from the English authorities. Ultimately, when Shaw was an infant, the family immi-grated to the United States.

A more recent counterpart of these early rebels raised in politically embattled families is Margaret Thatcher, the first woman prime minis-ter of Great Britain. Anyone who ever watched Thatcher take on her political opponents with unapologetic delight could not help but be struck by her exhilaration. Thatcher thrived on being attacked by her colleagues, a situation that would make most women want to crawl under the nearest chair. Verbally routing those with "unenlightened" views was her mission. She made no effort to soften her articulate, aggressive speaking style. When Thatcher applied for her first job, she was turned down. Her evaluation by the interviewer read: "This young woman has much too strong a personality to work here."

Thatcher made it clear in her autobiography that a preeminent value of her parents was to uphold what they considered to be right and true, even if their position was unpopular. Her family was, quite literally, nonconformist: they were Methodists in an overwhelmingly Episco-palian society. In addition, they were conservatives on issues that placed them in the minority even within this dissenting religious group. As Thatcher succinctly described it, "We were the odd family out"—a great source of family pride and solidarity. Thatcher's father, who was also her political mentor, repeatedly drove home the importance of independence:

> When I said to my father that my friends were able to go out for a walk . . . and I would like to join them, he would reply: "Never do things just because other people do them." In fact, this was one of his favorite expressions.

Thatcher, rather self-righteously, quoted "some verses which I still use in off-the-cuff speeches because they came to embody for me so much of what I was brought up to feel":

> *One ship drives East, and another drives West,*
> *By the self-same gale that blows;*
> *'Tis the set of the sail, and not the gale,*
> *That determines the way she goes.*

As with many other women who have upended social conventions regarding feminine roles, Thatcher's difficult position with regard to the larger society was consistent with her immediate family's beliefs and values. Even rebels require a strong social support system—otherwise the social opprobrium is too profoundly isolating.

Of the women reformers who did not come from reform-minded, middle-class families, many had grown up in families that left them disillusioned with the status quo. These women were raised in such blatantly inadequate or destroyed families that they rejected the traditional domestic model of womanhood out of hand. Typically the father was absent, abusive, ineffective, or punitive to the daughter. Such women experienced their fathers as unreliable at best and destructive at worst. Families of this kind produced young women with little trust in male protection and an abiding sense that they must fend for themselves— no matter what the social cost. Traditional femininity—based on the notion of ingratiating oneself to a man with the expectation of lifetime support from a husband—seemed futile or unsafe to them.

Margaret Sanger, the founder of the birth control movement, was raised in a problematic family of this type: she was one of eleven children. Her mother literally worked herself to death, while her father "took little or no responsibility." The father was frequently critical of Sanger and her sisters while favoring the brothers. At one crucial juncture he locked Sanger out of the house; the times when he provided support to her were erratic. Sanger had seen firsthand the potentially devastating impact of taking a subordinate, self-effacing, feminine role and wanted no part of it. From early on she realized that an adversarial stance was the only one that would save her from sinking into a position like her mother's.

Sanger became something of a contrarian, and in her recollections of her childhood she described how at school, even when economic issues were discussed, she'd seize upon the unpopular position: "The other students had automatically accepted the cause of solid money. I espoused free silver." When Sanger joined the Socialist Party, she chose Local Number Five, "itself something of a rebel in the [social party] ranks." The magazine Sanger founded was called *Woman Rebel,* and in it she defined a woman's duty as "[t]o look the world in the face with a go-to-hell look in the eyes: to have an idea, to speak and act in defiance of convention." This was not a woman who wanted to "fit in."

It is important to note, however, that Sanger nearly always had a robust social support system. Her first husband was enthusiastic about her work, encouraging her and doing domestic duties to give her time for her writing. Sanger's sister Ethel often worked with her and even went to jail for the cause of birth control. Sanger had affairs with powerful established men such as Havelock Ellis, who helped her materially and intellectually. Sanger's sister Nan, and even her critical father, provided important contributions by standing in as foster parents for her children when she could not care for them. Her work was heroic, but she was hardly alone in her crusade.

Most of the groundbreaking women of the last two centuries, like Sanger, had a combination of unusual circumstances: a family that laid the groundwork for their rebellion, and the talent or charisma to cre-

ate a circle of devoted supporters. Even when their position represented a radical departure from the larger culture, these women had
encouragement in their personal and community lives.

Whether leading the way toward new women's rights as Margaret
Sanger did or simply getting a job outside the home, women of the
nineteenth and early twentieth centuries lived in a society in which their
position was constantly shifting. Massive legal, economic, political,
medical, and technological changes required constant new formula-
tions of their roles. Multiple new feminine personae arose and came
in and out of favor: social reformers, suffragettes, flappers, idealized
homemakers, factory workers, pink-collar workers. Women's efforts
to seize new opportunities for themselves and integrate these depar-
tures into the cultural notion of femininity proceeded along multiple
tracks. Many women chose to subtly and quietly work to broaden the
purview of "femininity." Others boldly rejected the status quo, creating new models of female initiative and power.

CONTEMPORARY WOMEN AND MASTERY

By the mid-twentieth century, many of the legal and political obstacles
to women's participation in society had been overcome. Undergraduate education was widely available to women; they had even begun to
go to professional schools in small numbers. In 1972 further progress
was made with the passage of Title IX of the Educational Amendments
Act, prohibiting sex discrimination by educational institutions that
received aid from the federal government.

At midcentury the most blatant discrimination against women
occurred in the workplace. The Federal Equal Pay Act was finally passed
in 1963; the groundbreaking 1964 Civil Rights Act outlawed employment discrimination; but the workforce remained largely segregated
by gender, with most working women remaining in jobs at the low end
of the pay scale. Nearly all the professions, with the exceptions of
nursing, social work, and teaching, remained overwhelmingly male-
dominated. Women's participation in society had expanded up to this
point but little further: most middle-class women remained in their

domestic roles as wives and mothers. Those who had jobs were, for the most part, in poorly paid or in relatively low-status, service-oriented areas of employment.

The publication of Betty Friedan's *The Feminine Mystique* in the mid-1960s coincided with several major historical and cultural events: the wide dissemination of birth control techniques, the new generation of privileged baby boomers who were already challenging many middle-class mores, and rising divorce rates. Protests against the Vietnam War both arose from and further promoted the questioning of traditional authorities and belief systems. Perhaps most important, the civil rights movement sensitized the nation to discrimination against underprivileged groups. Much as the suffrage organizations of the nineteenth century arose in the context of abolitionism, the women's movement of the 1960s and 1970s arrived on the heels of the civil rights movement.

Friedan's thesis was that women had fallen victim to the cultural dictum that they could "find fulfillment only in sexual passivity, male domination, and nurturing maternal love." "Self-esteem in women, as well as in men," she believed, could "only be based on real capacity, competence and achievement; on deserved respect from others rather than unwarranted adulation." The book provided a manifesto for a rapidly growing women's movement that demanded that women be given equal access to the workplace at every level.

The convergence of events produced a swift and massive transformation of women's lives. In fact, such a fundamental social reorganization has probably never occurred so rapidly, except perhaps in such time-limited crises as war. Sexual mores, the distinctive dress codes for the two sexes, marital norms, employment rates for women, and access to previously male-dominated professions all radically changed over the next decades. In 1960 only 19 percent of married women with preschool children were employed. By 1995 that figure had climbed to 64 percent.

Women have more options now than in any prior historical period. Young women are increasingly pursuing goals in the public sphere. Women are assuming new professional roles, particularly in the years prior to marriage and childbearing. By the mid-1980s women were

applying to graduate programs in the humanities as well as to professional schools in medicine, law, accounting, and business in equal or
greater numbers than men. Nearly all the professions in the United
States have seen a substantial rise in the percentage of women in their
ranks—even if the women remain clustered at the lower echelons of
many career tracks. From 1960 to 1995, for example, the percentage
of physicians who were women rose from 9 to 25 percent, while women
lawyers went from 5 to 26 percent of the profession. During the 1990s
60 percent of families had both husband and wife working, and in
40 percent of families both were working full-time.

CHANGING GENDER ROLES

In tandem with these changes came a massive rethinking of gender
roles. Many of the newer theories of gender minimized the contradictions that arise when women (or men) try to combine traditional masculine and feminine traits. You can be a leader whose style is nurturing
and inclusive, and you can be a caretaker who is proactive, confident of
your beliefs, and effective. Reading contemporary gender theories, you
might think that the conflicting demands that accomplished women
had struggled with in the past no longer existed.

Young women are, in fact, increasingly endorsing both sets of attributes. To combine traditionally masculine and feminine qualities has
become, at least nominally, a cultural ideal and, as such, is receiving
enthusiastic endorsements from a surprising variety of sources. The
business community, for example, has embraced the use of more "feminine," group-oriented structures in workplaces previously dominated
by more competitive "masculine" ones. "People skills" is a ubiquitous buzzword. The most popular book at Harvard Business School
extolls "the virtues of interconnectedness"—shades of Carol Gilligan.

In fact, no one seems to have a good word for the traditional binary
system of gender roles. It is arguable that the examination and break-
down of the mutually exclusive, dual gender system is the dominant
cultural theme of our time. Studies of bisexuality, androgyny, homosexuality, and other forms of gender role "deviance" are a focus in

humanities departments across the country; college catalogs abound in courses on cross-dressing in Shakespeare and "queer studies."

In the art world, critiques of sexual stereotypes are prime material for every genre, from Adrienne Rich's poetry to Judy Chicago's feminist installations to Cindy Sherman's photographs cataloging female personae to Jeffrey Eugenides's best-selling novel *Middlesex,* about a hermaphrodite raised as a female but genetically a male. Diane Middlebrook's biography, *Suits Me: The Double Life of Billy Tipton,* recounts the tale of a transsexual woman who led her entire adult life, including marriage, disguised as a man; *Newsweek* hailed the book as "the paradigmatic biography of our time."

The popular media, always quick to exploit any cultural trend, has hurried to add gay or bisexual characters to sitcoms and major motion pictures. Comedies like *The Birdcage* depict charming gay families, while earnest tragedies like *Philadelphia* expose discrimination against gays. In *The Crying Game,* a surprise independent film hit, the female protagonist is revealed to be a male transvestite, while the critically acclaimed movie *Boys Don't Cry* tells the true story of a girl who tried to pass herself off as a boy.

The question at the present time, then, is what conflicts, if any, remain for women who attain professional skills and venture into the public sphere. Do the notions of traditional masculinity and femininity still have powerful legacies in the culture, and if conflicts remain between these two ideals, how can women best deal with them? Women are coping with massive changes that have occurred in every aspect of their lives. What works for them and what proves disastrous as they gain access to work opportunities that were never available to them before?

A spate of new books, including *I Don't Know How She Does It; The Bitch in the House: 26 Women Tell the Truth about Sex, Solitude, Work, Motherhood, and Marriage;* and *The Price of Motherhood,* attests to the fact that merging traditional "masculine" and "feminine" roles remains overwhelmingly problematic—and exhausting. In each of these books the young woman author seems stunned by the unexpected complexities involved in trying to retain one's identity and goals while combining motherhood, marriage, and work. In fact, at times this project seems downright impossible. As the popular joke goes, a contemporary woman must "act like a lady, think like a man, and work like a dog." Somehow the pieces don't fit together into a coherent, feasible reality, particularly for young married women with children. But even for older women of accomplishment, the social agendas they seek to fulfill are often in conflict.

Accomplished women often try out one persona after another in an effort to meld the requirements of the two gender roles. Public figures as different as Hillary Rodham Clinton and Madonna have morphed from one identity to another trying to get it right. Clinton changed her hair color, makeup, eyewear, haircut, clothing style (dresses or pantsuits), and even her name multiple times. Should she keep her maiden name, assume her husband's name, or insert her maiden name before her married name? She veered between being a policy wonk and dispensing chocolate chip cookie recipes. She eventually opted for a position of political power—but only after "proving" her femininity by supporting her husband through his humiliatingly public infidelities. One wonders if she could have been elected senator from New York if she had chosen to divorce him.

In a similar fashion, Madonna has switched from being the "material girl" and dominatrix to being a mystic and a traditional bride and mom. As she sings in the title track of her album *American Life,* "I tried to be a boy, I tried to be a girl, I tried to be a mess, I tried to be the best. I guess I got it wrong."

When women pursue types of mastery previously unavailable to them, they suddenly enter a bewildering terra incognita. Because they still are, in fact, pioneering new gender roles, their choices are frequently criticized by those around them, no matter what they choose. The inevitable social opprobrium elicited by such new ventures is uncomfortable and confusing to women, whether it comes from other moms at the PTA meeting or from colleagues at work or from their own families. I remember with horror the looks I received from other mothers at my children's nursery school when I, alone in the entire group, did not raise my hand to volunteer. They were asking us to take Tuesday or Thursday mornings off to prepare for the Spring Festival. At the time I was still a practicing internist. I could just picture trying to explain these absences to my covering colleagues, my residents, and my medical students, not to speak of my patients. There was no way I could possibly do it. I felt awful. I was letting down the school and missing out on what might have been a fun social experience. I even had the paranoid fantasy that it would affect the school's attitude toward my children.

"Not caring" about such criticism is rarely an option unless a woman has unusually strong, countervailing supports in place. Identity requires ongoing corroboration by others. As the philosopher Charles Taylor observes, "A person or group of people can suffer real damage, real distortion, if the people or society around them mirror back to them a confining or demeaning or contemptible picture of themselves." We need people in our immediate environment to think well of us so we can think well of ourselves. Being surrounded by well-intentioned but ambivalent or openly disapproving people is debilitating.

Forming a coherent, comfortable identity as a powerful woman clearly remains a problem, particularly for white, middle-class women. All too often they must improvise as they go, unsure about the eventual outcome for themselves, their work, their marriage, and their children. As Virginia Woolf remarked about the pioneering women writers in her era, "They [had] no tradition behind them, or one so short and partial that it was of little help."

DEVELOPING MASTERY IN THE CONTEXT OF MALE SUPPORT

Some women have been ingenious or lucky enough to find circumstances that bridge the masculinity-femininity divide. They have found situations that allow them to develop mastery within a protected environment that neutralizes painful questions about their womanliness. The most tried-and-true tactic for integrating femininity with mastery is to develop skills within a reassuringly traditional male-female relationship, the woman being in the subordinate, mentee role. An important (usually older) man in a girl's or woman's life encourages and/or instructs her. He could be a father, a teacher, a professor, a boss, or a husband. The ongoing male-female dynamic dramatically lessens the woman's vulnerability to doubts concerning her feminine identity. In such relationships the female often seeks to remain in a nondominant role—even as her status advances—further allaying fears of being desexualized.

The father-daughter relationship is the earliest and perhaps the prototypical relationship that protects female identity in situations of accomplishment. As girls go into their years of schooling, particularly in high school and beyond, male teachers can provide mentoring support that stabilizes sexual identity. The student mentee role can be a particularly reassuring one for girls and young women and can diminish the impact of disapproving male peers: being the eager understudy to a male teacher is a well-traveled route for young women. Sometimes there is an understated or even overt flirtatious element in such relationships.

In more general terms, the subordinate status that characterizes being a student may help explain women's rapid advances in the educational system. Being a student provides a unique blend of self-advancement while remaining in the one-down position; a student works to "please" the authority. For girls and women this situation has proved to be relatively comfortable and compatible with their feminine mandates. Women have excelled academically.

Women in entry-level jobs often enjoy the role of "gal Friday," providing crucial support for their boss's career. Many women, for example, thrive in the early stages of legal training at the associate level but become progressively more dissatisfied as they advance through the ranks and must function more independently and competitively. In the scientific community, women often do exceptional doctoral theses and go on to work successfully as postdoctorate fellows in the labs of senior scientists. It is frequently at the stage where they must apply for their own grants and establish their own laboratories that they begin to falter.

Margaret Hennig and Anne Jardim, in their book on women managers, quote women executives as saying that their (male) bosses were the "make or break factor" in their work lives. The women likened their bosses to a father; one described her boss as her "supporter, her encourager, her teacher and her strength in the company." When the male bosses left or retired, the women found themselves less interested in their work.

It is at the stage when a woman no longer functions as the subordinate but must create an independent position for herself that she begins to fall behind professionally. Undoubtedly this pattern occurs for many reasons. There remains a huge amount of outright discrimination, but many women also feel an element of ambivalence and confusion as they lose their traditional female status as the adjunct to a more powerful figure.

For some women of accomplishment, the pressures on femininity produced by increasing responsibility at work are attenuated by a supportive husband. Partnership with an actively encouraging spouse is a factor commonly cited by accomplished women—as it has been for the last century and a half. The relationship renders derogatory sexual innuendos at work less credible; a woman can no longer be derided as unattractive, "spinsterly," and incapable of a "normal" relationship. A husband who supports his wife's career also lightens her workload at home. In one study by Catalyst, an organization that funds research on women in business, female corporate executives were asked how they had managed to balance personal life and career. The largest single response was that "having a supportive spouse [had] been key to their own ability to balance work and family responsibilities." Some of these women's comments were: "Married the right guy—not threatened by me, shares work." "Married a very forward-thinking husband, who is wonderfully attentive father." "You can't do without a spouse who's willing to work with you. And without a spouse who values it. . . . The first role he played was believing it was right, and entering into the marriage, the relationship and everything, under the assumption that I was going to work. . . . And the second role has been that he has always done his share of the tasks." One woman simply noted without further comment, "Married the right guy—the second time."

Ruth Bader Ginsburg, the second woman to reach the Supreme Court, has a classically supportive husband. Martin Ginsburg, a tax professor at Georgetown Law School, has been enormously encouraging about her career and has few qualms about his unusual role. On the practical front, he cooks for the family. As described in a *New York Times* profile, "Martin Ginsburg does indeed cook—he taught himself by reading Escoffier while serving in the Army at Fort Sill, Oklahoma— and he takes pleasure in challenging traditional sex roles by preparing elaborate banquets in the classical style for Justice Ginsburg's clerks, colleagues and friends. . . . As a general rule," Martin Ginsburg announced jokingly, "my wife does not give me any advice about cooking, and I do not give her any advice about law. This seems to work well on both sides."

Martin Ginsburg's humorous remark touches on an extremely important point. If a woman wishes to pursue an ambition, her male partner cannot simply pay lip service to equality in the relationship. If the great preponderance of domestic work and professional compromise are left to the wife, the final message is to endorse female subordination. All too commonly a woman has a husband who verbally encourages her career, but after their children are born, he continues his own career at full tilt while her career is indefinitely put on hold. For all his good intentions, his position is simply an updated version of conventional male hegemony.

A more radical and dramatic solution for a woman with a career is simply to reverse male-female roles: she has the high-powered career, while her husband has a less demanding job or is a full-time househusband. Increasingly, women are earning more than their husbands, and the financial logic of a wife's work taking precedence can become irrefutable. For some men this reversal comes as a huge relief—for one reason or another they are simply not interested in having a full-time career. A man may have other interests that he wants to pursue, a dislike of his profession, a psychological disability that prevents career advancement, or a general lack of career motivation. He may just take to the domestic life or simply grow used to a lifestyle that he couldn't support on his own.

A *Fortune* magazine poll of 187 women who participated in its

"Most Powerful Women in Business Summit" found that 30 percent had househusbands. And the women were clear on the importance of having such full-time support. Dina Dublon, the CFO of J.P. Morgan Chase, commented, "There is no doubt in my mind that the extent to which I can do this is because of his willingness to be at home."

The social stigma attached to this role reversal remains significant, although it is diminishing. The *Fortune* article noted that five years ago it was hard to get anyone to talk about such marriages: "Everyone was in the closet." Now there is much more discussion of the issue. Nonetheless, the women interviewed were extremely protective of their husband's socially anomalous position. Carly Fiorina, chairman and CEO of Hewlett-Packard, is quoted as saying, "Frank has been a huge source of support. He had a very successful career and has lots of interests outside of me and my career. He has been a rock for me; I am tremendously lucky. To describe him as a stay-at-home husband is not fair to him."

In my own psychiatric practice, I have noted an increasing number of marriages that demonstrate this type of role reversal, but in a much less dramatic form. Many, if not most, couples now need two full incomes to maintain their middle-class or upper-middle-class lifestyle. In some marriages it gradually becomes clear that the wife is more capable than the husband and that it is in everyone's best interest to make her career work. The husband will frequently have a solid job, one with limited possibilities for advancement but enough status for him to save face. The wife, who turns out to have more energy or talent or ambition than her husband, slowly takes on the more demanding career.

The psychological fallout from such an arrangement can be complex. Often both husband and wife are ambivalent about it. The wife will appreciate the career opportunities that come her way while resenting the financial and time pressures placed upon her. The husband may feel slightly humiliated but is often relieved to not have to compete aggressively in the job market. In my admittedly limited sample, these marriages ultimately appear to be no more or less stable than their more traditional counterparts.

DOWNPLAYING POWER AND SEXUALITY

Difficulties in integrating "masculine" initiative and authority with "feminine" mandates arise most starkly for women in professions that clearly provide status, authority, or power. At present women in such positions often rush for cover by (rather transparently) trying to spin their careers as purely self-sacrificing, caretaking tasks. The personal pleasures are downplayed; it's all about hard work for others' benefit. Women politicians, for example, because of their high visibility, are particularly vulnerable to the critique of self-aggrandizement or overweening ambition—and as a consequence, many go to extraordinary lengths to stress their altruistic motives. The psychologists Dorothy Cantor and Toni Bernay in *Women in Power* interviewed twenty-five women in elected office. The politicians and the authors alike both profess to believe that status and attention are simply serendipitous by-products of an elected women's expertise:

> The women we studied went for high-visibility, in-the-spotlight careers. . . . Do they need to feel the center of everyone's world . . . We think not . . . these women claim the spotlight and recognition for their political leadership and policymaking talent rather like musicians, who get the spotlight and are respected for their musical ability. This is different from the self-centeredness of adults whose overindulgent parents set no limits and thus led them to believe that the world revolves around them.

As so often happens in the defense of successful women, there is a scolding, self-righteous tone. God forbid that these women "went for high-visibility careers" in part because they enjoyed the publicity. The authors and their political subjects are at pains to convince us that sacrifice is the order of the day. They conclude their description of one senator, Olympia Snowe of Maine, by noting that "even when Snowe was suffering, she thought of somebody else."

Women politicians use another, related strategy to integrate their

"masculine" profession with traditional "feminine" roles: they carefully reframe their profession as an extension of women's position in
their immediate family. Nancy Adler, in a study of women leaders,
describes how former Turkish prime minister Tansu Çiller proposed
during her electoral campaign that she would be the "mother, sister
and daughter" of the Turkish people. Dominica's Eugenia Charles
referred to herself as a "mother of the people." Golda Meir was not
averse to being described as Israel's Jewish grandmother. Interestingly,
the family roles with which women politicians seek to identify themselves are all consanguineous and therefore asexual. The combining
of power and a women's sexual identity must be avoided. There is
no female equivalent of the former presidential candidate Bill Clinton,
a self-proclaimed Elvis wannabe, wiggling his hips and playing a mean
saxophone on *The Arsenio Hall Show*.

Women politicians work overtime to maintain an image that is
at once attractive and womanly but not sexual. This is not a simple
task, and they must be constantly vigilant. A 2001 *USA Today* article
describes a meeting of the women U.S. senators:

> When [Senator Barbara] Boxer spots a picture of [Senator Barbara]
> Mikulski hanging among the restaurant's VIP patrons, she says,
> "Good hair!" In mock acknowledgment of the Holy Grail of fe-
> male politicians' existence, the other senators chime in: "Go-o-o-od
> hair." Laughingly, Mikulski declares: "In my office, hair is content."
> [Senator Hillary Rodham] Clinton cannot help blurt out: "In my
> life."
>
> For now, the female senators' dinners remain an oasis where poli-
> tics is put aside and where the incessant scrutiny of their public lives is
> a subject for commiseration and laughter. As the *USA Today* reporter
> and photographer prepare to leave, Mikulski, who has been worrying
> about details like a chaperone fretting over a clutch of debutantes,
> finally allows wine to be poured. "We're a little funny about booze in
> pictures," she explains.

Debutantes is an interesting choice of word for these middle-aged,
worldly, powerful, hardworking women. Amazingly, they are repre-

senting themselves as young (presexual?) innocents. God forbid that they actually drink in public or appear inelegantly coiffed—despite their grueling schedules.

Unfortunately, young women are acutely aware of the problem that women politicians face in combining femininity with power. One study of college students' ambitions found women to be "significantly more likely than men to anticipate relationship problems associated with the political leader role." Not surprisingly, these young women rated becoming a political leader lower than did their male peers.

BICULTURALISM AND FRAUDULENCE

For a woman training for or practicing a profession that prides it-self on its hypermasculine style, the issue of merging authority with the "feminine" supportive role is particularly bewildering. In law schools, for example, the teaching technique is purposely adversarial and competitive—making it hard for women to participate without being branded as "overly aggressive." This pedagogic technique tends to reduce female participation, and the educational benefit of such a combative format is far from clear. The use of this approach—a virtual caricature of masculinity—even in actual legal practice is also questionable. Today the vast majority of litigation cases end in settlements arrived at by mediation. Nonetheless, the professional legal culture celebrates the adversarial, take-no-prisoners stance at every level of training and practice.

When placed in such exaggeratedly masculine environments, many professional women must switch between a tough persona at work and a more sensitive, pliant one at home in order to fulfill the expectations of both milieus. This phenomenon has been dubbed "biculturalism." In essence, women shuttle back and forth between two dissimilar cultural contexts. Articles on professional women often visually represent the incongruity of their dual roles by photographing them in formal work attire—a suit, a crisp blouse, pumps, stockings, jewelry, a briefcase—awkwardly clutching a drooling, sprawling toddler. This Dr. Jekyll and Mr. Hyde act can leave a woman understandably exhausted and confused about her actual identity—the split between the responses required of her in these two situations is uncomfortable.

An eminent woman lawyer I interviewed gave a vivid portrait of her discomfort with what she described as a "testosterone-driven profession":

> At the time that I became a lawyer, I felt that individuals had to stand up for certain principles against the powers that be. . . . The Vietnam war and the civil rights movement were all happening. Mostly I became a lawyer as an outgrowth of that movement. But jockeying for legal power in the larger society almost meant you abnegated your own self. I was totally in the service of this world out there and not at all about my individual destiny as a human being. My little self was more interested in art history and literature and history and was a more scholarly, softer and subdued person. The self that I put on to be in this larger world was like armor. And I went with the armor, but I'm sorry that I did that. It still doesn't feel like me. Maybe many more men are comfortable with that kind of a dichotomy between what you do and what you are or maybe what they do is what they are.

Women deal with this type of role confusion in many ways. A friend told me about a highly successful woman colleague who, after each of several large promotions, immediately got pregnant—as if to reassure herself that her feminine-maternal identity was still intact. Last I heard she was up to four children.

Another study of women in the business community found that women frequently feel the need to be secretive about their split life—adding yet another stress. Women executives described leading "a double life" and using "smoke and mirrors" to avoid any perception at their jobs that family duties might intrude upon their work lives. Many career women are scared to keep pictures of their children on their desks for fear that their colleagues will question their commitment to work. They worry about leaving early to pick up their children, even if they have arrived at work at dawn to make sure their work gets completed. "These are the women," one researcher noted disapprovingly, "who become gentlemen."

At home, things are not much better. A woman must pretend that she is as domestic and as available to her husband, her children, and the larger community as the housewife next door. This wearying charade goes on in most working women's lives. I vividly recall my own Herculean efforts to get enough done at work to rush to a mothers' luncheon at school or parent (read: mother) get-together.

In her effort to deal with the fragmented sense of self that biculturalism produces, a woman may resort to pure denial. She may decide that her "work self" is an act and that her more traditional feminine role is her "real self." To preserve a culturally accepted sexual identity and consolidate a coherent sense of herself, she minimizes or distances herself from her achievements. Sadly enough, often after heroic efforts, a woman may feel compelled to disown her own success.

While the feelings of fraudulence commonly expressed by women of accomplishment reflect a true underestimation of their capabilities, they are also a way to cope with contradictory expectations. When singled out for promotion, praise, or public attention, many women cannot internalize the affirmation because it threatens their sense of self-effacing femininity. So instead they feel fraudulent. As the psychoanalyst Ethel Person has noted, "The successful woman protects her 'femininity' by denying the authenticity of her success." Such women tenaciously cling to pictures of themselves as timid, incompetent souls mistakenly thrust into positions of power.

The "fraudulence" syndrome is so pervasive in accomplished women's lives that it is readily apparent even at a conference for feminist leaders. One author describes the scene in a paper entitled "Feeling Like a Fraud":

> Seventeen women in a row spoke from the floor during a plenary session and all seventeen started their remarks with some kind of apology or disclaimer. . . . Ironically enough, all of us had been funded to attend the conference because we supposedly know something about Women's Leadership. Yet we seemed to share a feeling of illegitimacy.

The denial of competence and authority by accomplished women is a virtual commonplace. Madeline Kunin, for example, was the first woman to be elected governor of Vermont (and only the third Democrat elected to this position since the Civil War); she was the deputy secretary of education in the Clinton administration and later ambassador to Switzerland. Yet during this distinguished career she has suffered from "the great imposter syndrome." In her 1994 autobiography she admits to a "chronic symptom of female insecurity: feeling like a fraud." In a 1997 profile in *The New York Times* the interviewer reported that Kunin insisted that "the feeling [of fraudulence] no longer existed. . . . But then she talk[ed] about having to do a 'careful dance' in her job." For Kunin, the defensive, self-defeating denial of competence has been supplanted by a realistic vigilance. She is aware that she needs to recognize and gracefully deflect the resentment her achievements are likely to elicit.

The biculturalism women experience as they climb the professional ladder in male-dominated professions is exacerbated by their minority status. A person who differs in an obvious way from the majority is scrutinized and judged differently from his or her peers. Henry Louis Gates Jr., the chairman of the Afro-American Studies department at Harvard, has vividly described the burden of being "the other" and bearing the "freight of being iconic." The socially anomalous individual is inevitably seen as a representative of his or her minority group. As Gates notes, "It follows you everywhere like your own shadow. It isn't a thing of your making, and it won't succumb to your powers of unmaking."

Numerous studies have suggested that women, or members of any other group that represent fewer than 15 to 25 percent of the individuals in a given work situation, feel socially isolated and self-conscious. Being an "outsider" is inevitably a stressful and disorienting situation; the minority members have to function with the majority's cultural rules in order be professionally validated.

Pure numbers make a huge difference in women's comfort level. One woman lawyer from a large firm described it this way:

It's not something very concrete. But I still feel it's a man's world. I hope I don't say this bitterly, but it just seems like that's the way it is. It's about who feels very confident about their being in this world and on an equal basis with all the other lawyers.

First of all there are many, many, many more men in the higher or more public positions, whether it's partners in big law firms or prosecutors or people running the government at all the levels. Think about it—who are the women in these positions? You can conjure up a few, but there are hardly any. And who are in the most prominent positions? It's all men with a couple of exceptions.

I go to the bar association and I'm always conscious of this. You'll see a panel of people and there'll be no women on it. Where are the women? So you always feel that you're the one who's not in the club.

But there is this group of women in my field who meet; among them are a few of the rare women who hold very high-level jobs. And when you're together and have lunch or go to a meeting, it's a different kind of energy and different sensibility and you have this sense of empowerment. It just comes from the feeling that, hey, we're all women and we're all in these high positions.

Only when a critical mass is reached do women feel that they can be accepted as individuals in their own right and with their own style.

CHOOSING "DEVIANCE"

Now as in the past, a small but hardy group of women openly refuse to do the "careful dance" mentioned by Madeline Kunin. Unlike women who deny or disguise their abilities, these women embrace cultural "deviance" for a wide variety of personal reasons. Opposing the status quo is, by definition, socially punishing. It requires a combination of powerful motivation and some form of supportive community within the larger society. Specific cultural, economic, or social conditions permit such openly rebellious women to confidently pursue a life of accomplishment outside the cultural norms.

Like the early women's rights activists, a portion of the women who choose this path grew up in politically radical families that endorsed their daughters' unconventional beliefs. Some of the parents of such women, for example, were leftists during the 1930s and 1940s. Also as in the past, some women reject traditional femininity because their experiences with fathers and/or husbands have left them deeply wary of dependence on men. Such a woman will have no wish to allow a male partner to define her life; her determination to have direct control over her own fate makes her unwilling to adopt the romantic plotline that is the basis for most white, middle-class women's lives.

Social class can also be an important factor. Paradoxically, women with the greatest educational opportunities, career options, and financial resources are often ambivalent about fully utilizing these resources. Women from lower- or lower-middle-class backgrounds, on the other hand, often have fewer inhibitions about their achievements. Early studies of adolescent girls, as we have seen, found that many of the most ambitious and self-confident white girls came from less affluent backgrounds. The researchers hypothesized that these girls' experiences gave them little reason to picture marriage as the road to financial or social stability. Much like their black counterparts, they were convinced that they would be the major financial support for their families. They concluded that they themselves were the most reliable agents of their own advancement.

More recent studies of women law students discovered that young women from working-class and poor backgrounds participate in classes at a higher rate than their elite female classmates from prestigious colleges. Asked in one study to explain their fearlessness in class, a woman explained, "If we came from Ivy League schools, we'd be concerned with doing things right." The author of the study, Catherine G. Krupnick, a professor of education at Harvard, suggests:

> These working-class women had grown accustomed to challenging societal prescribed roles during their struggles to gain admission to law school. Once they were in law school, they were not about to give it up. In other words, these women had socialized themselves to be successful, active participants who took charge of their education as they had taken charge of the course of their lives and careers.

These young women never had the belief (or illusion) that they would be defined by and cared for by a male partner.

Gloria Steinem, herself from a downwardly mobile middle-class family, has made similar observations, comparing the working-class women from her high school with her Smith College classmates. Her contemporaries from East Toledo, she noted, had had children early on and by their forties were "full of rebellion, humor, energy, and a certain earthy wisdom that seemed to say, 'I'm myself now—take it or leave it.' " Some of these women had organized a sex discrimination lawsuit, while others had recently defeated a local anti-abortion ordinance. Several were working on the campaign of a woman mayoral candidate (she won and was the first woman to hold this position in Toledo). A number of women had started their own businesses.

Her classmates from Smith College, according to Steinem, were more ambivalent about their lives. Some of the women had, in fact, been active in politics, business, or other ventures. But to Steinem they seemed "more apologetic and self-blaming; more distant from themselves. If divorced, they were more likely to have lost their identity along with their husbands. If married, they seemed more identified with their husband's careers." As Steinem summed it up, the Smith women were much more likely to begin their sentences with "It's probably only me but . . ."

Perhaps the apotheosis of the unapologetic, antiromantic working-class woman is Roseanne Barr, the most successful female comedian of our time. Barr herself received no education past ninth grade and had her first child at age eighteen. She went on to have jobs as a maid, window dresser, and cocktail waitress. In her skits Barr typically lampoons male assumptions of their superiority and middle-class women's collusion with these beliefs. The divide between middle-class notions of femininity and the reality of women's lives is the basis of Barr's humor. Her trademark persona, the Domestic Goddess, is a broad parody of traditional feminine virtues. Here is a sample of her notes for a comedy routine from her early career:

> Boys like a good listener. Boys like to win at games. Boys like to think they're smarter than you. Boys don't respect a girl who gives in to them, so you go around practicing virginal behavior: being docile, being quiet, a gracious loser. But that's only till you get a man. Then

you must . . . spend all your time trying to change him from someone who'd want to live with a stupid loser with no sex drive.

For Barr, as for many women from this social milieu, the payoff for adhering to white, middle-class notions of femininity seems pitifully small. Being called "unfeminine" seems a price well worth paying in exchange for the opportunity to pursue personal goals.

Ethnic groups vary enormously in their expectations for women. The vast majority of cultures have advocated extremely restricted and domestic activities for them, but a few have long histories of women being a part of the workforce. Historically, not unlike the black community, Jewish communities have promoted an unusually worldly role for women. Although in theory Jewish women were assigned a subordinate, low-status position, the reality of Jewish life in eastern Europe was somewhat different. These women were allowed to obtain divorces long before Christian women. Perhaps more important, men in Jewish communities often devoted their lives to scholarship, while their wives coped with the gritty reality of commercial life in both the Jewish and gentile worlds. Wives commonly ran not only the household finances but the finances of the family business as well. As Mark Zborowski and Elizabeth Herzog observe in *Life Is with People: The Culture of the Shtetl*:

> Clearly, although the woman's life is home-centered, it is by no means home-limited. She does the buying and often the selling. She is familiar with the market place and with the merchants who frequent it. Therefore, on the whole, women have a better command of the local language than do the learned men. . . . The learned [Jewish] men handle the local language haltingly, if at all. . . .
>
> The earning of a livelihood is sexless, and the large majority of women, even among the [upper class], participate in some gainful occupation, if they do not carry the chief burden of support. The wife of a "perennial student" is very apt to be the sole support of the family. The

problem of managing both a business and a home is so common that no one recognizes it as special. The economic area is more nearly an extension of the woman's domain than of the man. . . .

If anyone is sheltered it is the scholarly man. Women and even girls move about freely.

The authors summarized the male and female places in the Jewish community: "Both men and women feel, 'Mine is the real work of the world.' " I suspect that this is a somewhat idealized view of shtetl life. But even so, the acceptance of middle-class women working as local merchants and overseeing the economic transactions of the family is striking for this era. It would certainly help explain the disproportionate representation of Jewish women in many previously all-male venues, including the Supreme Court and the Senate. They have also been at the forefront of women in academic institutions, the media, law, and medicine. They have been heavily represented in the feminist movement. For both men and women from this tradition, acceptance of women who practice skills in the public sphere may not require a radical transformation of values. Perhaps Martin Ginsburg and Leonard Woolf, both of whom were unusually accepting of their wives' careers, were influenced by this cultural history.

PART FOUR

CAREERS, MARRIAGE, AND FAMILY

Be wary of marriage, of motherhood, of men.
Don't necessarily avoid them, but be careful.
—SIMONE DE BEAUVOIR, *The Second Sex*

CHAPTER ELEVEN

THE CURRENT DILEMMA

O ver the last two centuries, as women's role in society has end-lessly been reconfigured, it became increasingly clear that in important new ways, women's and men's interests did not coincide. In the small farm households where most men and women lived prior to the industrial revolution, women were economically crucial to the family unit. But as production moved outside the home, middle-class women's contributions became more circumscribed, centering chiefly on child care, even as women's life spans extended well beyond this phase of life and women bore fewer children.

Historically, the marital quid pro quo was vastly unequal. Men had the upper hand—they held the dominant position, and their wives were their dependents. But at least the arrangement had clear bene-fits for each party, even if those benefits were not fairly distributed. The women provided child care and kept the household, while the men provided the bulk of financial support. In the twentieth century new difficulties with this division of duties arose. Women, despite their in-creasing education and many decades of life following motherhood, had severely restricted options at nearly every turn. They also remained totally reliant on their husbands for their social and economic well-being. In addition, many men who now worked at a distance from their homes resented providing lifetime support for a wife who, after the chil-dren were raised, often played a less central role in their lives. Divorce became increasingly common as the economic, biological, and geo-graphical underpinnings of the family underwent seismic shifts.

As William Goode pointed out in *Rethinking the Family*, in the last fifty years our society has moved slowly but inexorably "towards less personal long-term investments in the collectivity of the family." This

is a fact that, although we may not like or approve of it, is increasingly
the case. As the divorce rate increased, men in particular withdrew
financial, emotional, and time commitments from their children. Increasing numbers of children from all socioeconomic classes were con-
ceived out of wedlock, with little or no paternal participation in child
care. Divorced fathers all too commonly provided inadequate child
support and saw little of their children. Fathers who remained in their
families often were required to work increased hours outside the
home.

The conflicting interests of couples became more exposed as divorce
became increasingly common. What was good for the husband's career,
for example, would not necessarily benefit the wife's or the children's
lives in the long run or even the short run. In a typical scenario a husband or wife might wish to relocate for a job promotion, despite the
fact that it would uproot the children from their schools and terminate
the spouse's work life. Or one member of a couple might want to work
long hours to further their job opportunities, even if it reduced time
spent with the family. Although there were many situations in which
husbands' and wives' interests complemented each other, in many others their agendas were only partially complementary or were not complementary at all. Men's and women's interests have always been at
odds to a significant extent—"the war between the sexes" is an age-old
comic trope. In the past, however, women were by necessity invested in
their husbands' careers: men provided the economic foundations of
women's lives. However, as the possibility of divorce, at every stage
of adult life, became a powerful reality, the economic interests of husbands and wives were no longer as closely or firmly linked.

Many factors have conspired to place the separate interests of men
and women in stark relief: the poverty rates that are higher for women
than for men, the lack of enforcement of alimony payments, the workplace structure that fits the male life cycle while penalizing women
with children, and the relative lack of male participation in the household despite women's increasing financial contributions. The romantic
notion of a woman's life being predicated on a male provider has been
severely and, most likely, irreparably damaged. Only 3 to 7 percent of
households in the United States currently are composed of a nonwork-

ing mother and a father who provides the financial support for the family. Far from being the norm, this family structure is an anomaly.

Recent findings in the field of molecular biology have coincidentally provided an wonderfully apt scientific metaphor for the frequent lack of congruence between men's and women's interests. Dr. Shirley M. Tilghman, a scientist who is now the president of Princeton University, discovered in her genetic research that even in the fertilized ovum, the first moments of conception, there is a male-female struggle, in this case over whether paternal or maternal genes will determine the size of the fetus. As Natalie Angier describes the probable origin of this molecular tussle:

A mammalian father has one aspiration—that his offspring grow as big and strong as possible in the womb, to give them a head start in life. The mother, it so happens, has a slightly different plan. She wants the healthy offspring as well, but she also wants to preserve her future fecundity, which means that any one embryo must not be permitted to grow so cumbersome that it weakens or depletes her.

What appears at first glance to be the straightforward, common goal for a couple—to produce a healthy child—turns out, on the biological level, to have somewhat different optimal outcomes for the woman and man involved. The molecular dance that Tilghman discovered seems to echo the complexity now evident in many of the male-female ventures that we previously took for granted.

Where does this leave contemporary women? Increasing opportunities for women, evolving over many decades, have slowly advanced through the different stages of women's lives, starting with girlhood and working up to young womanhood. Access to grammar school education for girls was followed by access to high school and college educations. By the early twentieth century a few women had gained admission to graduate and professional schools, and in the 1970s women began to graduate from these programs in significant numbers. By the 1980s and 1990s women were assuming places in the lower ranks of many professions in ever greater numbers.

Currently, the time when women become second-class citizens, when their options are radically reduced in comparison to those of men, has been pushed yet later into their lives. Girls and women still receive less favorable treatment than their male counterparts throughout their childhoods and on into their early twenties and thirties—but less than in the past. Many young, middle-class women have experienced a shift toward more equal opportunities right up to their early careers and marriages.

Women now experience the most powerful social and institutional discrimination during young adulthood, after they have left the educational system and started pursuing their ambitions. At the age when women most frequently marry and have children, they must decide whether to try to hold on to their own ambitions, or downsize or abandon them. Often a young woman must make this decision at the moment when she is just learning to be a parent, with all its attendant fears, pleasures, and insecurities—and around-the-clock work.

The lack of adequate social support, ongoing career opportunities, and financial protection for women who provide child care is the contemporary version of the many previous barriers that women have faced. And as with all prior obstacles, it has proved stressful, confusing, and painful. In all such transitions, there are no easy solutions. Institutional changes and cultural norms lag behind social realities. The complex issues that arise in early adulthood, concerning both the pursuit of a career and the structuring of a family, are currently the most pressing ones facing women.

There is, however, good news. Enough information now exists about the outcomes of various options so that women can make educated decisions and have a clearer idea of what lies ahead. This was not the case a generation ago. At that time, for example, when I had my first child, I asked the head of pediatric psychiatry at the hospital where I worked how my child would be affected if I continued to work full-time. He paused, then accurately but rather coldly stated, "We simply do not know." Now, twenty years later, we have a great deal more information about the outcomes of choices that women make—how they impact their children, marriages, health, self-esteem, and economic well-being.

CHAPTER TWELVE

CAREERS

So that when I ask you to earn money and have a room of your own, I am asking you to live in the presence of reality, an invigorating life, it would appear.

—VIRGINIA WOOLF, *A Room of One's Own*

PROS AND CONS OF PURSUING A CAREER

Taking on real, remunerated work is, all too often, stressful and exhausting for women who simultaneously must do the lion's share of child care and household duties. It is particularly striking, therefore, that the available studies demonstrate that, in virtually every area of their lives, women benefit from participation in the workplace. Those work situations that provide advancement opportunities and prestige further enhance the positive impact of work outside the home.

As middle-class women have been allowed into the labor force, particularly the skilled workforce, they have increasingly chosen to be employed outside the home. Women's portion of the labor market has grown steadily over the last century, and the jobs employing them have increased at a greater rate than those employing men. By 1995 over two-thirds of married women worked for a wage and 64 percent of married women with preschool children were working. Undoubtedly many women work because of financial need, but there is a great deal of evidence that given the choice, most women prefer to have employment.

One investigation in which 201 gifted women were interviewed found that "more women who worked reaped satisfaction from that

experience than the homemakers did from their work at home."
Another study reported that only 21 percent of working mothers say
that they would like to leave their jobs to stay home with their children, while 56 percent of homemakers, given the chance to start over,
said that they would choose to have a career. While in 1943, 61 percent of women stated that they preferred not to hold a job, by 1979, as
more work opportunities opened up, only 5 percent of women held
this view.

Counterintuitively, workers with young children put in more, rather
than fewer, hours at the workplace than those without children! One
possible explanation for this finding derives from medical studies of
stress hormones. Investigators have found that employed mothers are
significantly *less* stressed during their time at work than at home. This
may help explain why these women linger at the workplace. Some
researchers have humorously dubbed this finding the TGIM phenomenon: Thank God It's Monday.

It's been found that women in all socioeconomic groups prefer to
work outside the home, even those who have no financial incentive to
do so. In fact, the higher the income bracket of working parents, the
longer the children are left to child care. The more prestigious and high
paid the job, the more time men and women choose to devote to it. As
Jared Bernstein, a labor economist at the Economic Policy Institute,
has observed, "Opportunity keeps drawing women into work regard-
less of how much their husbands make." We may like to think that we
value the family and we may like to emphasize its rewards, but this is
not how men or women vote with their feet.

Medical studies strongly endorse the benefits of work outside the
home. Employed women are healthier than their homemaker peers,
despite the pressure of their added responsibilities. They have lower
blood pressure, lower cholesterol levels, and lower weight. Rosalind
Barnett and Caryl Rivers note in *She Works/He Works:*

> Few facts are as well-documented as the good physical and emotional
> health of women on the job. . . . Among social scientists, the question
> of whether work is good for women isn't even much argued anymore.

Researchers are delving into just what it *is* about work that affects women's health.

Psychologically, working women have less depression than their domestic counterparts, and they have, astonishingly, been reported to have less anxiety. The work factors that adversely affect women's health are the same as those that affect men. They involve a loss of control over their environment: few advancement possibilities, discrimination, poor physical work conditions, and hostile corporate cultures.

Unfortunately, the benefits that accrue to women pursuing careers do not come early or easily. Unlike their male peers, at the present historical moment every choice that a young woman makes exacts a steep price. What works best for her early in adulthood can ultimately lead to a worse outcome in her later life and vice versa. It is a complicated trade-off and one that young women need to look at carefully.

In their mid-twenties, at the time when families typically have young children, the more traditional homemakers actually fare better than their work-oriented peers. At this early age the women are "typically still excited about being married and having children and intensely involved in all the gratifications and responsibilities of early child-rearing." Judith Birnbaum, who studied a cohort of young women, reports that at this early life stage women who pursue careers are "far more troubled with self-doubt and [have] low self-esteem during their twenties and early thirties."

The twenties and early thirties are a sizable portion of the prime years of life for a career woman to have to suffer through, plagued with self-doubt, in the hope of later rewards. The miserable bargain is, however, precisely the one necessary for what have been dubbed the "front-loaded" professions. Careers in law, medicine, and business require years of often brutally intensive training. Women who choose these professions must agree to a painful trade-off: the loss of many of their potential childbearing years, in exchange for the pursuit of their career.

When women arrive at their mid-thirties, however, the relative gains and losses shift dramatically—career women are doing much better than the homemakers. A comparison of homemakers with married women professionals and with unmarried women professionals twenty-five years after their college graduations found that the homemakers had "the lowest self-esteem and the lowest sense of personal competence, even including childcare and social skills." Perhaps counter-intuitively, this study also found the marital happiness of the career women to be dramatically higher by midlife than that of the homemakers. This enhanced marital happiness may be a direct benefit of the women's careers; it has been shown that for both men and women, the less time individuals spend on low-control tasks, the better the quality of their marriages.

HOW CAREER CHOICES GET MADE

Given the problematic alternatives that women face, how do they currently make the decisions that create their future lives? Endless research has scrutinized the psychological variables believed to be crucial to such choices: self-esteem, locus of control, self-efficacy, a mother who works, a hostile mother, an encouraging or distant father, birth order, and on and on. The evidence suggests that specific developmental factors have a significant impact on a woman's achievements. The most important of these factors, at any life stage, are the opportunity to develop a skill and the recognition of that skill by family, peers, mentors, employers, and social contacts. In the presence of these elements, women's ambitions expand and gain momentum. In their absence—particularly after women marry and have children—they fade. Young women's career choices are continuously reshaped by the availability or dearth of work opportunities and the support provided or withheld by their husbands, mentors, and employers. Ambitions remain malleable—capable of growth or extinction—by their very nature.

In *Hard Choices* Kathleen Gerson describes following the life trajectories of two groups of women. One group began their young adulthoods wanting to remain "on the domestic track," and the other had work aspirations. Gerson concluded, "Remarkable change is more common than stability." In the group that started out with "non-domestic early aspirations and expectations," fully 63 percent became homemakers as adults. Among those whose original goals centered on purely domestic roles, the number who shifted their orientation was similarly large. Early life plans were carried out only when circumstances reinforced them. Unexpected social constraints and opportunities usually caused ambitions to be heightened, reformulated, or abandoned.

Two-thirds of the originally home-oriented women whose career aspirations *increased* over time experienced unexpected work promotions that permitted them to leave female-dominated, dead-end jobs and move on to more challenging positions. The majority of these women happily seized the opportunities. In Gerson's words, "Access to work offering a sense of accomplishment, upward movement towards a goal and significant material and emotional rewards critically influenced the process of developing strong ties to the workplace, heightened work aspirations, and a growing ambivalence towards domestic pursuits. . . . Both ambition and self-confidence grew." For other women in this group practical constraints pushed them toward a career orientation: unstable marriages, economic necessity, or disillusionment with homemaking. The group of women that moved in the opposite direction—away from career orientation and toward a homemaking role—faced a different set of limitations and opportunities. Among the obstacles to career development were geographical moves and a husband's lack of support for his wife's work.

One longitudinal study that compared the impact of aspects of personality (such as self-definition and "need for achievement") with life circumstances (such as marriage and children) found that the latter factors were ultimately more powerful: "The results strongly indicate that a woman's family situation sets some limits on her career activity. Career persistence and career type were both strongly negatively predicted by marriage and children in this study." The authors found that women who had strong self-definition and were achievement oriented nonetheless had great difficulty pursuing a career after they had a family. Typically, they turned away from their career and toward "freelance" activity in the home. In most cases, faced with conflicts between the husband's and the wife's ambitions and the need for child care, couples decide to limit the wife's career and expand the husband's. In the baby boom generation, the first large cohort of women to aspire to careers and to attend professional schools in significant numbers, fewer than 20 percent of the college-educated women managed to have children and maintain a career into their late thirties and early forties.

Henry Etzkowitz, Carol Kemelgor, and Brian Uzzi, the authors of *Athena Unbound: The Advancement of Women in Science and Technology*, describe a typical woman scientist facing this situation:

> For a man to decide not to take his career seriously is like admitting he takes drugs. For a woman to say she puts her family ahead of her career is considered a virtue: the pressures are all in that direction. The women are told, "Isn't this wonderful. You are giving up your career to sacrifice for your husband." The pressures come from society, relatives, to some extent from the men involved, the parents of the husband.

As the authors go on to conclude, "Professional identity is inextricably linked to a 'social identity' in which the esteem of others provides recognition and serves to enhance self-esteem." If a woman's career engenders disapproval from her husband, family, and social contacts, her ambition is unlikely to flourish or even survive.

BAD JOBS

Despite the hardships that career women experience toward the beginning of their work lives, eventually they benefit in terms of satisfaction, self-esteem, economic status, and physical and mental health. The data support the notion that women with careers eventually reap the rewards of their labors. This picture may seem an unrealistically rosy to many of us. As we well know, careers frequently entail grueling schedules, conflicting priorities, and at times uninspiring goals. Women, like men, often find their work alienating or boring. Many women have been made miserable by the corporate rat race, the legal profession's point-lessly long hours, or other rigid, stressful careers.

But the available studies do not claim that a career is an unalloyed boon for women; they are only saying that, for the majority of women, it appears to be the best of their present options. And no one is saying that the available options are particularly good at this historical moment. Social roles are in great flux, and our institutions, private and public, do not acknowledge or support this changing reality. Given the satisfactions that a career potentially affords—the community avail-able at the workplace, the high value that our society places on work, the low value it places on child care, and the financial difficulties that middle-class women without work skills often ultimately face—a career is often the best of women's several problematic choices.

There is no question, however, that a career can present painful dif-ficulties. These problems chiefly come in two forms. Women are asked to pursue a career in a manner designed to fit men's life cycle, with no provision for child care—an unfair, exhausting, and often virtually unachievable endeavor.

Equally problematic, many of the employment opportunities in our economy lack the emotional rewards that people seek. Most peo-ple, and certainly most women, do not have "blind ambition"—that is, they do not crave advancement at any price. They are ambitious because the rewards they derive from ambition's two interdependent components, skill and recognition within a community, fulfill basic hu-man needs.

An ambition succeeds to the extent that these two elements are real-ized. Some of the jobs that are available in the present corporate economy have little besides a salary to offer. They fail to provide a challenge, satisfaction, recognition for accomplishments, or for that matter even security. They are demoralizing to men and women alike.

This isn't a problem with ambition, it's a problem with much of the current work environment. Many authors conflate the issue of women having careers with women having bad jobs. In *When Work Doesn't Work Anymore: Women, Work, and Identity*, Elizabeth Perle McKenna describes how women pursuing their ambitions often, ultimately, feel that their careers are not worth the effort. She suggests that the women's jobs prevent them from enjoying other, more valuable aspects of their lives. McKenna tells us the story of how she changed her priorities and gave up her own career to have a more meaningful personal life.

It should be noted in passing that when McKenna gave up her career as a publishing executive, she had options that may not be available to many of her peers. In her late thirties, after successfully pursuing her own ambitions for many years, she married a man with "a big job." She also, of course, gave up one career for another and became an author, a job that requires mastery and provides her with ample recognition.

But what is particularly interesting about the book is McKenna's many interviews with unhappy career women. These demoralized women repeatedly complain not about the amount of work expected of them or even the stress of their crowded lives. What they miss is a community and appropriate affirmation. The problem isn't their ambition; it's the miserable job that they're stuck in that doesn't come anywhere near fulfilling their ambition. Here are some typical stories McKenna relates:

> Jane's career was marked by an orderly, steady progression to increased responsibility, larger jobs and new publishing houses . . . publishing houses were being bought by larger and larger media corporations. . . . For Jane it signaled the end of the community and therefore the end of communal purpose. "The work became increasingly purposeless," she said with sadness. . . . For Jane, as the recognition and shared sense of purpose dissolved, her motivation and joy in the work began to flag. Jane began to feel undervalued and unappreciated.

Here is "Ellie's" unhappy experience:

> I looked to my work for love and approval, recognition and attention. Which, for a long time I got. But in the end the joke was on me. . . . One day I saw the bonus grid in my boss's office. Right on the other side of my box, the guys above me were making a fortune. I saw that they were only stringing along the appropriate number of females to keep the field diverse. It wasn't that I was valuable or important to the team.

McKenna says of her own old job:

My profession was changing rapidly and objectively—and not for the good. The positions that had once looked like destinations of security and recognition were starting to look like first-class deck chairs on the *Titanic*.

What is the moral of this tale? McKenna's conclusion is that women should abandon their careers for more personal, domestic satisfactions. She does not advise them to find or create a work situation that better provides the "security and recognition" that she herself desires and apparently found in her career before her workplace changed. Yet that is the choice that she ultimately made in becoming a writer.

According to McKenna, women need to ignore the values of the culture around them and follow their bliss—their own inner compass. They should give up on the conventional quest for success and focus more on family and friendship. She quotes Anna Quindlen saying, "When I'm on my deathbed, I'm not going to say to myself, 'Gee, everyone out there really thought that I was a success.' I'm going to have to say to myself, 'Did I do what I wanted to do with my life?' And if the answer is no, God help you."

Quindlen is trying to help women sort out what is most meaningful to them. But this is actually rather tough advice, coming as it does from one of the most celebrated women in America. The choices she has made do not seem to have ignored conventional notions of success; her career actually exemplifies ambition at its most rewarding. Quindlen does, however, raise an important question. To what extent can or should our values be independent from those of the people and culture around us? Like everyone else, I would like to believe with McKenna that one can trust one's "inner hand," "risking an entire culture's recognition and approval," and go happily on one's way. Who would not choose to believe that we can all forge ahead to realize our deepest values unperturbed by the disapproval, disregard, and lack of financial support from those around us? Unfortunately, everything that we know about the intensely social nature of human beings suggests that this scenario is highly unlikely. We need the affirmation of those within our communities; our ambitions provide one of the most productive and satisfying road maps for achieving it. Neither Quindlen or McKenna "risked the entire culture's recognition and approval," as McKenna so blithely advises other women to do.

She also ignores the fact that in our highly work-centered society, careers are often a source of enduring relationships and not some socially barren interlude in our "personal" lives. Many of my colleagues, for example, are among my closest friends and have been so for many years. We trained together and have shared our experiences ever since. I speak with, e-mail, or have lunch with them on a daily basis. We share family events. We even have a monthly "study group" dinner that is, in reality, a thinly veiled excuse for gossiping and exchanging news. My work provides me with a rich network of friendships. In our country with its diverse, mobile population and without shared religion, geographical continuity, or even extended families, work may often provide one of the only sources of community.

The underlying question that McKenna raises is whether our society provides adequate opportunities for the realization of ambitions. It is an important issue, though not one particular to women. One factor, however, does make the choices available to unhappily employed, married women distinctly different from those available to men. Such women, particularly those with children, sometimes have the financial option of quitting their jobs, staying home, and being supported by their husbands. The immediate benefits of leaving a miserable job to take care of one's children are self-evident.

Quitting a job, taking a part-time job, or doing freelance, unstructured projects at home works well for some women. These choices, however, entail risks as well as benefits. A woman making such a decision needs to consider how it will play in the long run. She may discover that she does not thrive in her new domestic life. She will be totally financially dependent on her husband, and it will very likely be impossible for her to rejoin the workforce at anywhere near the same level that she left it, if at all. At the same time it advances her husband's work situation, since he now has the support of a full-time homemaker, making it ever less practical for him to change or cut back on his career. For a large number of women, the decision to quit their professional lives early on effectively ends their careers.

WORKING FOR YOURSELF

Many of the most interesting, influential, and well-paid careers are structured in a way that makes their personal cost to women prohibitive. Companies effectively exclude women from advancing by holding women's children hostage; women can succeed only if they give up important parenting functions. These companies have inflexible schedules, no child care, inadequate personal days for family events, and schedules that preclude any real life outside of work. Many large companies, particularly at the upper reaches, are unresponsive to the childcare needs of families. Obviously it is discriminatory to have women raise society's children and, for their efforts, be excluded from many of its most challenging and satisfying occupations and roles. This, however, is commonly the case.

One option for a woman who, understandably, chooses to leave full-time employment is to become a contract worker—a professional who takes on freelance assignments or limited outsourced work from established companies. As more highly trained women have joined the job market looking for work that allows them to spend time with their families, companies have been quick to make use of this pool of relatively cheap, trained, talented workers. Sometimes the arrangement is the woman's choice; at other times a company will push employees off the payroll or provide "buyouts," only to rehire the women later on a limited contract with no benefits and no chance of career advancement. For women, this type of situation can gain greater time flexibility and reduced pressure, while providing some income and allowing them to continue to practice their skills. But obviously, they pay a high price in terms of job security and future opportunities.

An increasing number of women choose to bypass the women-unfriendly structures of the traditional work world by starting their own businesses. Having her own company allows a woman a less rigid schedule and a work culture that feels comfortable. For many women it is the fantasy solution to all work/family problems—have a career completely on your own terms. This appealing resolution shows up repeatedly in upbeat fictional accounts of career women trapped in the vise of conflicting priorities: home vs. work. The movie *Baby Boom* has this happy denouement; the protagonist quits her corporate job to start a gourmet baby food business out of her home, which instantly becomes a huge success. Owning your own small company seems like the perfect solution, having your cake and eating it, too.

According to the Center for Women's Business Research, in 2003 an astonishing one out of eleven women in the United States was a business owner. Between 1975 and 1985 American women went from owning only one-twentieth of all small businesses to owning one-fourth. From 1997 to 2002 the number of female-owned companies grew by an estimated 11 percent compared with 4 percent of all privately held firms. The growth in revenues from female-owned companies rose at a significantly higher rate than the average for all firms; one study calculated that companies that were 50 percent or more owned by women had annual revenues of $2.3 trillion in 2002. Clearly these small businesses owned by women represent a burgeoning part of our current economy. The data suggest a brave new world of women entrepreneurs forming a sort of parallel economic universe, a corporate counterculture.

This optimistic vision, unfortunately, does not tell the whole story. It is unclear whether the new, small, female-owned businesses are a positive development, or if they simply represent an inadequate fallback position for women excluded from the workplace.

Certainly the growth rates of these new enterprises and their rising profits suggest that women are becoming successful in their ventures. Many of these companies, however, remain tenuous and minimally profitable. Women-owned businesses tend to be tiny, home-based operations; 85 percent are sole proprietorships, and most are unincorporated businesses. Owners of home businesses run the risk of isolation, since they fail to provide the opportunity for contact with a workplace community. Approximately 69 percent of women-owned firms have less than

$25,000 in annual receipts—hardly an adequate income to support a family. Only 2 percent produce over a million dollars in yearly receipts, compared with approximately 5 percent of all businesses. Few of these small firms provide minimum health insurance, disability, paid sick days, paid vacations, retirement supplementation, or other basic work-related benefits. To what extent these fledgling businesses will eventually provide women with a viable alternative to the more conventional workplace remains to be seen. For now, despite their many drawbacks, they are among the only options that allow women flexible hours and control over their work environment.

PURSUING AMBITIONS THAT AREN'T REMUNERATED

Why, in the quotation at the beginning of this chapter, did Virginia Woolf stipulate that women should pursue interests that "earn money"? It seems like a rather crass suggestion. Why not pursue a pastime strictly for its own sake if one has the luxury to do so? I suspect that the point Woolf is making is that money is the currency, so to speak, through which society expresses what it values. Most skills that are admired by others are ultimately paid for. It is the least ambiguous sign of appreciation and certainly the most quantifiable. And of course, money provides a certain amount of independence. But money is far from the only form that recognition can take.

Some women, if they can afford it, choose to avoid the workplace entirely and pursue their interests in unpaid positions. Typically, they function as volunteers in a variety of community institutions or organizations based on a special interest such as local history, land use, education, or politics. Women who make this choice frequently provide services to our society that we would be much the poorer without. They provide an important part of the social fabric.

For the women involved in them, such unpaid activities can be as gratifying as any other type of ambition, and like other ambitions, the amount of satisfaction that they provide rests on specific factors. Ideally, the work is based within an appreciative community that extends beyond the immediate family; the community has some stability; and the project requires and develops skills, whether they involve organizational expertise or a depth of knowledge in a particular area. Women who pursue unremunerated ambitions that fit these parameters often find them deeply satisfying.

The drawbacks are that this type of unpaid activity can be marginalized and undervalued, and it can fail to provide stable institutions in which to participate. A woman, for example, who volunteers as a docent in a museum, telling visitors about the artwork, usually will not be considered a real part of the staff. Compared to a curator, for example, she will have no official authority; she will not help determine museum decisions or shows; and it is unlikely that she will be included in many museum functions. Women on the volunteer staff of a hospital routinely get shunted to the gift shop to work as clerks or pull wagons of flowers to patient rooms. Women who play valuable roles at their children's schools, in the PTA, are moved out of these positions when their children move on to the next level of education, so that any potential for a sustained involvement is cut short. Raising money for worthy organizations can be a time-consuming and thankless task and often doesn't lead to further opportunities. Women are commonly appointed to such positions on the basis of their family wealth or connections, with little consideration of their capability.

Unremunerated projects also frequently fail to truly test people's capabilities and therefore fail to challenge and develop them. Too often a minimal level of competence will be tolerated, because the volunteer's willingness to donate time more than compensates for it. Or the volunteer nature of the unpaid enterprise will make constructive criticism seem harsh and pointless. A group of writers who read one another's unpublished works will not bring to the task the same sharp analysis as an editor whose livelihood depends on finding talented writers. Part of the attraction of nonremunerative work is the avoidance of this type of tough, bottom-line evaluation. But the price of avoiding it can be dilettantism.

Volunteerism offers both the benefits and drawbacks of functioning outside the tough but vital commercial world. In the world of unpaid work, there is typically less honing of skills, a more free-form community, and less public appreciation. And there are purely practical difficulties. Such enterprises require financial support from a source other than work—usually a working husband. This may or may not turn out to be a dependable arrangement. Job insecurity, illness, and divorce can all make the choice a risky one. On the positive side of the balance sheet, volunteer work offers less critical evaluation by peers or bosses, less time commitment, and definitely less stress than regular employment. It can provide women with work that feels more meaningful than a conventional job. Such activities have historically provided many women with rewarding alternatives to the workplace, but often at the price of more challenging, appreciated, and influential roles.

CHAPTER THIRTEEN

MARRIAGE

It is a myth that couples marry only for love. But while factors such as timing, the desire for children, financial stability, and religion play a role in many marriages, how many young people probe seriously the professional ambitions and family commitments of their prospective spouse? How many women stop to consider the traditional pressure to marry "successful" men and look at whether the very factors that account for their beloved's success are compatible with their vision of a balanced family life?
—ANDREA GABOR, *Einstein's Wife: Work and Marriage in the Lives of Five Great Twentieth-Century Women*

Marriage, at its best, is one of life's great pleasures. It can provide companionship, sexual satisfaction, new interests, someone to share daily tasks with, economic benefits, and of course, a helpmeet to raise children. No one would dispute that when all goes well, marriage is a boon to both people involved. Those marriages that do not end in divorce can provide financial and emotional support for women, particularly to those with young children at what is probably the most vulnerable time of a woman's life. Having a partner to help out with the daunting task of supporting and caring for children is undoubtedly one of the prime historical reasons for the creation of this institution. Marriage remains our culture's gold standard for a successful adult relationship, even as its foundations—biological as well as economic—have been radically altered.

Marriage is also the keystone of white, middle-class adult female identity. Without marriage, a woman is still perceived as incomplete.

The social assumption is that an unmarried woman is single, not by choice, but because no man wants her as a partner. Being a "singleton," in the argot of Helen Fielding's screenplay and best-selling novel, *Bridget Jones's Diary,* remains a humiliating public mark of rejection and failed sexual identity for white, middle-class women. The main character in the book, a young single woman, vividly describes her plight: "Homosexuals and single women in their thirties have a natural bonding: both being accustomed to disappointing their parents and being treated as freaks by society." At a party with family friends, she is pummeled with comments about her unsatisfactory marital status: "So you *still* haven't got a feller!" "How does a woman manage to get to your age without being married?"

The book's plot is loosely based on Jane Austen's *Pride and Prejudice,* and it's striking how smoothly Austen's early-nineteenth-century plot adapts to women's current marital situation. The social imperative that a woman must marry has apparently lost little of its ferocious strength. A woman's identity remains heavily defined by her relational status. An unmarried woman is presumed to be unhappy or, in the pitying language of women's magazines, "unfulfilled," despite significant amounts of evidence to the contrary.

As a result of this ancient social imperative, marriage has a huge payoff for women. It provides them with social confirmation that they have assumed the feminine role our culture endorses. The need to receive this validation is an overwhelmingly powerful incentive for women to marry. The woman who never marries, like the woman who doesn't have children, lives with a penumbra of unanswered questions hovering around her: What happened? Can she still be happy? Does she feel cheated? Is there something wrong with her? No woman wants to go through life trailing this dismal shadow.

Once a woman is married, however, she discovers that she has made a complicated bargain. Marriages nearly always contain within them conflicting interests and needs—and limited resources. How the resources are distributed to meet these divergent priorities often determines the quality and fate of a marriage. Both parties must be able to accept the accommodations made for their own and their mate's wishes and needs. Each party inevitably incurs some losses as well as gains.

As Phyllis Rose remarks in her book about Victorian couples, *Parallel Lives,* a successful marriage does not require that resources or tasks be identically or even equally divided. What is crucial for a marriage to work is that the husband and wife agree on the arrangement. If a wife or husband wants to stay at home to be a homemaker and their spouse concurs, all is well.

Problems can arise, nonetheless, if a partner unilaterally decides to change the ground rules during the course of the marriage. A husband may decide to get a divorce and contest paying minimal alimony; a wife may decide to restart her career while the children are still young. In one couple I know, the wife, a successful professional, decided to quit her job and be supported by her husband while she raised the children, much to his chagrin. He had vicariously enjoyed her career in the arts and had depended on her salary. The inevitable reality is that, as spouses go through their lives, their priorities can change. It is crucial for a woman to factor this uncertainty into her plans and to be cautious about relinquishing her own goals for an unclear future.

Difficulties also occur in a marriage if the husband and wife come to realize, too late, that they had unrealistic expectations. Such misconceptions are common. The nitty-gritty issues of marriage are rarely discussed in any detail prior to the wedding. There are no honest, direct explorations and negotiations about the tough decisions that will inevitably arise. Highly charged questions are frequently passed over with well-intentioned blandishments. A premarriage "plan" frequently goes something like this: both members of the couple want to have work they love, and both want children. The couple pays well-intentioned lip service to sharing parenting and household duties: over two-thirds of college men and women have been found to endorse "equal emphasis on family and career." The couple may agree that the woman will "take some time off" to care for the children when they are little. The unspoken assumption is that she will jump back into the job market when she wishes with no serious, irreversible consequences.

This "agreement" easily breaks down when the couple is faced with real-life choices in which one member's potential gain will be the other's loss. One spouse gets a more time-consuming job than the other and become less available for "family time"; the first child arrives, and neither parent has enough flexibility at work to be home evenings when the babysitter leaves. Suddenly the couple must make decisions with no real plan in place. Under the immediate and overwhelming pressures of the situation, with no road map, couples usually fall back on traditional roles—whether or not this is actually what either partner signed up for.

It's extremely hard for any woman, at this moment of clashing interests, to resist the pressure to assume the "feminine" supportive role. If she does not take this role, she risks incurring not only social disapproval but the anger of a husband who has frequently assumed that his career would take precedence. At this point most women take on more household and/or child-care tasks, while their husbands expand their careers. All too frequently the first casualty of a marriage with children is the wife's ambitions. Her life choices are made by default instead of being actively chosen.

Unfortunately, it is precisely at this difficult period in women's lives, more than any other, that they need to consider their own long-term needs and wishes. They have to work against their lifelong training to assume the traditional, subordinate, "feminine" role. Otherwise they will reflexively absorb any losses to protect their husband from disappointment or themselves from their husband's anger. Being "nice" and minimizing conflict is most women's impulse in such situations, but their "supportive" stance often results in compliance with the status quo. It's the easier path to take in the short run, but it may not be what ultimately works out best for the wife—or any member of the family— over the long run. A woman at this juncture must at least evaluate the less socially condoned alternative: that her husband also compromise or reshape his goals and commitments.

Marriages that, under personal and professional pressures, slip into traditional "masculine-feminine" roles are an unequal bargain for the majority of women. Over the past century massive changes in the structure of the family have occurred; today the most common type of household in the United States is one in which both members of a married couple work, whether or not there are children. In 1990 40 percent of households had husbands and wives who worked full-time. Currently, in 25 to 30 percent of families the wife earns more than the husband. Yet old marital conventions, based on men as the sole breadwinner and more privileged member of the couple, remain in place. Right up to the present time, wives commonly assume a supportive role toward their husbands, and in most cases the support is not fully reciprocated. For a woman to place her own interests on par with those of her husband is still considered aggressive, unusual, unfeminine, and risky behavior. As one contemporary sociologist succinctly summarized the situation:

> Family role differentiation assigns distinctive responsibilities, rights, and activities to husbands and wives. Although these roles have many minor variations, they typically have differentiated a *provider and leader role* from a *childrearer and follower role*.

Even in the most "modern" marriages, where the wife has a career that she deeply enjoys and at which she is successful, the husband's job, almost without exception, takes priority. Some women have referred to this ubiquitous phenomenon as "the marital glass ceiling." Just such a scenario was vividly illustrated in an article by the writer Lois Smith Brady that appeared in the *New York Times* Styles section. I had been an admirer of Brady's eccentric, shrewd, and often touching weekly marriage columns for years and wondered why she had stopped writing. I found out the answer in this article, which she published several years after leaving her job:

> In 2001, after nine years of writing the Vows column every week since its inception, I moved to Aspen, Colo., where my husband had gotten a great job. It was a perfect example of how marriage is like a three-legged race. For better or for worse, you are tied to someone else, and once in a while you have to go—or in my case be dragged—in the direction of your partner.

I did not want to move, even though I was able to keep writing columns occasionally.

There are lots of things I miss about attending 52 weddings a year. I miss hearing the big dreams of brides and bridegrooms. . . . Now, like many couples who have appeared in Vows, I'm living the day-to-day life of a spouse and a parent, juggling work, children, problems and mysteries. It's nothing like being a bride. You blend into the crowd; you never wear white, since by noon you're covered with jelly stains. It can be as humbling as being passed by a unicyclist on a narrow steep hiking trail.

Brady tries to put a humorous spin on the events—unicyclists and three-legged races—but her resentment comes through. As she notes in her article, which traces the subsequent lives of the couples she watched getting married, "Brides and bridegrooms always glow. But these updates of couples are stories of the afterglow, or in some cases the aftermath."

Brady's own situation is echoed in one of the wedding follow-up stories she recounts. Eight years into their marriage, this couple too was "humbled." But *humble* has different meanings for the husband and wife. The husband gave up weekends in Paris; the wife relinquished her ambitions:

At first, their marriage was glamorous rather than dark. She was a managing director at Bear, Stearns; he a partner at Forstmann Little. On vacations, they did things like fly to Paris for a few days. . . .

They don't do that anymore. They now have three children. . . . "Having kids is a humbling experience," said Mr. Klinsky, who currently manages his own private equity fund.

It was especially humbling for Ms. Klinsky. After their first son was born, she couldn't decide what she wanted to be—a working mom or a non-working mom. That decision was pretty much made for her. "I came back to work after my maternity leave and there was a guy in my seat," she said. "Do you stay and fight it or do you accept it and head out to the playground?"

Not surprisingly, as a vulnerable new mother with no support for continuing her work, Ms. Klinsky headed for the playground. As Ms. Klinsky and Lois Smith Brady might both confirm, the pressure from husbands or employers to assume traditional marital roles is often intense. Women are asked to relinquish or subordinate their ambitions, but if they do so, they can precipitate a cascade of long-term, often unforeseen consequences.

Marriage, as it is currently constituted, is such a powerful cultural ideal and so central to most women's life plans that it is startling to realize the price it commonly extracts from them. The resources of most marriages are unequally distributed between the couple. A woman typically gives her husband's goals priority and in doing so automatically assumes a greater emotional dependence on the marriage, a greater long-term financial risk, and a larger workload. As a consequence, she pays a price in terms of her physical and emotional health.

Virtually no one questions the fact that for men—those creatures always depicted as being reluctantly dragged to the altar—marriage is largely a win/win proposition. Married men, compared to their single peers, are healthier, happier, professionally more successful, and financially better off; they typically earn 10 to 40 percent more than their unmarried brethren. Marriage also does wonders for men's mental health. George Vaillant, in his longitudinal study of male Harvard graduates, *Adaptation to Life,* found that a long-term marriage was virtually synonymous with the absence of individual pathology in men. Married men are also much healthier than their "singleton" peers; single men have a dramatically higher mortality rate than married men.

This thriving male cohort reports having more "positive emotional states" at home than at work—while women report the opposite. Men report higher marital satisfaction than women. The ending of a marriage is, not uncommonly, disastrous for men; of all demographic groups, the highest suicide rate is among men who are divorced or widowed.

The many advantages that accrue to a married man persist whether or not his marriage has the added time constraints imposed by a wife who works and by children. Husbands of working mothers with children have been found to remain happy, despite the many stresses that their wives are experiencing. These men also report that their wives are doing fine, even when their wives report the opposite. In fact, employed fathers have fewer depressive or angry moods than their wives or employed men without children. For men, wives and children are a surprisingly unalloyed boon.

The advantages of marriage for women are nowhere near as clear. Throughout the last several decades a hot debate has raged over the ways women may or may not benefit from marriage, other than the social validation they receive. On one side are books pointing out the drawbacks of marriage, such as Jessie Bernard's *The Future of Marriage* and Ann Crittenden's *The Price of Motherhood;* on the other are books such as *Creating a Life* by Sylvia Ann Hewlett, *The Case for Marriage* by Linda Waite and Maggie Gallagher, and *Is the Marriage Debate Over?* by James Q. Wilson and Janet C. Gornick. What emerges from all the research is that although marriage confers some benefits on women who marry and remain married, for a majority of women it also entails significant losses.

Married women work harder than married men, single men, or single women. As has been endlessly chronicled, they do a disproportionate amount of the child care and household work, even if they are working full-time and even if they have a larger income than the husband. Amazingly, one study found that when men are unemployed, their portion of the housework and child care still rarely exceeds 30 percent. Husbands believe that they are doing equal amounts of housework when they do 36 percent of it, and feel that the division of labor is unequal only when their wives do over 70 percent of the domestic work. One study found that women do 81 percent of the cooking, 78 percent of the cleaning, and 63 percent of the bill paying— and we haven't even gotten to child care. And many women do this while working full-time. It's little wonder that their ambitions take a backseat. Sheer survival becomes the goal.

As Rosalind Barnett and Caryl Rivers discovered in their studies of married couples, it is not only the hours of domestic work that distinguishes the male and female contributions to the home. It is also the type of tasks that each performs. The "high-demand and low-control" work—transporting children to and from appointments, cooking, doing laundry, grocery shopping—is stressful, has a negative impact on health, and is largely done by wives. The "high-control work" that is not time-pressured—such as making house repairs, doing lawn work, and keeping up the car—are largely done by men and have no ill effects on health.

Encouraging new evidence, however, suggests that married men are starting to do a more significant share of the housework. A Louis Harris poll in the late 1990s reported that over the past twenty years, the time women spend on home chores has decreased by about half an hour per day, while for men it increased by nearly an hour. A similar investigation by the Families and Work Institute found that men are currently putting in almost 75 percent as much time as women on general household duties. These trends suggest that major changes in family structures are occurring quickly. I suspect that these shifts are a response to women's increasing financial contributions to the family. It's a development that makes it difficult for husbands to defend continued nonparticipation in child care and household duties.

In terms of women's mental health, physical health, and finances, marriage is at best modestly beneficial and at worst detrimental. Women who are unmarried have a slightly higher mortality rate than women who remain in their marriages. (This statistic does not include women who marry and then divorce or become widowed.) There are new studies, however, that suggest that marital "caretaking" exacts a toll on women's health. Conventional wisdom in the past held that all relationships, known as "social supports," had health benefits, causing reduced rates of illnesses such as congestive heart failure and even cancer. Medical research lent support to these beliefs.

Several years ago a review of such studies discovered that they included few women. When women participated in studies of "social supports," the results were very different. Two large studies were carried out, one in Canada and one in the United States sponsored by the National Institutes of Health. Both discovered that men with "social supports" following a heart attack did indeed have significantly better outcomes than those who did not. For women, however, the opposite was true. After a heart attack women with the most "social supports," in the form of relationships, had a worse prognosis. One of the researchers suggested, "It may be that for women after a heart attack, the more social support they receive, the more they are expected to give, and the more burden they have." A separate study discovered that, following coronary bypass surgery, married women were four times more likely to be depressed than were single women. These findings have large medical implications since depression is a serious risk factor in cardiovascular disease.

It's even unclear whether marriage confers greater happiness on women than being single does. Some studies suggest that single women are happier than married women. Others have found that married women are happier than unmarried women, while a recent investigation reports that marital status is irrelevant to a woman's happiness. According to this report, an individual's temperament, plain and simple, is the most powerful determinant of mood—irrespective of marital status.

Financially, marriage is clearly riskier for women than for men. Ann Crittenden, in *The Price of Motherhood*, describes how most mothers must cut back or altogether drop their careers because of male-oriented workplaces that make no provisions for married women with children. Crittenden calculates the "forgone income" from job loss for each college-educated mother at approximately one million dollars. To make matters worse, because our government does not recognize homemaking as legitimate "work," it does not provide social insurance plans for this almost exclusively female type of labor. It hardly comes as a surprise, then, to find that American women over sixty-five are twice as likely as their male counterparts to be poor.

The financial benefits of marriage for women who remain married can be real but are hardly compelling. In *The Case for Marriage*, Linda Waite and Maggie Gallagher state that for married women with children, the chief financial advantage is security in old age. Married couples save more than single people, and spouses tend to leave their assets to each other. Since women outlive their husbands by an average of seven years, the payoff for women is additional income in the last few years of their life.

A financial disparity between married men and women, however, is most glaring in the 50 percent of marriages that end in divorce. A study of divorced couples in Los Angeles County, for example, found that the wives' standard of living was reduced by 27 percent, while that of their husbands increased by 10 percent. In the many marriages in which divorce occurs after children are born, the situation is even grimmer. In forty-seven of the fifty states, married women with children do not have an unequivocal right to half the family assets after divorce. Consequently the spouse who cares for the children, usually the mother, is nearly invariably worse off after a divorce. In such cases, an average mother and child who were not poor before the divorce will see a 50 percent drop in their income, while the husband's income will rise. It says something about the quality of marriage for women that despite these astonishing statistics, two-thirds of divorces are initiated by women.

In conventional marriages women are expected to provide the emotional support required for their husbands' career advancement, with little or no expectation that it will be reciprocated. Daniel Levinson, in *The Seasons of a Man's Life*, gives a rather chilling description of how this works. Women provide the home team that boosts the early phase of the husband's career:

> Now [at ages twenty-two to twenty-eight], a man has more fully carried out the termination of pre-adulthood and is actively building his first adult life structure. He seeks a woman who will appreciate his emerging aspirations and want to share his planned life with him. . . .
>
> Like the mentor, the special woman is a transitional figure. During early adulthood, a man is struggling to outgrow the little boy in himself and to become a more autonomous adult. The special woman can foster his adult aspirations while accepting his dependency, his incompleteness and his need to make her into something more than (and less

than) she actually is. Later, in the Mid-Life Transition, he will be more complete in himself and will have less need of the actual and the illusory contributions of the special woman.

So much for the "autonomous man," and so much for signing on as the "special woman." Levinson's use of the phrase "transitional figure" to describe the young wife foretells the fate of many such marriages. Unfortunately, in my practice I see all too many women whose husbands, in midlife, decide that they have no need for what Levinson calls their wives' "actual and illusory contributions." These women supported their husbands' difficult early careers, raised the children, and sacrificed or downsized their own careers—and were then told that their services were no longer needed.

Sylvia Ann Hewlett, in her 2002 book, *Creating a Life,* admonishes women about the risks of careers. She describes, from a different vantage point, the same phenomenon as Levinson, quoting a woman interviewee about what Hewlett dubs the "Wow factor":

[Men] find oxygen in the form of women who will coddle their egos and make them feel like a king or some other kind of superior being.

What any hard-driving, high-performing individual wants at the end of a fourteen-hour day is a partner who says, "Wow, you're amazing." Or, "Wow, what a killing you made today, you must be exhausted—let me rub your back/get you a drink/cook your supper."

Hewlett, like Levinson, goes on to note that the "Wow factor" is "particularly powerful in the early years of a career, which is precisely when most ambitious men get married." According to Hewlett, speaking through her interviewee, these men don't want career women who are too tired to provide for their outsize emotional needs.

Hewlett's book carries this much-publicized message: "Nowadays, the rule of thumb seems to be that the more successful a woman, the less likely it is she will find a husband or bear children." Hewlett, a board member of the Institute for American Values, warns us that achievement per se lowers a woman's chance of marriage.

A reanalysis of Hewlett's data, by economist Heather Boushey, using a larger sample, revealed that Hewlett's conclusion was not accurate. Among the cohort of women who work full-time, there is no difference in marriage or fertility rate between high achievers and low achievers. In other words, achievement per se has nothing to do with marital statistics. Fully 81 percent of high-achieving women and 83 percent of all other women working full-time had married.

Hewlett, however, does make an important point. Our society often makes it painfully difficult for women with careers to lead the full lives that their male peers do. A larger proportion of high-income women than high-income men are unmarried or childless. The stresses on women who pursue careers are enormous. The choice, too frequently, is whether to painfully conform to the conventional professional timetable and possibly forgo children or to go with a more traditional marriage scenario, often with later problematic consequences.

Hewlett recommends that "women cut through the anxiety and skepticism around marriage and figure out that giving priority to establishing a stable, loving relationship early on might be well worth the effort even if this involves surrendering part of one's own ego." In essence Hewlett is saying, Give up the struggle to have your own ambitions; don't take any risks; just suck it up and go with the system. It's less painful.

What Hewlett doesn't address is that there are large risks involved in whatever choices women make. That, unfortunately, is the current reality. Hewlett acts as if every wedded couple gallops off into the sunset to endless marital bliss. Yet evidently at least 50 percent of American men and women are unable to sort out which spouse will be able to sustain a "stable, loving relationship."

The career-oriented husband, the "good provider" that Hewett would have women seek out and marry, has long been the social and sexual ideal. For many women, the idea of being financially supported by their husbands so that they can provide child care is understandably attractive. Women need, however, to understand the potential downside of this arrangement, at a time when there is little provision for women to rejoin the work world.

An article in *New York* magazine about such career-driven husbands quotes a psychiatrist who warned a young woman about her upcoming marriage. He was concerned that her future husband would be unavailable to her or their potential children if he pursued his high-powered career. "She said, 'I love him. . . . There's something powerful and macho and sexy, almost, about [such career-obsessed men].' " Years later, in the midst of a divorce, the woman returned to the therapist. She explained the understanding on which the relationship was based: "I was working on Wall Street, too. . . . We had common interests. I just wanted a family. Mark used to say the most important thing was family."

This kind of marriage has built-in strains: the husband usually receives recognition for his accomplishments and financially supports the family. The wife's tasks are neither highly respected by the community nor directly remunerated, a fact that inevitably shifts all the power and many of the rewards to the husband. And as Hewlett herself points out, young parents tend to separate and divorce more than older parents. The woman who marries young has an excellent chance of also divorcing young—with or without children and often without satisfying or even remunerative work.

To add insult to injury, giving up ambitions early in life to hunker down and get a husband is not as easy as Hewlett would have us believe. Hewlett's implication is that women are too picky. They should take what they can get, while they can still get it. Would that it were so simple. A newsweekly article on women and careers quoted, as representative, a twenty-eight-year-old teacher trying desperately to put her life together. The teacher stated what all too many women express in their twenties or thirties while trying to find a partner: "I'm just waiting to date someone who isn't a jerk." Most women, in my experience, are not throwing over attractive potential mates for their do-or-die ambitions.

Hewlett advises women to quickly grab the golden ring of marriage, as though marriage and children, in and of themselves, safeguard a happy future. Yet despite the popularity of large weddings for those who choose marriage, marriage itself as an institution is on the wane. In 1998 the marriage rate was the lowest in the United States in forty years—8.3 couples per 1000. Children of divorcees are less likely to marry than their peers; divorced adults living with a mate are also less willing to remarry. The percent of children born out of wedlock has risen dramatically, not because of women giving birth without a partner but because of the large number of cohabiting couples who have bypassed marriage. This practice, according to *The New York Times,* "has become so commonplace that it is practically the norm." It includes all ages, races, and income groups. Clearly the perception of marriage "on the ground" is not as rosy as its advocates would have us believe.

Given the many problems inherent in traditional marriages, women and men have begun to devise a host of less traditional relationships. Recently two class reunions underscored for me how varied couples and families have become. The first was a reunion of the women from my college class, and the second was a gathering of women from my medical school class. In both groups virtually all of the women had clearly struggled with issues about relationships, families, and careers. They were a broad mix of women in every possible marital situation: women in long-term marriages, some happier than others; women who were divorced and single, divorced and remarried, or divorced and in a nonmarital relationship, and women who had never married but were in a long-term relationship. A number of women were happily single, and others were unhappily single. Most had children. Two had had children out of wedlock. One was in a gay couple. Many, but not all, had careers. Nearly equal numbers had pursued their original career, dropped out of the work world, and radically altered their career path.

These women had had to create their own solutions to the conflicted agendas our society imposes on contemporary women. They did so thoughtfully and with a great deal of effort. My classmates had arrived at the best solutions they could devise, and most seemed fairly content with their present situation. But it had been hard for most of us, with many choices and uncertainties. It would have been tempting for my cohort to romanticize the clear roles our mothers had accepted, except that we all knew the limitations and regrets that many of those lives had entailed. The fact is, it's never been easy for women, even—or particularly—when they had fewer choices. And despite the many positive changes that have occurred in women's lives, it's still not easy now.

My current psychiatric practice gives me an unusually intimate look at many contemporary marriages. My impression is that they are, for pragmatic reasons, much more fluid than in the past. The flexibility is a response to the instability of the workplace and to the possibilities inherent in a dual-career marriage. Not infrequently a husband is "downsized" and the wife has to step up or restart her career. A wife's career may prove to be more lucrative than her husband's, and he may find that he enjoys having a job rather than a career, with extra time for his avocations. A husband or wife may have a problem with alcohol or depression, necessitating that the other partner provide more support for the family. Marital arrangements shift and are reformulated.

Despite the current strains and uncertainties, I suspect that the ultimate outcome of women's evolving careers will be salutary for marriage. Many couples get used to a lifestyle that is available only if both spouses work. There is more economic interdependence—it now takes two incomes to support the typical middle-class household. When a husband and wife are both working, each may be able to take greater career risks and even time off. In my own marriage, my husband and I have, at times, taken turns supporting the family. When I went back to do a second residency, he had to take over financially. When he was finishing writing a book, it was my turn.

Like marriages two hundred years ago, marriages today may be working partnerships, albeit more equal ones than those of the past. Women are contributing ever larger amounts of financial support to their families. Working couples may also be able to avoid the slow divergence of interests that can occur when only one member is employed. Men and women no longer exist in emotionally and geographically separate worlds.

Women need to look carefully at the couples around them and search for models that correspond to their goals and seem to work well. There is no single successful type of marriage or relationship. The idea that one can just fall in love and then passively allow things to fall in place is at best wishful thinking and at worst willful ignorance. In any long-term relationship there will be unpredictable events, but some key factors can be foreseen. The number of hours involved in each spouse's line of work and the flexibility of those hours powerfully shape the structure of a marriage. There is only so much give in any system. If one spouse has long hours and little flexibility, it is overwhelmingly likely that the other spouse will not be left with sufficient time for his or her own ambitions. If a husband or wife has a high-pressure, all-consuming job, the other will undoubtedly have to pick up the slack, particularly if children are involved. Women need to be thoughtful and purposeful when establishing a serious relationship. The results of our planning, given the current social constraints and life's inevitable twists and turns, will likely be imperfect and incomplete. But they will keep us moving in the right direction, preserving an awareness of our deepest needs and goals. Understanding the likely outcomes of choices we make early in adulthood is essential for women; they will define much of our future lives.

CHAPTER FOURTEEN

CHILDREN AND CAREERS

What is needed is across-the-board recognition—in the work-place, in the family, in the law, and in social policy—that some-one has to do the necessary work of raising children and sustaining families, and that the reward for such vital work should not be professional marginalization, a loss of status, and an increased risk of poverty.

— ANN CRITTENDEN, *The Price of Motherhood*

Childbirth and motherhood are the anvil upon which sexual inequality was forged.

— RACHEL CUSK, *A Life's Work*

CHILD CARE AND AMBITION ARE COMPLEMENTARY

In many ways, caring for children is the exact opposite of ambition. It occurs primarily within the nuclear family; it does not involve skills that require high levels of training, endless child-care manuals notwithstanding; and it provides extremely low levels of recognition. It's not just that our society does little to recognize mothering skills; children themselves, those constant companions of mothers, are often comically oblivious to their parents' lives and travails. If recognition is what you're looking for, motherhood is not the place to find it. Parenting provides a different set of pleasures: loving and being loved, seeing your children develop, sharing their experiences, taking on a new aspect of identity, entering into new communities, and many more. I need hardly say that it can be one of life's richest experiences.

Parenting and ambitions have very different benefits and constraints—in fact, they barely overlap. The two activities employ separate talents, provide different emotional rewards, have different requirements for mental and physical activity, provide separate adult communities, and call upon dissimilar personal resources. Precisely for this reason, they are highly complementary—as many men will happily tell you. Lives that consist primarily of parenting or career often feel unbalanced or limited. Half of the experiences that life can provide are missing. Like men, women have been found to be happier and healthier when they can participate in both spheres.

In contemporary America, however, having children creates the great divide between male and female adult roles. It is all too often the death knell for women's ambitions. Most women want adequate time to care for their children, particularly when they are small. But in our society women take on this role at significant personal cost. They are expected to do the vast majority of child care despite the lack of respect, social support systems, financial security, or financial remuneration. Women, unlike men, are asked to take on virtually all of the risks, stresses, and losses that child care entails. Few governmental policies are in place to realistically assure women that they can maintain a place in the workforce or reenter it once they take off more than a few weeks for child care. Women in the workforce with children are required to carry the same workload as men. In effect, women are treated not as equal to men but as identical to them. It is a charade of equality that effectively leaves women with a terrible choice: which of the two basic parts of their lives—family or career—do they wish to sacrifice?

For a few women this is an easy call: they have always wanted to be a full-time mother and can be supported by their husbands, or they are career-oriented and have an unusually good support system to provide child care. Most women are not so lucky. They face painful compromises no matter what they choose. Currently a woman with children has three main choices: abandon her career (for unemployment, lower-level work, or a part-time job), give up motherhood altogether for a career, or try desperately to do two full-time jobs: motherhood and career. Each option potentially entails its own major sacrifices—sacrifices that are required of women but not of men. Understandably, out of love, guilt, and worry and in response to social pressures, she will usually choose to downsize or eliminate her career.

On the first page of Allison Pearson's best-selling novel *I Don't Know How She Does It*, Pearson gives an unforgettable portrait of the exhaustion and frustration that many women experience as they try to pursue a career while being a mother. As the scene opens the protagonist is trying, after a long day's work, to be a good mom:

> Monday, 1:37 A.M. How did I get here? Can someone please tell me that? Not in my kitchen, I mean in this life. It is the morning of the school carol concert and I am hitting mince pies. No let us be quite clear about this, I am *distressing* mince pies . . . you can start a crumbly little landslide, giving the pastry a pleasing homemade appearance. And homemade is what I'm after here. Home is where the heart is. Home is where the good mother is, baking for her children.

By the end of the book—no surprise—the woman has abandoned her successful career and headed for a simpler country life with her sweet, ineffectual husband, whom her best friend has dubbed "Slow Richard." Having two children has completely thrown out of kilter the structure of this couple's lives. As is so often the case, the wife has made the wrenching changes in goals. But it's hard not to wonder why she, the partner with the high-paid, successful career, was the one to deconstruct her life and not her husband, a hapless architect at a firm where work has "slowed almost to a standstill." Why is it that women, no matter what their circumstances or talents, are usually expected to take primary responsibility for the children?

CHILD CARE IS HARD

As increasing numbers of writers are women with children, a new subject is being chronicled: mothers and their children—from the mother's vantage point. This close-up view of motherhood, by actual caretakers, is turning out to be radically different from the previous received wisdom delivered by the media and child-care manuals. What emerges is information hitherto ignored, suppressed, or denied. Child care is hard, at times brutal. Most people want children, and if they have them, they deeply love them. But being the primary caretaker is a whole different story.

Books about the confusion, deprivations, and ambivalence of motherhood—such as *Misconceptions* by Naomi Wolf, *A Life's Work* by Rachel Cusk, and *Life After Birth: What Even Your Friends Won't Tell You About Motherhood* by Kate Figes with Jean Zimmerman— are suddenly everywhere. In her latest novel the well-known author Anne Lamott describes the claustrophobia that many mothers feel at times:

> Mattie wanted to devour her children when she wasn't with them, but she could hardly tolerate their neediness when they were about. Ella clung to her like a starfish, and Mattie saw herself peel away her fingers.

Sandra Tsing Loh, in *The Atlantic Monthly*, describes her own experience of becoming a new mother:

> Day Six of the Baby, bent double over the bed, I found myself frantically cracking back the spine of each new "what to expect" book. Our newborn's mouth had been stretched in a screaming O for five hours. . . . Squatting on the bed, employing a four-part technique described somewhat differently in five books, I was trying to milk myself into a tiny rocking metal bowl.

Elissa Schappell, in a book of collected essays by women, describes putting her children to bed:

> I go get a towel and mop up the water. "Now, in your bunks, pirates," I say. "Please don't make me tell you again, mateys."
>
> I glance at my watch: 9:30. Already 9:30. And I still have work I want to do tonight. No, *ought* to do. . . .
>
> Wringing out the towel in the bathroom sink, I look at myself in the

mirror. . . . Anger makes me look old. My handsome young husband is out listening to music, talking with our friends, childless friends . . . not that he doesn't deserve it, but still, here I am in the domestic waste-land turning more and more shrewish by the moment.

As Rachel Cusk explains rather grimly in the introduction to her book on motherhood, "Looking after children is a low-status occupation. It is isolating, frequently boring, relentlessly demanding and exhausting. It erodes your self-esteem and your membership in the adult world."

These women are not opposed to caring for their children; most seem passionately devoted to them. Nor are these women saying that the time-consuming labor of child care is the only or even predominant experience of parenting. What their writings document is the large component of child care that consists of demanding, low-control, repetitive tasks. This aspect of child care undoubtedly accounts for the fact that virtually everyone who can afford some type of child care has it. It is the reason that full-time parenting, frequently praised as the most important and meaningful job in the world, is not one that men are lining up to do.

Parenting has many joys but also significant deprivations, and there is no reason why women should be the ones primarily burdened with its more depleting and relentless aspects. Most women with children want to parent but do not wish to have virtually sole responsibility for their children. They enjoy motherhood and love being with their children but also enjoy many other parts of their lives. Women, like men, have a wide spectrum of styles and talents; they should be allowed to create lives that reflect this variety.

CAN MEN BE CARETAKERS?

I used to think it was lack of training; now I think that it's that Y chromosome. [My husband] Dean is spectacular at spelling Kyr-gyzstan and remembering who won the 1976 World Series. Ask him the first name of Hugo's nursery school teacher and he's stumped. Ask him to remember to pick up cat food and it goes in

one ear and out the other; on really frustrating days he'll deny
ever being spoken to at all (note to self: don't say anything
important if the sports section is within ten feet).

So writes Kristin van Ogtrop in a book on contemporary women's
lives. In her humorous way, van Ogtrop is repeating a refrain that's
been with us for centuries or even millennia—men just aren't constructed to be nurturers or caretakers. They become all fuzzy-headed
and incompetent when faced with child-rearing tasks: scheduling children's dental appointments, or going to parent-teacher meetings, or
making up the lunch bags, or folding the wash. It goes right by them; it
must be a testosterone thing. We women are left to do all the homemaking and child care by default; we're the only ones who care and are
capable enough to do it. That's just the way nature made us.

Van Ogtrop's conclusion is one that has been arrived at from any
number of different starting points: evolutionary psychology, folk wisdom, fundamentalist religion, anthropology. You might think, with so
many learned professions arriving at the same conclusion, that it must
be true. On the other hand, if you look back to see what the same or
similar august groups were saying about the behavior of blacks, Native
Americans, women, and children one hundred years ago, it might give
you pause.

The truth is that, at present, we can't conclusively answer the question of why women are almost always assigned a greater proportion of
nurturing tasks than men. It isn't clear to what degree this pattern
arises from genetics, from cultural norms that were arguably better
adapted to previous historical conditions, or from structures of dominance and subordination based on women's physical and reproductive
vulnerabilities. What the available evidence suggests is that men, whatever their "natural" proclivities, function quite competently when
pressed into service as caretakers. They rise to the occasion with surprising flexibility and skill.

In one illuminating study on this subject, the sociologist Barbara
Risman looked at what she called "reluctant" single fathers. These
were men who became single fathers not by choice but because their
wives died or deserted the family or ex-wives expressed no interest in

child-care responsibilities. In this group, as well as in control groups, Risman looked at the fathers' self-ratings on masculinity-femininity scales (the BSRI) and their homemaking abilities. She found that "responsibility for housework is better explained by parental role than sex. Primary parents, whether men or women (housewives or single parents) reported doing more housework than other parents." Single fathers, like single mothers but unlike married fathers, were serious homemakers. Single fathers also described themselves in the questionnaire with more "feminine" adjectives than did the other fathers and "femininity" was a factor that predicted close parent-child relationships. Single fathers, though not identical to single mothers in their attributes, took on many of the mothers' traits and tasks.

Risman's investigations are in line with multiple other studies that have compared single-parent homes with fathers to those with mothers. These studies have found minimal differences in parental satisfaction or child development; single fathers and single mothers do very near equally well. In one investigation, children living with their fathers actually did better than those who stayed with their mothers, due to the fathers' higher socioeconomic status. Once this factor was controlled for, the children who remained with their mothers had surprisingly little advantage. Single mothers and fathers do not differ in the number of meals that they eat with their children or in time spent with the children on other activities. Single dads appear to do a remarkably good job of "mothering" when no one else is there to do it for them.

Cultural changes that are presently occurring in our society, as more women work full-time, seem to corroborate these scientific findings. In those intact families in which the wives work, men are doing more household chores and child care than any time in the past. Working men are now taking off the same amount of time as working women to care for aging relatives. And in a new twist, in the face of rising unemployment, men are increasingly competing with women for traditionally "nurturant" female jobs such as nursing and public school teaching. When it is in their interest or unavoidable, men seem to be quite capable of developing caretaking skills.

Given these findings, it seems unlikely that men have relegated domestic duties to women solely on the basis of men's woeful lack of genetic ability in this area. Mothers may, indeed, be better at caring for infants, but it's hard to imagine a genetic proclivity for doing the laundry or going to the grocery store or driving to piano lessons. More likely, men enjoy having families and careers and skipping most of the drudge work. I suspect that husbands don't focus on PTA meetings and pediatrician appointments because they know that their wives will step into the breach. Who wouldn't pass on such tasks if given the choice?

THE PRE-NATE

A man is not a plan.
—SANDRA BARTY, a widow, quoted in *The New York Times*

Given the limited career options for women who assume the primary responsibility for child care, many women downsize their ambitions to have more family time. They may quit work entirely; they may discontinue their profession to take a part-time job; or they may hold on to their career in a less demanding position that offers fewer intellectual and professional opportunities. As I've noted, the lifetime income forgone by college-educated mothers is an estimated one million dollars, and this large sum doesn't even address the losses of the many women with postgraduate degrees.

The unspoken contract in these couples is that the husbands will share their future incomes with their wives. But what happens to these women if the marriage goes bad, as it does 50 percent of the time? Too often women find themselves in a bait-and-switch situation: suddenly one party decides to breach the agreement. In such cases women can find themselves with little in the way of career or financial support to fall back on. Marriage is not an equal financial partnership; women assume almost all of the economic risk.

Many years ago Margaret Mead distinguished between two profoundly different kinds of marriage: marriage prior to or without children and marriage with children. She pointed out that we usually don't separate these two types of partnerships; we assume that if a man and woman make a good couple, good parenting will follow. But in reality, a relationship that works well for two childless married adults may become highly problematic when it expands into a threesome or more—namely a family.

Mead suggested that couples should not make the decision to have children lightly; she went so far as to suggest that this phase of marriage have a separate type of contract. Providing child care and financial support for offspring, she pointed out, is a massive life commitment, perhaps *the* largest commitment we ever make. The promise to care for and support children throughout their childhood should not be vague or easily evaded—too much is at stake. The "solution" that Mead proposed is wonderfully innovative but probably unfeasible. She advocated a kind of "marriage insurance" that would compensate family members' losses in the case of divorce. "Like life insurance, for which most all families carefully budget their resources, marriage insurance would give a stronger base of security to the whole family," Mead suggested.

The idea is certainly thought-provoking in this age of divorce, but probably financially unworkable. One might wonder half-facetiously, however, whether women should consider an updated version of "marriage insurance." It could be called a "pre-nate." This would be a contractual commitment between a husband and wife to provide, in case of divorce, support for their children and compensation to the child-rearing spouse for lost income and career opportunities. There are obvious precedents for such an arrangement. In many couples where one member enters the marriage with significant assets, a prenuptial contract is arranged to protect those assets in case of divorce. In a similar fashion, many wives and husbands starting a family have significant assets that are potentially at risk; namely their training and careers. If the husband and wife agree that the wife should terminate or reduce her professional activities to care for the children, she should have some assurances that the children will not be financially penalized in the long run.

A contractual arrangement of this sort may seem ridiculously legalistic or cold-blooded. But one has only to look at what occurs in its absence—the frequent lack of child support provided by divorced non-custodial parents, 90 percent of whom are fathers—to realize that it may be the most sensible and compassionate alternative. Equally tragic is the fact that when there is no formal contract, there is no compensation for divorced spouses who gave up or reduced their careers to care for the couple's children. It is not particularly reassuring to realize that, as Ann Crittenden points out, "motherhood is the biggest risk for poverty in old age." The unequal, unspoken financial contract underlying most marriages with children should be made explicit. Openness about this crucial issue would encourage both men and women to make realistic decisions and commitments when creating a family.

THE FEMINIZATION OF FAMILIES

As white, middle-class women join the workforce in ever-greater numbers, debate rages endlessly about whether they are neglecting their children. The available evidence suggests they are not. The amount of time that white mothers spent in caring for their children, for example, nearly doubled between the 1920s and 1980s. Women today have also been found to spend as much or more time with their children than the largely unemployed mothers of the 1960s. Further good news is that in intact, dual-income families, children are getting more attention from their fathers than they did a generation ago; the total number of hours that the children spend with their parents has reached new highs.

Nonetheless, worrisome trends in child care have also arisen during the last half-century. Astonishingly, as women became wage earners, many men *reduced* their commitments to supporting or caring for their children, increasingly leaving both tasks to women. These are the fathers who leave or have never been in marriages. Of the babies born in our country now, one in five is born to a single mother. A generation ago the number was one in twenty. In the last thirty years the number of single-parent families has soared, and the vast majority of these households are headed by women. Approximately one in four children is now raised in a household without a father or stepfather. Between 1970 and 1995 the number of total households with children and two parents shrank from 40 to 25 percent. During the same period the number of single-parent households climbed.

The statistics on deadbeat dads are equally disturbing. Less than 50 percent of divorced men pay child support promptly and completely; roughly half rarely see their children within a few years of a divorce. Between 1960 and 1980 the average number of years that men spent in households with children declined overall. Some sociologists have dubbed this trend toward women carrying the entire responsibility for child-raising "the feminization of kinship."

WEIGHING THE OPTIONS

How have women reacted to this increased workload—the expectation that they will need, in many instances, to provide full child support *and* child care? The short answer is: with bafflement, denial, and anger. I suspect that this anger is one of the reasons so many young women, while embracing the freedoms that feminists fought for, resent feminism itself. These young women feel like a bad historical joke has been played on them: "Congratulations, girls, now you have the golden opportunity to do two full-time jobs rather than one." Many of these young women have seen their mothers struggle with the impossible stress of career plus children, and they want no part of it. Their position is understandable. The choices available to them may be better than two generations ago, but they're still highly problematic. The feminists of the 1970s and 1980s, unfortunately, only got women part of the way, and major obstacles must still be overcome before women receive fair treatment at work and at home.

One response to the double burden placed on women has been a dramatic decline in the birthrate (although this decrease certainly reflects other factors as well). In the United States, the birthrate, as of 2002, dropped so low that it was slightly under the number required to sustain the population. The fact that the birthrate was even this high was attributed to the influx of immigrants with large families. As one economist described the situation:

> The most fundamental changes of recent decades were the massive entry of married women into paid work and the steep decline in fertility. The other changes—in marriage and divorce, in training for higher level occupations, and in childrearing outside marriage—mostly derive from choices about work and fertility. For many women this is a joint decision, expressed as "I will take a paid job *and* have fewer children."

In Europe, where divorce is now more common than in the past and there is less immigration, the birthrate has fallen even more precipitously than in the United States. Countries such as Spain have birthrates approximately half that required to maintain their population. Astonishingly, in Germany, 39 percent of the most highly educated women are childless, as are nearly 25 percent of the women with less education. As one German bureaucrat explained to *The New York Times,* "The more money you make, the greater is the opportunity cost for having children." In an article on the declining birthrate in Italy, a woman suggests to the reporter that Italian women's low fertility reflects their distrust of Italian men: "When [the men] marry, they are not prepared to help out at home in ways that take pressure off of women, especially if those women want to have children." Governments across Europe are now scrambling to accommodate working women who have children, offering tax breaks, free nursery schools, free child health care, maternity and paternity leaves, and low mortgage rates.

In the United States, by contrast, the government has taken few steps to accommodate working women with children. Among the developed nations, ours stands out as one of the least supportive of working women and, for that matter, of all women and their children. The national policy has been virtually punitive. In America not only is the poverty rate higher for women than men, but one in five children lives in poverty. In Sweden, a comparably affluent country that has generous maternal and child benefits, no child lives in poverty. It's not hard to figure out which demographic group benefits from the American arrangement. It is certainly not women or children.

THE CHILDREN OF WOMEN WITH CAREERS

When I first began my medical career, I recall reading with amazement an article in the *Journal of the American Medical Women's Association* regarding the families of women doctors. It described a study comparing families of male and female physicians. Two observations were unforgettable to me. The first was that the (largely unemployed) wives of the male physicians had *more* hired help at home than the married women physicians did. (What does that tell you about career women's guilt?) The second was that everyone in the women physicians' families—husbands and children—were doing just fine, but the women physicians themselves were stressed and worried about their children. Twenty years later most contemporary women still are haunted by the idea that working mothers are worse mothers—even though men now believe that it makes no difference!

In the United States our psychoanalytically informed belief in the massive, irreversible influence of mothering has generated huge concern about the children of working mothers. As a result, over the last half century extraordinary amounts of research have been carried out looking for possible damage to children whose mothers work. Few areas of research have generated such interest.

The findings have been mixed but overall are reassuring. On the positive end, the children of working mothers appear to benefit from the increased financial resources of dual-income families. Girls with working mothers, as opposed to nonworking mothers, are reportedly more self-confident and get better grades; boys with working mothers are well adjusted, but sometimes have lower grade-school achievement, particularly if the mother has more than a forty-hour week. (Apparently if women stay home, the girls fare somewhat worse and the boys better.) One wonders if more paternal time at home might have helped these boys' school achievement.

By and large, the children of working mothers do just fine. Rosalind Barnett and Caryl Rivers, in *She Works/He Works,* report that when a panel of distinguished social scientists reviewed all the studies dealing with this issue for the National Academy of Sciences, they concluded: "There were no consistent effects of maternal employment on child development, because work is only one variable in a woman's life, and there are many others." Income, adequate child care, paternal and extended family help with child care, the mother's satisfaction with her work, and many other elements all were important determinants of outcome. Working versus not working did not seem to be the factor predictive of outcome. The sociologist Kathleen Gerson, in her study of the children of working and nonworking mothers, also found no alarming issues: "Children with working mothers (from all income groups) are no more likely to drop out, take drugs, break the law, or experiment with sex prematurely than children with non-employed mothers."

Among the massive number of studies in this area, very few have had any worrisome or even negative findings. Several recent studies suggest, however, that under specific circumstances, lack of adequate parenting may take a toll. Early infancy is one period where real concerns exist. A study by researchers from Columbia Teachers College has suggested that infants less than nine months old who are placed in group child-care facilities may have developmental delays by age three. It is certainly possible, if not likely, that the quality of early infant care has an impact on neural development.

If these studies are replicated, they will highlight the woefully inadequate U.S. governmental provisions for parents with newborns. Other Western nations, on average, allow new mothers to take ten months off from work. In this country women can expect six weeks of paid leave or, if they work for a large enough company, up to twelve weeks without pay. Such policies represent a significant public health problem; large numbers of new mothers are in the workforce, and many can't afford to leave their jobs even if they wished to.

A study by the National Institute of Child and Human Development also found potential detrimental effects of long hours in child care for some young children. In this investigation, the more time children spent in child care, the more likely they were to have behavioral problems such as aggression. Many experts believe that the issue is the quality of the care provided. Children who attend Head Start programs with relatively low child-to-caretaker ratios, for example, have less aggressive behavior than children attending other child-care facilities. It is distressing, but characteristic of the low priority our society and government places on child care, that an estimated 85 to 90 percent of child-care facilities in the United States are not of high quality.

Parenting, like marriage and so many other aspects of our culture, is in constant flux, and we, especially mothers, worry about the new family configurations. The scientific community has scrambled to keep up with these changes and keep us informed about their implications. To date, the research findings about working mothers are largely positive, but there are undoubtedly areas of concern that need to be addressed. The quality of child care available to most of the population clearly must be improved. Mothers and children make up the vast majority of the population, yet their needs are chronically underfunded. The costs of parenting are passed along from the government to corporations, from corporations to individual families, and within families to mothers. At present, the costs of child care—time, emotional energy, career opportunities, and financial security—are largely shouldered by women.

CONCLUSION

For women at this historical moment, absent unusual luck, talent, or financial support, there are no perfect solutions. Women and their ambitions are a work in progress. Today women have more opportunities than at any prior time but still are expected to fill an almost comically large number of roles. They have been given new options, but little effort has been made to lessen the family obligations that have historically been theirs. And to complicate matters further, some of women's socially condoned roles are in conflict with others.

Like immigrants and other social groups undergoing huge, rapid transitions, women find themselves caught between a traditional culture and a quickly evolving contemporary one. The transition generates an odd combination of creativity, hope, excitement, and discomfort. Nothing feels easy or natural. Whatever life decisions get made have a willed, experimental quality.

I wonder, at times, if women appreciate the dimensions of the social upheavals that they must navigate in order to reach some sort of emotional terra firma. The number, speed, and magnitude of changes in women's lives that have occurred over the last century are without historical precedent: women's life spans nearly doubled; birth control was discovered; women's legal, political, and educational rights were all won. Our society is still reeling from the alterations of basic male-female relationships for which these events laid the groundwork.

Women gained access to a whole new, vital aspect of life. They could freely pursue ambitions and were no longer automatically relegated to the role of love object or caretaker. As Virginia Woolf memorably wrote in an essay on the Brontës:

The drawbacks of being Jane Eyre are not far to seek. Always to be a governess and always to be in love is a serious limitation in a world which is full, after all, of people who are neither the one nor the other.

Prior to the last century nearly all women were in some sense Jane Eyres—living lives delimited by these two narrow venues.

The opportunities for mastery and recognition that have since become available to women have opened up a new world. Half of the spectrum of human experience, previously unavailable to women, is suddenly within their reach. At their best, women's new ambitions can help define, energize, reward, and expand their lives.

Women's ability to develop their ambitions, however, has remained problematic. Many of their gains have entailed losses for men. Valued social resources—such as time, money, recognition, and influence—are limited, and as women have asserted their right to equal access to such resources, they have been met with opposition. These highly valued commodities have not been relinquished without a bitter fight. This was true historically, and it is true now.

The conflicts between men's and women's interests have led to both subtle and overt attacks on women. Typically such attacks take the form of threats: women who pursue their ambitions will lose their femininity, their ability to have relationships, or their capacity to bear children. At times the attacks take the form of work discrimination, and sometimes they even include physical assault. The inevitable male-female role changes have been painful and disruptive for all concerned. But it is clear that women's roles cannot be reconfigured without altering men's lives in significant ways.

Some of these changes may ultimately benefit men. Many men would like to have more flexibility in the workplace and spend more time with their families. At present men are socially penalized for prioritizing family over work; they are the butt of endless jokes about househusbands. If men are to embrace changes in their balance of work and family, a society-wide shift in values is needed. Few people, male or female, wish to be segregated out of accepted work patterns and ghettoized in "mommy tracks."

Currently, our society views time spent away from work for child-birth and child care as an awkward, expensive digression from a "nor-mal" work life. Our model of a career trajectory is one that reflects the male life cycle. The rigid agenda of full-time, continuous participation in the workforce frequently precludes women from challenging, in-fluential, and remunerative jobs. The failure by our institutions to acknowledge the basic requirements of child care commonly sidelines women as well as men who wish to be good parents.

Yet there is no logical reason why a seamless work schedule is neces-sary. In many industrial societies men are asked to take two years of their young adulthood to participate in the military. During World War II this country accommodated a four-year hiatus in the normal career cycle of an entire generation of men. The work life of young adults can be reconfigured when it is a national priority.

The current, ongoing uncertainty about men's and women's roles makes it necessary for women to clearly understand their options, as well as the roadblocks they will likely face. What are ambitions about and how essential are they? Many cultural and personal forces are now pressuring women to relinquish their goals: why hold on to ambitions, those chimerical hopes for the future—half plan, half dream? Without a clear sense of the basic elements of life that such aspirations engage, they are all too easily abandoned.

Throughout their lives women are subtly discouraged from pursu-ing their goals by a pervasive lack of recognition for their accomplish-ments. Parents, peers, teachers, professors, bosses, and institutions all underrate work by females and therefore unwittingly withhold appro-priate praise and support. All too often girls and young women incre-mentally lose their early convictions about their abilities and talents. A belief in the likelihood of achieving their goals slowly fades and is sup-planted by aspirations for more socially available types of attention, particularly attention for sexual attractiveness.

The coup de grâce for many women's ambitions occurs when they have children. Up to this point girls and women experience a discour-aging absence of affirmation. After they have children, they can become the target of hostility and openly voiced social criticism if they do not follow the mandates of "femininity." It is assumed that they will subordinate their needs to those of others, particularly their husbands. The expectation is that a woman will sacrifice her career goals to those of her spouse and take on the responsibility for child care.

Despite women's increasing and economically necessary participation in the workforce, no one, from the federal government to community organizations to husbands, has been willing to assume the cost of providing the labor-intensive work of child and home care that women traditionally did for "free." Most men (and our government is run largely by men) believe that the work women do in the home is one of men's entitlements. They would like to believe that providing care for children is neither their problem nor their responsibility. A quick review of our national policies for women with children will confirm this unfortunate fact.

At present I have no "solutions" for individual women, only information and perspective on the life choices that they face. I do, however, have a recommendation for women collectively. The only way to reduce the conflicts that women now face is to alter our government's agenda. Women must begin to see themselves as a political constituency (one that forms the majority of voters) with a particular set of goals: the support of mothers in the workforce as well as mothers who choose to remain at home with their children. They must learn how to better apply political pressure in order to make sure their interests are prioritized as highly as those of men. Until they became politically involved in medical care, for example, women subjects were excluded from almost all of the research protocols supported by our government. Men's health was the unspoken goal; "women's diseases," such as breast cancer, were woefully underfunded.

Unless women, and particularly mothers, create more of a political presence, impetus for change will be insufficient. Precedents for this type of nonpartisan organization exist. In particular, there is one powerful lobby for a demographic group whose needs, like women's, differ from those of the working, middle-class male. This group has special financial, social, and medical needs that they actively advocate, despite the fact that its members do not even participate in the workforce. I am referring, of course, to the retired sector of our population, a politically diverse group that has effectively been organized by the American Association for Retired Persons, an organization which has enormous political clout. Women must become more aware of themselves as a group with the power to influence national policies. They will be able to fully share in the satisfaction that ambitions can provide only when they are confident that their children are well cared for.

We are all now embarked on a collective journey into largely unknown territory; radical reorganizations of family structures and work lives are continuing. Many of the ongoing social changes have benefited women. We are now thriving and productive in ways that were impossible to foresee only a decade or two ago: women are presidents of Ivy League colleges, editors of national magazines, astronauts, business owners, Supreme Court justices, surgeons, and presidential cabinet members. Change has come at a price, but I believe that it was well worth paying. My hope and expectation is that with each generation, the conflicts will lessen and the difficult decisions become fewer. But resistance to women participating in our society as equals to men will remain for a long time. To quote Virginia Woolf one final time:

> Even when the path is nominally open—when there is nothing to prevent women from becoming a doctor, a lawyer, a civil servant—there are many phantoms and obstacles, as I believe, looming in her way. To discuss and define them is I think of great value and importance; for thus only can the labour be shared, the difficulties solved.

NOTES

CHAPTER ONE: *What Is Ambition?*

7 "BE ABLE TO MAKE THINGS AND MAKE THEM WELL": Erik H. Erikson, *Childhood and Society* (New York: Norton, 1952), p. 259.

7 "THE ADDICTION TO BRIDGE": Robert White, "Motivation Reconsidered: The Concept of Competence," *Psychological Review* (1959), p. 313.

7 "IT IS CHARACTERISTIC": Ibid., p. 323.

8 "THE GREATEST PLEASURE IN YO-YOING": Frank Conroy, *Stop-Time: A Memoir* (New York: Penguin Books, 1967), p. 111.

12 "FURTHERMORE, FOUR OF THE OTHER FREQUENTLY MENTIONED": Sylvia Rimm with Sara Rimm-Kaufman and Ilonna Rimm, *See Jane Win: The Rimm Report on How 1,000 Girls Became Successful Women* (New York: Crown Publishers, 1999), p. 170.

12 "CATHER WENT OFF TO LINCOLN": Joan Acocella, "Cather and the Academy," *The New Yorker,* November 25, 1995, p. 60.

13 "I AM CONVINCED THAT IT WAS MY MISFORTUNE": Alice Miller, *The Drama of the Gifted Child: The Search for the True Self* (New York: Basic Books, 1981), pp. 43–44.

14 "FOR MANY YEARS I WROTE": Jamaica Kincaid, *My Brother* (New York: Farrar, Straus & Giroux, 1997), p. 191.

14 "THE PERFECT READER HAD DIED": Ibid., p. 193.

14 "FOR IS IT NOT A DESIRE": Ibid., pp. 152–53.

15 "RADICAL INDIVIDUALISM": Robert N. Bellah et al., *Habits of the Heart: Individualism and Commitment in American Life* (Berkeley: University of California Press, 1985), p. 21.

17 "I'M TRULY GLAD": Joyce Jensen, "As Anthologies Duel, Women Gain Ground," *New York Times,* January 30, 1999, p. B11.

17 "BEFORE THAT I HAD MADE MY LIVING": Virginia Woolf, *A Room of One's Own* (New York: Harcourt Brace and Co., 1989), p. 37.

CHAPTER TWO: *Distorted Ambitions*

20   "HUMANITY IS MALE": Simone de Beauvoir, *The Second Sex* (1952; repr. New York: Vintage Books, 1989), p. xxii.

20   "FOR THE YOUNG WOMAN": Ibid., p. 336.

20   "FROM NOW ON, I'M GOING TO TAKE YOU UNDER MY WING": Simone de Beauvoir, *Memoirs of a Dutiful Daughter,* translated by James Kirkup, (1958; repr., London, Weidenfeld & Nicolson 1959), p. 342

20   "BUT WHAT HE HIMSELF RECOGNIZED": Ibid., p. 343.

20   "AT THE AGE OF THIRTY": Jean-Paul Sartre, *The Words,* translated by Bernard Frechtman, (1964; repr., New York: George Braziller, 1964), p. 252.

21   "IDENTITY IS GROUNDED": Carolyn Heilbrun, *Writing a Woman's Life* (New York: Ballantine Books, 1988), p. 24.

21   "WHAT DOES IT MEAN": Ibid., p. 21.

21   "FOR A SHORT TIME": Ibid.

21   "THE CLEAREST FORM IN WHICH THE SEX DIFFERENCE": Elizabeth Douvan and Joseph Adelson, *The Adolescent Experience* (New York: John Wiley & Sons, 1966), p. 25.

22   " 'TALENTS' ARE RELATIVELY VAGUE": Ibid., p. 70.

22   "THIS GROUP INCLUDES ALL GIRLS": Ibid., p. 255.

23   "THE 'PERSONALLY MOBILE' [GIRLS] SHOW STATISTICAL DIFFERENCES": Ibid., p. 77.

25   "I BECAME PRIME MINISTER": Golda Meir, *My Life* (New York: G.P. Putnam's Sons, 1975), p. 379.

25   "I LET MY NAME STAY": Mary McCarthy, *Intellectual Memoirs: New York 1936–1938* (New York: Harcourt Brace Jovanovich, 1992), p. 58.

25   "TO THIS DAY": Ibid., p. 109.

25   "THE LOGIC OF HAVING SLEPT WITH WILSON": Ibid., p. 101.

26   "MAKING A CHOICE": Ibid., p. 58.

26   "I SHALL VOTE FOR THE COMMUNIST CANDIDATES": Edmund Wilson, *The Thirties: From Notebooks and Diaries of the Period* (New York: Farrar, Straus & Giroux, 1980), p. 213.

26   "I HAVE OFTEN BEEN CREDITED": Katharine Graham, *Personal History* (New York: Alfred A. Knopf, 1997), p. 505.

26   "WE WENT AFTER WOODWARD AND BERNSTEIN": Ben Bradlee, *A Good Life: Newspapering and Other Adventures* (New York: Simon & Schuster, 1995), p. 338.

27   "ALL OF US SEEK EVIDENCE": Ibid., p. 356.

27   "I SHOULD HAVE BEEN PLEASED": Graham, *Personal History,* p. 501.

27 "REDFORD IMAGINED I WOULD BE RELIEVED": Ibid., p. 502.

28 WHEREAS IN THE 1970S, THE U.S. CENSUS BUREAU: Adam Clymer, "Child-Support Collection Net Usually Fails," *New York Times*, July 17, 1997, p. A16.

28 FOR MOST OF THE 42.1 PERCENT: "Century of the Woman: USA Today Poll: Mothers, Daughters See Brighter Future," *USA Today*, February 17, 1999, p. 10A.

28 "WITHOUT EXCEPTION, THE GIRLS": Carol Gilligan, Nona P. Lyons, and Trudy J. Hanmer, eds., *Making Connections: The Relational Worlds of Adolescent Girls at Emma Willard School* (Cambridge, Mass.: Harvard University Press, 1990), p. 238.

28 "TO WORK FULL-TIME": Joy Fisher Hammersla and Lynne Frease-McMahon, "University Students' Priorities: Life Goals vs. Relationships," *Sex Roles* 23:1&2 (1990), p. 1.

28 "THERE HAS BEEN AN INCREASE IN THE VALUE": Robert Fiorentine, "Increasing Similarity in the Values and Life Plans of Male and Female College Students? Evidence and Implications," *Sex Roles* 18:3&4 (1988), p. 143.

29 "EQUAL EMPHASIS ON CHILDREN AND CAREER": Hammersla and Frease-McMahon, "University Students' Priorities," p. 1.

29 ONE RECENT STUDY OF 138 MEN: Barbara J. Risman, *Gender Vertigo: American Families in Transition* (New Haven, Conn.: Yale University Press, 1998), p. 70.

29 "WOMEN ARE ONLY SLIGHTLY MORE LIKELY": Ibid., p. 85.

30 "[THE SENATOR], LIKE MANY OF THE WOMEN": Rimm, Rimm-Kaufman, and Rimm, *See Jane Win*, p. 39.

30 "EVERYTHING HAS BEEN RATHER SERENDIPITOUS": Ibid., p. 35.

30 "LARINDA SPEAR IS CONCERNED": Charles Gandee, "Plunging Ahead," *Vogue* (January 1999), pp. 226–72.

31 "IT IS PERHAPS WORTH NOTING": Charles Gandee, "Of Maya Lin," *Vogue* (April 1995), p. 348.

32 "IT WAS [HER HUSBAND] WHO WENT INTO POLITICS FIRST": Michelle Green, "Pat Schroeder's Ambition to Be First Lady in the Oval Office Nears Moment of Truth," *People*, September 1987, p. 90.

CHAPTER THREE: *Avoiding Attention*

37 "TO GET A JOB AS A LAW PROFESSOR": Susan Estrich, *Sex and Power* (New York: Riverhead Books, 2000), pp. 126–27.

38 "FOR MIDDLE-CLASS AMERICAN WOMEN": Deborah Tannen, *Talking*

from Nine to Five: How Women's and Men's Conversational Styles Affect Who Gets Heard, Who Gets Credit, and What Gets Done at Work (New York: William Morrow, 1994), p. 38.

38 "GIRLS ARE SUPPOSED TO BE 'HUMBLE' ": Ibid., p. 42.

39 "THE DESIRE TO HAVE AN IMPACT": Judith Jordan, "A Relational Perspective on Self-Esteem," *Work in Progress* 70 (1994), p. 8.

39 "NONE OF THEM TALKED OF THE NEED": Margaret Hennig and Anne Jardim, *The Managerial Woman* (New York: Anchor Press/Doubleday, 1977), p. 7.

39 "WOMEN SEE CAREER AS PERSONAL GROWTH": Ibid., p. 14.

41 "WORKED FOR YEARS": Natalie Angier, "A Lifetime Later, Still in Love with the Lab," *New York Times*, April 10, 2001, p. C1.

42 "DR. DAVID BALTIMORE, THE PRESIDENT": Ibid., p. C6.

42 "THERE HAVE TO BE MANY MORE OF US": Ibid., p. C6.

42 "THE TYPICAL CHICAGO [GROUP] HIGH-SKILL GIRL RESPONSE": Carol Cronin Weisfeld et al., "The Spelling Bee: A Naturalistic Study of Female Inhibition in Mixed-Sex Competition," *Adolescence* 18:71 (fall 1983), p. 705.

43 "IT SEEMS THAT FEMALES ALTER THEIR BEHAVIOR": Ibid., p. 706.

43 "HAD LOWER EXPECTATIONS": Joan B. LaNoue and Rebecca C. Curtis, "Improving Women's Performance in Mixed-Sex Situations by Effort Attributions," *Psychology of Women Quarterly* 9 (1985), p. 337.

43 GIRLS DO BETTER IN MATH CLASSES: Sally Reis, "We Can't Change What We Don't Recognize: Understanding the Special Needs of Gifted Females," *Gifted Child Quarterly* 31:2 (1987), p. 88.

43 GIRLS IN SINGLE-SEX PAROCHIAL SCHOOLS: Valerie E. Lee and Anthony S. Bryk, "Effects of Single-Sex Secondary Schools on Student Achievement and Attitudes," *Journal of Educational Psychology* 78:5 (1986), p. 386.

43 "THE CORRELATION BETWEEN WOMEN ACHIEVERS": Elizabeth M. Tidball, "Perspective on Academic Women and Affirmative Action," *Educational Record* (Spring 1973), p. 134.

44 "TEND TO HAVE LESS INFLUENCE": Cecelia L. Ridgeway, "Status in Groups: The Importance of Motivation," *American Sociological Review* 47 (1982), p. 78.

44 THEY ACTUALLY RECEIVE LESS ATTENTION: Carolyn M. Callahan, "An Update on Gifted Females," *Journal for the Education of the Gifted* 14:3 (1991), p. 295.

44 "I DON'T BELIEVE THAT I AM GIFTED": Betty A. Walker, Sally M. Reis, and Janet S. Leonard, "A Developmental Investigation of the Lives of Gifted Women," *Gifted Child Quarterly* 36:4 (1992), p. 202.

45 ONE REVIEW OF THIRTY STUDIES: Nancy Eisenberg and Randy Lennon,

"Sex Differences in Empathy and Related Capacities," *Psychological Bulletin* 94:1 (July 1983), p. 100

45 ANOTHER REVIEW OF SEVENTY-FIVE STUDIES: Sara E. Snodgrass, "Women's Intuition: The Effect of Subordinate Role on Interpersonal Sensitivity," *Journal of Personality and Social Psychology* 49:1 (1985), p. 147.

45 "NO SEX DIFFERENCES WERE EVIDENT": Eisenberg and Lennon, "Sex Differences in Empathy," p. 100.

46 "WHEN LEADERSHIP-SUBORDINATE ROLE": Snodgrass, "Women's Intuition," p. 152.

46 "DON'T BE A LOUD, KNEE-SLAPPING": Ellen Fein and Sherrie Schneider, *The Rules: Time-Tested Secrets for Capturing the Heart of Mr. Right* (New York: Warner Books, 1995), p. 19.

46 "LOOK INTO HIS EYES": Ibid., p. 64.

46 "OF COURSE, THIS IS NOT HOW YOU REALLY FEEL": Ibid., p. 23.

CHAPTER FOUR: *Femininity*

48 "BEAMING BETTY CROCKERS": Camille Paglia, *Sex, Art and American Culture* (New York: Vintage, 1992), p. 5.

48 THE MOST FAMOUS AND WIDELY USED: Sandra L. Bem, "The Measurement of Psychological Androgyny," *Journal of Consulting and Clinical Psychology* 42:2 (1974), p. 156.

49 A FREQUENTLY CITED STUDY: "The Effects of Sex and Sex-Role on Achievement Strivings: Dimensions of Similarity and Difference," *Journal of Personality* 53:2 (June 1985), pp. 286–305.

49 THE PERSONAL ATTRIBUTES QUESTIONNAIRE: Gail Hackett, Donna Esposito, and M. Sean O'Halloran, "The Relationship of Role Model Influences to the Career Salience and Educational and Career Plans of College Women," *Journal of Vocational Behavior* 35 (1989), p. 168.

49 "QUALITIES OF SUBMISSIVENESS": Inge K. Broverman et al., "Sex-Role Stereotypes: A Current Appraisal," in *Women and Achievement: Social and Motivational Analysis*, edited by Martha Mednick, Sandra Schwartz Tangri, and Lois Wladis Hoffman (New York: John Wiley & Sons, 1975), pp. 36–37.

50 "DOES A WOMAN ALONE": Jane Smiley, "Just Like a Woman," *Harper's Bazaar*, January 2002.

50 THE BSRI ADJECTIVES THAT DESCRIBE MASCULINITY: Bem, "The Measurement of Psychological Androgyny," p. 156.

51 ALTHOUGH IN RECENT YEARS: Darhl M. Pedersen and Barbara L. Bond, "Shifts in Sex-Role After a Decade of Cultural Change," *Psychological Reports* 57 (1985), p. 47.

51 "SOLICITING THE RESPONDENT'S": Fiorentine, "Increasing Similarity in the Values and Life Plans," p. 154.

52 "MORE LIKELY THAN BOYS TO RANK POPULARITY": John P. Hill and Mary Ellen Lynch, "The Intensification of Gender-Related Role Expectations During Adolescence," in *Girls and Puberty: Biological and Psychological Perspectives,* edited by Jeanne Brooks-Gunn and Anne C. Pedersen (New York: Plenum Press, 1983), p. 211.

53 "AROUND 6:30 MOST WEEKDAY MORNINGS": Stuart Elliot, "An Anomaly on Madison Avenue," *New York Times,* February 19, 1997, p. C1.

53 "SHELLEY LAZARUS—WIFE FOR ALMOST 27 YEARS": Peter Truell, "The Wall Street Soothsayer Who Never Blinked," *New York Times,* July 27, 1997, p. C1.

54 "WHEN ASKED TO IMAGINE THEIR LIVES": Gilligan, Lyons, and Hanmer, *Making Connections,* pp. 170–71.

55 "MORE AND MORE CASES": Tamar Lewin, " 'Collegiality' as a Tenure Battleground," *New York Times,* July 12, 2002, p. A12.

58 IN THE BLACK COMMUNITY: Vonnie C. McLoyd and Debra Joze Fowitz, "Sizing up the Future: Predictors of African American Adolescent Females Expectations about Their Economic Fortunes and Family Life Course," in Bonnie J. Ross Leadbetter and Niobe Way, eds., *Urban Girls: Resisting Stereotypes, Creating Identities* (New York: New York University Press 1996), p. 355.

58 DESPITE THE MANY SOCIOECONOMIC: American Association of University Women, *Shortchanging Girls, Shortchanging America* (Washington, D.C.: AAUW, 1994), p. 9.

58 "SIGNIFICANTLY LOWER DROPOUT RATES": American Association of University Women, *How Schools Shortchange Girls: A Study of Major Findings on Girls and Education* (Washington, D.C.: AAUW Educational Foundation and National Education Association, 1992), p. 48.

59 THEY RECEIVE LESS REINFORCEMENT: Ibid., p. 70.

59 "I DON'T HAVE ANY DESIRE TO MARRY": Ena Gunderson, "Oprah, Tina Bask in Kinship, Bliss on Tour," *USA Today,* p. D1.

60 IN THE LATE 1990S: Debbie Becker, "Coach Asks School to Play Fair," *USA Today,* December 18, 1996, p. 1.

61 "RIDICULED ABOUT THEIR SEXUALITY": Lani Guinier, Michelle Fine, and Jane Balint, "Becoming Gentlemen: Women's Experiences at One Ivy League School," *University of Pennsylvania Law Review* 143:1 (November 1994), p. 50.

61 "IN THE SKIT SHE WAS PLAYED BY A MAN": Malcolm Gladwell, "The Healy Experiment," *Washington Post Magazine,* June 21, 1992.

61 "THE EYES OF CALIGULA": *Miami Herald,* January 25, 2003, p. 2.

61 "SIZZLING SEXUAL CHARM": Ibid., p. 2.

61 "THE ICE MAIDEN": Youssef M. Ibrahim, "A Prize Emerges in Merill's British Deal," *New York Times,* November 28, 1997, p. D1.

62 "THEY HATED THE UNRELENTING RIDICULE": Marlise Simons, "Frenchwomen on the Ballot Face Down Voter Sexism," *New York Times,* May 23, 1997, p. A6.

62 KELLY FLINN, A GRADUATE FROM THE U.S. AIR FORCE ACADEMY: Susan Chase, "The Woman Who Fell to Earth," *Elle,* January 1998.

62 "MANY EXPERTS ON WOMEN'S CONDITION": Susan Faludi, *Backlash: The Undeclared War Against American Women* (New York: Doubleday, 1991), p. 78.

63 "I CARVE OUT A SLICE OF MY DAY": Barbara Kantrowitz and Pat Wingert, "The Parent Trap," *Newsweek* (January 29, 2001), p. 51.

64 "THE SOUL OF CHILDHOOD": Ibid., p. 51.

64 "DESPITE A 50% INCREASE IN THE NUMBER OF WORKING MOTHERS": Pat Wingert, "Parents Today Make More Time for Quality Time," *Newsweek,* May 21, 2001, p. 53.

64 "UNCONTROLLABLE BY ANY": Francine Du Plessix Gray, "Du Plessix Gray Highlights 'Third Age,' " *New York Business Women's Calendar* 2:5 (May 1997), p. 1.

64 "THIRD AGE": Ibid., p. 1.

64 "WOMEN . . . WHEN THEY ARE OLD": Nancy B. Katreider, *Dilemmas of a Double Life: Women Balancing Careers and Relationships* (Northvale, N.J.: Jason Aronson, 1997), p. 27.

66 "AUTONOMY IS A SYMBOL OF EFFICIENCY": John Gray, *Men Are from Mars, Women Are from Venus: A Practical Guide for Improving Communication and Getting What You Want in Your Relationships* (New York: HarperCollins, 1992), p. 17.

66 "[MEN] EXPERIENCE FULFILLMENT": Ibid., p. 16.

66 "LOVE, COMMUNICATION, BEAUTY, AND RELATIONSHIPS": Ibid., p. 18.

66 "INSTEAD OF BEING GOAL-ORIENTED": Ibid., p. 19.

67 "IN CONTRAST TO MALES, FOR WHOM IDENTITY": Gilligan, Lyons, and Hanmer, *Making Connections,* p. 163.

67 "ACHIEVEMENT BEHAVIOR OF BOTH GIRLS AND BOYS": Aletha Huston Stein and Margaret M. Bailey, "The Socialization of Achievement Orientation in Females," *Psychological Bulletin* 40:5 (November 1973), p. 348.

67 "WOMEN NEED TO LEARN THE ART OF EMPOWERMENT": Gray, *Men Are from Mars,* p. 145.

67 "HERE ARE SOME EXAMPLES": Ibid., p. 27.

68 "TO PRACTICE GAINING": Ibid., p. 28.

68 "LOVING TRUST, ACCEPTANCE": Ibid., p. 145.

68 "BY RANDOMLY TALKING": Ibid., p. 36.

68 PERHAPS SURPRISINGLY, MEN: Rosalind C. Barnett and Caryl Rivers, *She Works/He Works: How Two-Income Families are Happier, Healthier, and Better Off* (New York: HarperCollins 1996), p. 185.

69 THE FINDINGS OF ONE META-ANALYSIS: Lawrence D. Cohn, "Sex Differences in the Course of Personality Development: A Meta-Analysis," *Psychological Bulletin* 109:2 (1991), pp. 252–66.

69 "OVERLY ATTACHED, UNINDIVIDUATED": Nancy Chodorow, *The Reproduction of Mothering* (Berkeley: University of California Press, 1978), p. 93.

69 "[T]HE MOST IMPORTANT CHANGE IN MEN'S POSITION": William J. Goode, "Why Men Resist," in *Rethinking the Family: Some Feminist Questions,* edited by Barrie Thorne and Marilyn Yalom (Boston: Northeastern University Press, 1992), p. 298.

CHAPTER FIVE: *Why Is Recognition So Important for Ambition?*

75 "IDENTITY FORMATION EMPLOYS A PROCESS": Erik H. Erikson, *Identity: Youth and Crisis* (New York: Norton, 1968), pp. 22–23.

75 "[IDENTITY] REFERS TO MEANINGS ATTACHED TO THE SELF": Diane Mitsch Bush and Roberta G. Simmons, "Gender and Coping with the Entry into Early Adolescences," in *Gender and Stress,* edited by Rosalind C. Barnett, Lois Bieuer, and Grace K. Barodi (New York: Free Press, 1987), p. 190.

75 "THE DATA CONSISTENTLY SUPPORT THE PRINCIPLE": Morris Rosenberg, "The Self-Concept: Social Product and Social Force," in *Social Psychology,* edited by Ralph H. Turner (New York: Basic Books, 1981), p. 597.

76 FROM CHILDHOOD RIGHT UP: Leadbetter and Way, *Urban Girls,* p. 361.

77 "TOOK A KEEN INTEREST": John Lahr, "The Player Queen," *The New Yorker,* January 21, 2002, p. 62.

77 "THE TURNING POINT IN DENCH'S AMBITION": Ibid., p. 62.

78 "SHE CLAIMS NOT TO BE 'GOOD AT MY OWN COMPANY' ": Ibid., p. 65.

78 "I HAVE TO HEAR THE AUDIENCE COMING IN": Ibid., p. 65.

78 "SELF-CONSCIOUSNESS EXISTS IN ITSELF": G.W.F. Hegel, in *The Philosophy of Hegel: Hegel's Basic Writings,* edited by Carl J. Friedrich (New York: Modern Library, 1954), p. 399.

79 "WHY ARE SOME PEOPLE MOTIVATED TO LEARN": Howard Gardner, *The Disciplined Mind: Beyond Facts and Standardized Tests, the K-12 Education That Every Child Deserves* (New York: Penguin Books, 1999), p. 76.

79 "WHAT ENHANCES MOTIVATION?": Ibid.

80 "YOUNG CHILDREN IMITATE ACCURATELY": Albert Bandura, *Social Learning Theory* (Englewood Cliffs, N.J.: Prentice-Hall, 1977), p. 32.

80 "THE TENDENCY TO STRIVE FOR A MASTERY": Howard A. Moss and Jerome Kagan, "Stability of Achievement and Recognition Seeking Behaviors from Early Childhood Through Adulthood," *Journal of Abnormal and Social Psychology* 62:3 (1961), p. 504.

81 IN THEIR STUDIES OF MOTIVATION: Carol S. Dweck and Elaine S. Elliot, "Achievement Motivation," in *Handbook of Child Psychology,* vol. 4, edited by P. Mussen and E. Hetherington (New York: John Wiley, 1983), p. 657.

81 "THE MOVEMENTS OF EXPRESSION": Joseph LeDoux, *The Emotional Brain: The Mysterious Underpinnings of Emotional Life* (New York: Simon & Schuster, 1996), p. 111.

82 "THE CHILDREN FROM WHOM INTELLECTUAL GROWTH WAS EXPECTED": Robert Rosenthal and Lenore F. Jacobson, "Teacher Expectations for the Disadvantaged," *Scientific American* 213:4 (April 1968), p. 20.

82 "THE EXPLANATION WE ARE SEEKING": Ibid., p. 23.

83 "THE GOAL . . . IS TO FEEL POWERFUL": David C. McClelland, *Power: The Inner Experience* (New York: Irvington Publishers, 1975), p. 17.

83 "THE SOCIAL WORLD MAKES ITSELF FELT": Joseph Verhoff, "Assertive Motivations: Achievement Versus Power," in *Motivation and Society,* edited by Abigail Stewart (Washington, D.C.: Jossey-Bass Publishers, 1982), p. 100.

84 "AN INTERESTING RESULT IS THAT MEN": Ibid., p. 115.

85 "MY DYING TUTOR": Richard B. Sewall, *The Life of Emily Dickinson* (Cambridge, Mass.: Harvard University Press, 1974), p. 403.

85 "WOULD YOU HAVE TIME": Ibid., p. 555.

85 "YOUR LETTER GAVE NO DRUNKENNESS": Ibid., p. 554.

86 "NECTAR AND AMBROSIA": Arnold H. Modell, *The Private Self* (Cambridge, Mass.: Harvard University Press, 1993), p. 141.

86 "IN GENERAL I MISS YOU BADLY": Jonathan Winson, *Brain and Psyche: The Biology of the Unconscious* (New York: Anchor Press/Doubleday, 1985), p. 100.

87 "THIS IS THE FIRST OFFICIAL RECOGNITION": Ibid., p. 122.

88 "PERCEIVED THEMSELVES AS SPECIAL": James L. Bowditch and Anthony F. Buono, *A Primer on Organizational Behavior,* 4th ed. (New York: John Wiley & Sons, 1997), p. 13.

88 "IT SOON BECAME EVIDENT": Rosenthal and Jacobson, "Teacher Expectations for the Disadvantaged," p. 23.

88 AN ARTICLE IN THE *HARVARD BUSINESS REVIEW*: Frederick Herzberg, "One More Time: How Do You Motivate Employees?" *Harvard Business Review,* 46:1 (Jan.–Feb. 1968), p. 56.

89 "MONEY IS NOT A MOTIVATOR": Rosabeth Moss Kantor, *Men and Women of the Corporation* (New York: Basic Books, 1977), p. 129.

89 "THAT EVERY PERSON COUNTS": Jack Welch, "Jack Welch Denies Old

Economy / New Economy Dichotomy," transcript of *The Charlie Rose Show,* March 16, 2001.

90 BLOOD LEVELS OF TESTOSTERONE: Deborah Blum, *Sex on the Brain* (New York: Viking Penguin, 1998), p. 227.

91 "ENHANCES SECURITY, COURAGE, ASSERTIVENESS": Peter D. Kramer, *Listening to Prozac* (New York: Viking, 1993), p. 134.

91 IF THE MONKEY THEN RECEIVES: Ibid., p. 212.

92 "SELF-ESTEEM (READ SEROTONIN) KEEPS RISING": Robert Wright, "The Biology of Violence," *The New Yorker,* March 13, 1995, p. 74.

92 "WHEN YOU GO THROUGH THE PSYCHOTHERAPY LITERATURE": Donald F. Klein and Michel Thase, "Medication vs. Psychotherapy for Depression," *Progress Notes* 8:2 (1998), p. 45.

94 "LEARNING, INCLUDING LEARNING THAT RESULTS IN DYSFUNCTIONAL BEHAVIOR": Erik R. Kandel, "Biology and the Future of Psychoanalysis: A New Intellectual Framework for Psychiatry Revisited," *American Journal of Psychology* 156 (1999), p. 460.

97 IT COMES AS NO SURPRISE: Klein and Thase, "Medication vs. Psychotherapy for Depression," p. 44.

98 "THE PROBLEM THAT HAS NO NAME": Betty Friedan, *The Feminine Mystique* (New York: Dell, 1963), p. 15.

CHAPTER SIX: *Unequal Rewards*

100 "QUINTESSENTIALLY MACHO": Carol Kaesuk Koon, "A Theorist with Personal Experience of the Divide Between the Sexes," *New York Times,* October 17, 2000, p. F1.

100 "ALL 15 OF THE TEACHERS GAVE MORE ATTENTION TO BOYS": Lisa A. Serbin and Daniel K. O'Leary, "How Nursery Schools Teach Girls to Shut Up," *Psychology Today* (December 1975), p. 102.

100 "NURSERY SCHOOL CLASSROOM TEACHERS": Ibid., p. 102.

101 "TEACHERS PRAISE BOYS MORE THAN GIRLS": Myra Sadker and David Sadker, "Sexism in the Schoolroom of the '80s," *Psychology Today* (March 1985), p. 54.

101 "TEACHERS BEHAVE DIFFERENTLY": Ibid., p. 56.

101 "THE TEACHERS OVERWHELMINGLY": Ibid., p. 57.

101 "THE TEACHERS SWITCHED FROM POSITIVE RATINGS": Stein and Bailey, "Socialization of Achievement Orientation in Females," p. 349.

101 A DIFFERENT STUDY FOUND: Callahan, "Update on Gifted Females," p. 295.

102 "BOYS RECEIVED MORE OF ALL FOUR": AAUW, *How Schools Shortchange Girls,* p. 69.

102 "TEACHERS INITIATE 10% MORE COMMUNICATIONS": American Association of University Women, "Equitable Treatment of Girls and Boys in the Classroom" (Washington, D.C.: AAUW Educational Foundation, 1992), p. 3.

102 "ALTHOUGH THE GIRLS STUDYING GEOMETRY": "Girls' Math Achievement: What We Do and Don't Know," *Harvard Education Letter* 2:1 (January 1986), p. 1.

102 IN ANOTHER STUDY OF TEACHER RESPONSES: Callahan, "Update on Gifted Females," p. 295.

102 "MAKE SURE THAT THE QUALITY OF THE WOMEN'S EDUCATION": Catherine G. Krupnick, "Unlearning Gender Roles: Meadows College Prepares for Men," *Gender and Public Policy: Cases and Comments* (Boulder, Colo.: Westview Press, 1993), p. 137.

103 "ONE OF THE MALES CONTRIBUTED": Ibid., p. 141.

103 "[W]HEN THE STUDENTS WERE GIVING ORAL PRESENTATIONS": Ibid., p. 147.

103 "AFFIRM STUDENTS OF THEIR OWN SEX": Bernice R. Sandler, Mary De Mouy, and Roberta M. Hall, "The Classroom Climate: A Chilly One for Women?" (Washington, D.C.: American Association of University Women Education Foundation, 1982), p. 2.

103 "THERE IS EVIDENCE THAT WOMEN STUDENTS": Helen M. Berg and Marianne A. Ferber, "Men and Women Graduate Students: Who Succeeds and Why?" *Journal of Higher Education* 54:6 (1983), p. 631.

103 "THEY ARE HIRED IN LOWER-LEVEL JOBS": Ibid., p. 631.

103 "MALE JOB APPLICANTS TEND TO BE SELECTED": Ibid.

104 "TWO GROUPS OF PEOPLE WERE ASKED": Sandler, De Mouy, and Hall, "Classroom Climate," p. 4.

104 "[T]HE TRAINED FEMALES RECEIVED": Virginia Valian, *Why So Slow? The Advancement of Women* (Cambridge, Mass.: MIT Press, 1998), p. 130.

104 MY FAVORITE IS ONE THAT SHOWS: Eleanor Maccoby, "Gender and Relationships: A Developmental Account," *American Psychologist* 45:4 (April 1990), p. 517.

105 "THE 3 JULY ISSUE PROVIDES AN INTERESTING ILLUSTRATION": Donna E. Stewart, "Where Are the Women?" *Psychiatric News*, August 21, 1998, p. 14.

CHAPTER SEVEN: *Pseudo-Recognition: Historical and Contemporary*

107 "IT IS ONE THE MORE STRIKING FACTS": Ruth Bernard Yeazell, ed., *The Death and Letters of Alice James* (Boston: Exact Change, 1997), p. 3.

107 "DESPITE HER APPARENT WISH": Ibid., p. 6.

107 " 'THOUGH SHE NEVER SAID SO' ": Ibid., p. 8.

107 "I DON'T SEE HOW WHEN I GET HOME": Ibid., p. 9.

108 "I'VE KEPT JOURNALS SINCE I WAS IN ELEMENTARY SCHOOL": Katherine Hart, "Thirty-Single," *Elle* (February 2001), p. 98.

109 "WHAT FIRE, WHAT EASE": "Lady Wortley Montague," http://darkwing.uoregon.edu/rbear/montagu.

109 "THE INJURY DONE ME BY THAT PRINTER": "Katherine Philips," http://www.usask.ca/english/phoenix/philipsbio.htm.

111 "BEGIN HERE. IT IS RAINING": May Sarton, *Journal of Solitude* (New York: W.W. Norton & Co., 1973), p. 11.

112 "A MAN OF MY OWN AGE": Kennedy Fraser, *Ornament and Silence: Essays on Women's Lives* (New York: Alfred A. Knopf, 1997), p. xiv.

112 "ARE MORE LIKELY TO BE SHOWN": Dinitia Smith, "Media More Likely to Show Women Talking About Romance Than at a Job, Study Says," *New York Times*, May 1, 1997, p. B15.

113 "WE ARE WHERE WE HAVE ALWAYS BEEN": Ibid.

114 IT WEIGHED IN AT 4.9 POUNDS: Marci McDonald, "Not-So-Rosie Times for Women's Mags," *U.S. News & World Report*, June 18, 2001, p. 35.

114 "IT'S BEEN PROVEN THAT WEDDINGS SELL": Amy M. Spindler, "The Wedding Dress That Ate Hollywood," *New York Times*, August 30, 1998, Section 9, p. 1.

114 THE WEIRD THING ABOUT WEDDING BOOKS: "Book Currents," *The New Yorker*, June 1, 1998, p. 26.

116 "WHEN THE MARRIAGE ENDS": Timothy McDarrah, "The Real First Wives Club," *Manhattan File*, September 1996, p. 108.

CHAPTER EIGHT: *Parents, Mentors, Institutions, and Peers*

119 "GIRLS REVEALED A SIGNIFICANT": Carol C. Nadelson, "Women in Leadership Roles: Development and Challenges," in *Adolescent Psychiatry: Developmental and Clinical Studies*, vol. 14, edited by Sherman Feinstein (Chicago: University of Chicago Press, 1987), p. 35.

119 "EXTREMELY CLOSE RELATIONSHIPS": Hennig and Jardim, *Managerial Woman*, p. 76.

119 "IF THE FATHER APPROVES": Stein and Bailey, "Socialization of Achievement Orientation in Females," p. 361.

119 A LONGITUDINAL STUDY: Nadelson, "Women in Leadership Roles," p. 35.

119 "THE BEHAVIOR AND PERCEIVED ORIENTATION": Gerson, *Hard Choices*, p. 46.

119 "ADULT ACHIEVEMENT IN FEMALES": Stein and Bailey, "Socialization of Achievement Orientation in Females," p. 358.

119 "NO RELATIONSHIP HAS BEEN FOUND": Margaret Mooney Marini, "Sex Differences in the Determination of Adolescent Aspirations: A Review of Research," *Sex Roles* 4:5 (1978), p. 732.

120 A LATER STUDY, HOWEVER: Nadelson, "Women in Leadership Roles," p. 34.

120 "PARENTAL ENCOURAGEMENT HAD NO SIGNIFICANT IMPACT": Diane Mitsch Bush, "The Impact of Family and School on Adolescent Girls' Aspirations and Expectations: The Public-Private Split and the Reproduction of Gender Inequality," in *Gender Deviance and Social Control,* edited by J. Figuerira-McDonough and R. Sarri (Beverly Hills, Calif.: Sage, 1986), p. 269.

120 "BETWEEN THE LIFESTYLE CHOSEN": Sally Reis, "The Need for Clarification in Research Designed to Examine Gender Differences in Achievement and Accomplishment," *Roeper Review* 13:5 (1991), p. 194.

120 "IN MOST CASES, THE [STATISTICAL] RELATIONSHIPS": E. E. Maccoby and J. A. Martin, "Socialization and the Context of the Family: Parent-Child Interaction," in *Handbook of Child Psychology: Volume 4, Socialization, Personality, and Social Development,* series edited by P. H. Mussen, volume edited by E. M. Hetherington (New York: Wiley, 1983).

120 "STUDY AFTER STUDY [SHOWED] THAT PAIRS": Judith Rich Harris, *The Nurture Assumption* (New York: Free Press, 1998), p. 36.

121 "TAKEN ALONE, EARLY CHILDHOOD EXPERIENCES": Gerson, *Hard Choices,* p. 65.

122 "ALTHOUGH THE INFLUENCE OF MOTHERS": Sue C. Whistler and Susan J. Eklund, "Women's Ambitions: A Three Generational Study," *Psychology of Women Quarterly* 10 (1986), p. 361.

122 "ELEANOR CRAVED HER MOTHER'S APPROVAL": Blanche Wiesen Cook, *Eleanor Roosevelt: Volume 1, 1884–1933* (New York: Penguin Books, 1992), p. 70.

122 "I ADMIRED SOME OF [THE FAMILY'S] FRIENDS": Ibid., p. 100.

123 MENTORS WILL OFTEN PROVIDE: Gerson, *Hard Choices,* p. 44.

123 "EMOTIONAL SUPPORT, SUCH AS . . . REASSURANCE": Monica Higgins and David A. Thomas, "Constellations and Careers: Towards Understanding the Effects of Multiple Developmental Relationships," *Journal of Organizational Behavior* (2001), p. 225.

124 "THE MENTOR RELATIONSHIP IS ONE OF THE MOST COMPLEX": Daniel Levinson, *The Seasons of a Man's Life* (New York: Alfred A. Knopf, 1978), p. 97.

124 "THE MENTOR FOSTERS THE YOUNG ADULT'S DEVELOPMENT," Ibid., p. 99.

124 "I THINK TWO REASONS WHY I KEPT GOING": Elaine Seymour and Nancy M. Hewitt, *Talking About Leaving: Why Undergraduates Leave the Sciences* (Boulder, Colo.: Westview Press, 1997), p. 62.

124 "PRESERVING THE SELF-CONFIDENCE": Ibid., p. 271.

124 "PERFORMANCE, ATTITUDE, OR BEHAVIOR": Ibid., p. 30.

125 "THE MALE STUDENTS RECEIVE INFORMAL 'MENTORING' ": Henry Etzkowitz, Carol Kemelgor, and Brian Uzzi, *Athena Unbound: The Advancement of Women in Science and Technology* (Cambridge, Eng.: Cambridge University Press, 2000), p. 72.

127 "WHILE THE QUALITY OF ONE'S PRIMARY DEVELOPER": Higgins and Thomas, "Constellations and Careers," p. 223.

127 "I HAVE HAD MUCH HELP ALONG THE WAY": Daniel L. Schacter, *Searching for Memory: The Brain, the Mind, and the Past* (New York: Basic Books, 1996), p. xi.

128 "I ALSO WANTED TO THANK": Joseph LeDoux, *The Emotional Brain: The Mysterious Underpinnings of Emotional Life* (New York: Touchstone, 1996), p. 10.

128 A STUDY OF LAW SCHOOL STUDENTS IN THE 1990S: Guinier, Fine, Balint, "Becoming Gentlemen," p. 3.

129 "COMPARED TO MEN, WOMEN ON AVERAGE EXPERIENCED": Gerhard Sonnert and Gerald Holton, "Career Patterns of Women and Men in the Sciences," *American Scientist* 84 (1996), p. 66.

129 "ON THE MARGINS IN REGARD": Ibid., p. 68.

130 "MEN STOOD IN THE HALLWAYS": Ibid.

130 A STUDY OF WOMEN PROFESSORS: Helen Astin and Christine M. Cress, "A National Profile of Academic Women in Research Universities," in *Equal Rites, Unequal Outcomes: Women in American Research Universities,* edited by Lilli S. Hornig (New York: Kluwer Academic/Plenum Publishers, 2003), p. 2.

133 SUE WHISTLER AND SUSAN EKLUND: Whistler and Eklund, "Women's Ambitions," p. 353.

134 "A SIGNIFICANT LOSS BY [COLLEGE] SOPHOMORE YEAR": Seymour and Hewitt, *Talking About Leaving,* p. 9.

134 A RARE LONGITUDINAL STUDY: Sharon Rae Jenkins, "Need for Achievement and Women's Careers Over 14 Years: Evidence for Occupational Structural Effects," *Journal of Personality and Social Psychology* 53:5 (1987).

135 "A CRITICAL MAKE OR BREAK FACTOR": Hennig and Jardim, *Managerial Woman,* p. 126.

135 "HER SUPPORTER": Ibid., p. 129.

135 "EVERYONE SEEMED TO LOOK AT ME IN A NEW WAY": Ibid., p. 142.

135 "WHEN THEY ARE BLOCKED FROM ORGANIZATIONAL RECOGNITION":
Kanter, *Men and Women of the Corporation*, p. 147.

136 "SOURCE OF OPPORTUNITY BLOCKAGE": Ibid., p. 139.

136 "WHY DON'T WORKING PARENTS": Arlie Russell Hochschild, *The Time Bind: When Work Becomes Home and Home Becomes Work* (New York: Metropolitan Books, 1997), p. 27.

136 "WOULD HAVE TO EXPLORE THE QUESTION": Ibid., p. 249.

137 "IN ESSENCE, [THE EMPLOYEES] DENIED THE NEEDS": Ibid., p. 211.

137 "AN URGENCY OF DEMANDS": Ibid., p. 17.

CHAPTER NINE: *Developing Skills*

141 "SOMETHING TO FILL AND EMPLOY": Lytton Strachey, *Eminent Victorians* (New York: Modern Library, 1918), p. 136.

144 "PAST EXPERIENCES CREATE CERTAIN EXPECTATIONS": Bandura, *Social Learning Theory*, p. 18.

144 HIGH-ACHIEVING SCHOOLGIRLS: Richard L. Luftig and Marci L. Nichols, "Assessing the Social Status of Gifted Students by Their Age Peers," *Gifted Child Quarterly* 34 (November 1990).

144 GIRLS WITH GOOD ACADEMIC RECORDS: Blum, *Sex on the Brain*, p. 215.

144 TO MAKE MATTERS EVEN MORE: Veronica F. Nieva and Barbara A. Gutek, "Sex Effects on Evaluation," *Academy of Management Review* 5:2 (1980), p. 273.

146 WHEN CONFRONTED WITH A NEW TASK: Carol S. Dweck, Therese E. Goetz, and Nan L. Strauss, "Sex Differences in Learned Helplessness: An Experimental and Naturalistic Study of Failure Generalization and Its Mediators," *Journal of Personality and Social Psychology* 38:3 (1980), p. 441.

146 FEMALES CHALK THEIR SUCCESSES UP: Stein and Bailey, "Socialization of Achievement Orientation in Females," p. 356.

146 "ARE MORE LIKELY TO CONDEMN": David B. Ryckman and Percy Beckham, "Gender Differences in Attributions for Success and Failure Situations Across Subject Areas," *Journal of Educational Research* 81:2 (November/ December 1987), p. 120.

147 IN TASKS THAT WOMEN: LaNoue and Curtis, "Improving Women's Performance in Mixed-Sex Situations," p. 337.

147 SIMILARLY, IN A GROUP: Robert W. Lent and Gail Hackett, "Career Self-Efficacy: Empirical Status and Future Directions," *Journal of Vocational Behavior* 30 (1987), p. 353.

147 SEVERAL STUDIES HAVE SUGGESTED: Carol S. Dweck, "The Role of Ex-

pectations and Attributions in the Alleviation of Learned Helplessness," *Journal of Personality and Social Psychology* 31:4 (1975); and Barbara G. Licht, Sandra R. Stader, and Cynthia C. Swenson, "Children's Achievement-Related Beliefs: Effects of Academic Area, Sex, and Achievement Level," *Journal of Educational Research* 82:5 (May/June 1982).

147 IN ONE REVEALING STUDY: Wendy Wood and Stephen Karten, "Sex Differences in Interaction Style as a Product of Perceived Sex Differences in Competence," *Journal of Personality and Social Psychology* 50:2 (1986).

149 A SENSE OF CAPABILITY: Robert Levine, Michal-Judith Gillman, and Harry Reis, "Individual Differences for Sex Differences in Achievement Attributions," *Sex Roles* 8:4 (1982).

149 "MONTHS AFTER [MY DAUGHTER'S] BIRTH": Rachel Cusk, *A Life's Work: On Becoming a Mother* (New York: Picador, 2001), p. 144.

149 "OWEN, WHO IS SIX": Kristin van Ogtrop, "Attila the Honey I'm Home," in *The Bitch in the House: 26 Women Tell the Truth About Sex, Solitude, Work, Motherhood and Marriage,* edited by Cathi Hanauer (New York: William Morrow, 2002), p. 159.

150 "MASCULINE" CHARACTERISTICS HAVE BEEN: P. T. P. Wong, G. Kettlewell, and C. F. Sproute, "On the Importance of Being Masculine: Sex Role Attribution and Women's Career Achievement," *Sex Roles* 12:7–8 (1985).

150 ONE STUDY INVOLVING THIRTEEN THOUSAND WOMEN: Barnett and Rivers, *She Works/He Works,* p. 27.

150 IN WOMEN, IDENTIFICATION WITH "MASCULINE": Wong, Kettlewell, and Sproute, "On the Importance of Being Masculine," p. 767.

150 YOUNG WOMEN WITH NONTRADITIONAL SEX-ROLE: Stein and Bailey, "Socialization of Achievement Orientation in Females," p. 351.

151 IMPORTANTLY, WOMEN WHO DESCRIBED THEMSELVES: Wong, Kettlewell, and Sproute, "On the Importance of Being Masculine," p. 762.

151 IN CONTRAST, WOMEN WHO CHIEFLY: Blum, *Sex on the Brain,* p. 215.

151 IN FACT, HOMEMAKING: Maurice M. Ohayon and Alan F. Schatzberg, "Using Chronic Pain to Predict Depressive Morbidity in the General Population," *Archives of General Psychiatry* 60 (January 2003), p. 45.

152 "NEED TO BE AWARE OF THE FEELINGS": Snodgrass, "Women's Intuition," p. 147.

152 "BECOME HIGHLY ATTUNED TO THE DOMINANTS": Jean Baker Miller, *Towards a New Psychology of Women* (Boston: Beacon Press, 1976), p. 10.

152 THE REFUSAL TO UNDERSTAND: Jessica Benjamin, *The Bonds of Love* (New York: Pantheon Books, 1988).

153 "PILOTS INFLUENCE DECISIONS": Joseph Berger, Bernard P. Cohen, and Morris Zelditch, "Status Characteristics and Social Interaction," *American Sociological Review* 37:3 (1972), p. 241.

153 "IT [IS] THE PRACTICE OF NICENESS": Malcolm Gladwell, *The New Yorker,* December 23 & 30, 2002, p. 58.
Animal ethnography: Blum, *Sex on the Brain,* p. 78.

154 "LIKEABILITY'S RELATIONSHIP": Ridgeway, "Status in Groups," p. 85.

154 A SMILEY FACE IN THE CAPITAL *P:* Green, "Pat Schroeder's Ambition to Be First Lady," p. 90.

154 "BY THIS I MEAN THE CAPACITIES FOR WORK": Karen Horney, *Feminine Psychology* (New York: W.W. Norton & Co., 1967), p. 228.

155 "[O]NE USUALLY FINDS WIDESPREAD": Horney, Ibid., p. 228.

155 IN ORDER TO HAVE AN IMPACT: Ridgeway, "Status in Groups," p. 78.

155 "AMONG STEINEM'S REQUESTED": *New York* magazine, July 7, 1997, p. 10.

156 "WE WANT OUR GIRLS TO BE STRONG": Amy Bloom, "Why Can't a Woman Be More Like a Man? And Vice Versa," O, *The Oprah Magazine* 3:10 (October 2002), p. 114.

156 "DON'T START A DEBATE WITH A MAN": Patti Mancini, "The Politics of Power: Getting to the Top and Staying There," *Vital Speeches of the Day* (November 1989), p. 661; speech delivered at Women in Management conference, Los Angeles, April 1, 1989.

157 "FOR MAGGIE WEINREICH": Kathleen Deveny, "We're Not in the Mood," *Newsweek,* June 30, 2003, pp. 41–46.

158 "THESE [EDUCATIONAL] INSTITUTIONS": Barbara Ehrenreich and Deirdre English, *For Her Own Good: 150 Years of the Experts' Advice to Women* (New York: Anchor Books/Doubleday, 1978), p. 128.

159 "THOSE WHO HAVE ALWAYS BEEN HOSTILE": Anna Quindlen, "Not So Safe Back Home," *Newsweek* (April 7, 2003), p. 72.

CHAPTER TEN: *Combining Femininity and Mastery*

163 CERTAIN DEBT STRUCTURES: Robert Max Jackson, *Destined for Equality: The Inevitable Rise of Women's Status* (Cambridge, Mass.: Harvard University Press, 1998), p. 31.

164 GEORGE SAND AND GEORGE ELIOT: Phyllis Rose, *Writing of Women: Essays in a Renaissance* (Middletown, Conn.: Wesleyan University Press 1985), p. 92.

165 "I HAVE AN INTELLECTUAL NATURE": Strachey, *Eminent Victorians,* p. 136.

167 "I MIGHT, IN TIME": Lois W. Banner, *Elizabeth Cady Stanton* (Boston: Little, Brown & Co., 1980), p. 50.

167 "I FORGED THE THUNDERBOLTS": Ibid., p. 59.

168 "WE HAD TALKED THIS OVER": Margaret Bourke-White, *Portrait of Myself*, excerpted in *Written by Herself, Autobiographies of American Women: An Anthology*, edited by Jill Ker Conway (New York: Vintage Books, 1992), p. 440.

168 "I WAS RELIEVED": Ibid., p. 445.

168 "HE WAS TOO DEMANDING": Margaret Mead, *Blackberry Winter: My Earlier Years*, excerpted in Conway, *Written by Herself*, p. 304.

168 "RESENTMENTS ENTER MOST PRECISELY": Dodie Kazanjian, "Excellence Has No Sex," *Vogue*, December 2001, p. 107.

169 "LIKE LEE KRASNER": Andrea Gabor, *Einstein's Wife: Work and Marriage in the Lives of Five Great Twentieth-Century Women* (New York: Viking, 1995), p. 182.

171 "EVERYONE KNOWS THE POPULAR CONCEPTION": Strachey, *Eminent Victorians*, p. 131.

173 "THESE [SLAVE] NARRATIVES": Conway, *Written by Herself*, p. ix.

174 "THOSE WHO ARE REALLY EARNEST": "Biography of Susan B. Anthony," http://www.susanbanthonyhouse.org/biography.html.

175 "THIS YOUNG WOMAN": Margaret Thatcher, *The Path to Power* (New York: HarperCollins, 1995), p. 61.

176 "WHEN I SAID TO MY FATHER": Ibid., p. 6.

176 "SOME VERSES WHICH I STILL USE": Ibid., p. 7.

177 "TOOK LITTLE OR NO RESPONSIBILITY": Margaret Sanger, *An Autobiography*, excerpted in Conway, *Written by Herself*, p. 551.

177 "THE OTHER STUDENTS HAD AUTOMATICALLY": Ibid., p. 554.

177 "ITSELF SOMETHING OF A REBEL": Ibid., p. 560.

177 "[T]O LOOK THE WORLD": Ibid., p. 570.

179 "FIND FULFILLMENT ONLY": Friedan, *Feminine Mystique*, p. 43.

179 "SELF-ESTEEM IN WOMEN": Ibid., p. 315.

183 "A PERSON OR GROUP OF PEOPLE": Charles Taylor, *Multiculturalism and the Politics of Recognition* (Princeton, N.J.: Princeton University Press, 1992), p. 25.

183 "THEY [HAD] NO TRADITION": Woolf, *A Room of One's Own*, p. 76.

185 "SUPPORTER, HER ENCOURAGER": Hennig and Jardim, *Managerial Woman*, p. 129.

185 "HAVING A SUPPORTIVE SPOUSE [HAD] BEEN KEY": Catalyst, *Women in Corporate Leadership: Progress and Prospects* (New York: Catalyst, 1996), p. 49.

185 "MARRIED THE RIGHT GUY": Ibid., p. 49.

186 "MARTIN GINSBURG DOES INDEED COOK": Jeffrey Rosen, "The New Look of Liberalism on the Court," *New York Times Magazine*, October 5, 1997, p. 63.

187 "THERE IS NO DOUBT": Betsy Morris, "Trophy Husbands," *Fortune,* October 14, 2002, p. 80.

187 "EVERYONE WAS IN THE CLOSET": Ibid.

187 "FRANK HAS BEEN A HUGE SOURCE": Ibid.

188 "THE WOMEN WE STUDIED WENT FOR HIGH-VISIBILITY": Dorothy W. Cantor, Toni Bernay, and Jean Stoess, *Women in Power: The Secrets of Leadership* (Boston: Houghton Mifflin, 1992), p. 143.

188 "EVEN WHEN SNOWE WAS SUFFERING": Ibid., p. 248.

189 "WHEN [SENATOR BARBARA] BOXER SPOTS A PICTURE": Kathy Kiely, "9 . . . 13 . . . Just Keep Counting," http://www.usatoday.com/news/washington, August 1, 2001.

190 "SIGNIFICANTLY MORE LIKELY": Hillary M. Lips, "College Students' Visions of Power and Possibility as Moderated by Gender," *Psychology of Women Quarterly* 24 (2000), p. 39.

191 "A DOUBLE LIFE": Catalyst, *Women in Corporate Leadership,* p. 53.

191 "THESE ARE THE WOMEN": Guinier, Fine, and Balin, "Becoming Gentlemen," p. 5.

192 "THE SUCCESSFUL WOMAN PROTECTS HER 'FEMININITY' ": Ethel Spector Person, "Women Working: Fears of Failure, Deviance and Success," *Journal of the American Academy of Psychoanalysis* 10:1 (1982), p. 78.

192 "SEVENTEEN WOMEN IN A ROW SPOKE": Peggy McIntosh, "Feeling Like a Fraud," *Work in Progress* 18 (1985), p. 1.

193 "CHRONIC SYMPTOM": Elaine Sciolino, *New York Times,* October 4, 1997, p. A5.

193 "THE FEELING [OF FRAUDULENCE]": Ibid., p. A5.

193 "IT FOLLOWS YOU EVERYWHERE": Michiko Kakutani, "Coping with the Idea of Representing One's Race," *New York Times,* January 28, 1997, p. C10.

195 "IF WE CAME FROM IVY LEAGUE SCHOOLS": Guinier, Fine, and Balin, "Becoming Gentlemen," p. 33.

195 "THESE WORKING-CLASS WOMEN": Ibid., p. 34.

196 "FULL OF REBELLION, HUMOR, ENERGY": Gloria Steinem, *Revolution from Within: A Book of Self-Esteem* (Boston: Little, Brown & Co., 1992), p. 112.

196 "MORE APOLOGETIC AND SELF-BLAMING": Ibid., p. 114.

196 "BOYS LIKE A GOOD LISTENER": John Lahr, "Dealing with Roseanne," *The New Yorker,* July 17, 1995, p. 59.

197 "CLEARLY, ALTHOUGH THE WOMAN'S LIFE": Mark Zborowski and Elizabeth Herzog, *Life Is with People: The Culture of the Shtetl* (New York: Schocken Books, 1952), p. 131.

198 "BOTH MEN AND WOMEN FEEL": Ibid., p. 141.

CHAPTER ELEVEN: *The Current Dilemma*

201 "TOWARDS LESS PERSONAL": Goode, "Why Men Resist," p. 296.
203 "A MAMMALIAN FATHER": Natalie Angier, "Fighting and Studying Battle of the Sexes with Men and Mice," *New York Times,* June 11, 1996, p. C11.

CHAPTER TWELVE: *Careers*

205 "MORE WOMEN WHO WORKED REAPED": Sally M. Reis, "The Need for Clarification in Research Designed to Examine Gender Differences in Achievement and Accomplishment," *Roeper Review* 13:4 (1991), p. 195.
206 ANOTHER STUDY REPORTED: Barnett and Rivers, *She Works/He Works,* p. 111.
206 WHILE IN 1943, 61 PERCENT OF WOMEN: Nancy E. Betz and Louise F. Fitzgerald, *The Career Psychology of Women* (Orlando, Fla.: Academic Press, 1987), p. 5.
206 THIS MAY HELP EXPLAIN: Nathan Childs, "More Stress, But Higher Well-Being: Good News, Bad News for Working Moms," *Clinical Psychiatry News* (June 1997), p. 18.
206 AS JARED BERNSTEIN: Louis Uchitelle, "A Middle Way: More Moms Find a Balance for Job and Family," *International Herald Tribune,* July 6–7, 2002, p. 9.
206 "FEW FACTS ARE AS WELL-DOCUMENTED": Barnett and Rivers, *She Works/He Works,* p. 25.
207 "TYPICALLY STILL EXCITED": Judith Abelew Birnbaum, "Life Patterns and Self-Esteem in Gifted Family-Oriented and Career-Committed Women," in Mednick, Tangri, and Hoffman, *Women and Achievement,* p. 397.
207 "FAR MORE TROUBLED WITH SELF-DOUBT": Ibid., p. 397.
208 "THE LOWEST SELF-ESTEEM": Ibid., p. 398.
209 "REMARKABLE CHANGE IS MORE COMMON": Gerson, *Hard Choices,* p. 67.
209 "ACCESS TO WORK": Ibid., p. 80.
209 "BOTH AMBITION": Ibid., p. 86.
209 ONE LONGITUDINAL STUDY: Abigail J. Steward, "Personality and Situation in the Prediction of Women's Life Patterns," *Psychology of Women Quarterly* 5 (1980), p. 195.
209 "THE RESULTS STRONGLY INDICATE": Ibid., p. 198.
210 IN THE BABY BOOM: Ann Crittenden, *The Price of Motherhood: Why the Most Important Job in the World Is Still the Least Valued* (New York: Henry Holt & Co., 2001), p. 32.

210 "FOR A MAN TO DECIDE": Etzkowitz, Kemelgor, and Uzzi, *Athena Unbound*, p. 135.

210 "PROFESSIONAL IDENTITY IS INEXTRICABLY": Ibid., p. 248.

212 "JANE'S CAREER WAS MARKED": Elizabeth Perle McKenna, *When Work Doesn't Work Anymore: Women, Work, and Identity* (New York: Delacorte Press, 1997), pp. 32–34.

212 "I LOOKED TO MY WORK": Ibid., p. 65.

213 "MY PROFESSION WAS CHANGING": Ibid., p. 92.

213 "WHEN I'M ON MY DEATHBED": Ibid., p. 91.

CHAPTER THIRTEEN: *Marriage*

221 "HOMOSEXUALS AND SINGLE WOMEN": Helen Fielding, *Bridget Jones's Diary* (New York: Penguin Books, 1996), p. 24.

221 "SO YOU *STILL* HAVEN'T GOT": Ibid., p. 11.

222 "EQUAL EMPHASIS": Hammersla and Frease-McMahon, "University Students' Priorities," p. 1.

224 "FAMILY ROLE DIFFERENTIATION": Jackson, *Destined for Equality*, p. 251.

224 "IN 2001, AFTER NINE YEARS": Lois Smith Brady, "Vows Revisited: The State of the Unions," *New York Times*, June 1, 2003, Section 9, p. 1.

225 "BRIDES AND BRIDEGROOMS": Ibid., p. 6.

225 "AT FIRST, THEIR MARRIAGE": Ibid.

226 MARRIED MEN, COMPARED TO THEIR SINGLE PEERS: Elise Harris, "Can Marriage Be Saved? An Unsentimental Case for Matrimony," *Lingua Franca* (November 2000), p. 29.

226 HAPPIER, PROFESSIONALLY MORE SUCCESSFUL: Sylvia Ann Hewlett, *Creating a Life: Professional Women and the Quest for Children* (New York: Miramax Books, 2002), p. 189.

226 GEORGE VAILLANT, IN HIS LONGITUDINAL STUDY: Jerry M. Lewis, "For Better or Worse: Interpersonal Relationships and Individual Outcome," *American Journal of Psychiatry* 155:5 (May 1998), p. 585.

226 MARRIED MEN ARE ALSO MUCH HEALTHIER: Linda J. Waite and Maggie Gallagher, *The Case for Marriage: Why Married People Are Happier, Healthier, and Better Off Financially* (New York: Broadway Books, 2000), p. 47.

226 MEN REPORT HIGHER MARITAL SATISFACTION: Barnett and Rivers, *She Works/He Works* p. 31.

226 THE ENDING OF A MARRIAGE: Andrew Solomon, *The Noonday Demon: An Atlas of Depression* (New York: Scribner, 2001), p. 259.

227 THESE MEN ALSO REPORT: Sarah Boxer, "One Casualty of the Women's Movement: Feminism," *New York Times*, December 21, 1997, p. 3.

227 IN FACT, EMPLOYED FATHERS: Childs, "More Stress, But Higher Well-Being," p. 18.

227 AS HAS BEEN ENDLESSLY CHRONICLED: Hewlett, *Creating a Life*, p. 88.

227 AMAZINGLY, ONE STUDY FOUND THAT WHEN MEN: Crittenden, *Price of Motherhood*, p. 24.

227 HUSBANDS BELIEVE THAT THEY ARE DOING EQUAL AMOUNTS: Valian, *Why So Slow?* p. 40.

227 AS ROSALIND BARNETT AND CARYL RIVERS DISCOVERED: Barnett and Rivers, *She Works/He Works*, p. 179.

228 A LOUIS HARRIS POLL IN THE LATE 1990S: Tamar Lewin, "Men Assuming Bigger Share at Home, New Survey Shows," *New York Times*, April 15, 1998, p. A18.

228 A SIMILAR INVESTIGATION: Ibid.

228 IN TERMS OF WOMEN'S MENTAL HEALTH: Waite and Gallagher, *Case for Marriage*. p. 51.

229 "IT MAY BE THAT FOR WOMEN": Bruce Jancin, "Greater Social Support Linked to More Cardiac Events in Women," *Clinical Psychiatric News*, March 2003, p. 48.

229 A SEPARATE STUDY DISCOVERED: Ibid.

230 A STUDY OF DIVORCED COUPLES: Waite and Gallagher, *Case for Marriage*, p. 119.

230 IN FORTY-SEVEN OF THE FIFTY STATES: Crittenden, *Price of Motherhood*, p. 6.

230 IN SUCH CASES, AN AVERAGE: Waite and Gallagher, *Case for Marriage*, p. 119.

230 "NOW [AT AGES TWENTY-TWO TO TWENTY-EIGHT], A MAN": Levinson, *Seasons of a Man's Life*, p. 108–109.

231 "[MEN] FIND OXYGEN": Hewlett, *Creating a Life*, p. 60.

231 "PARTICULARLY POWERFUL": Ibid., p. 61.

231 "NOWADAYS, THE RULE OF THUMB": Ibid., p. 41.

231 A REANALYSIS OF HEWLETT'S DATA: Barance Franke-Ruta, "Creating a Lie: Sylvia Ann Hewlett and the Myth of the Baby Bust," http://www.prospect.org/print/V13/franke-ruta-g.html, p. 3.

232 "WOMEN CUT THROUGH THE ANXIETY": Hewlett, *Creating a Life*, p. 198.

233 "SHE SAID, 'I LOVE HIM' ": Ralph Gardner Jr., "Married to the Market," *New York*, June 15, 1998, p. 28.

233 "I'M JUST WAITING": Susan H. Greenberg, "Time to Plan Your Life," *Newsweek*, January 8, 2001, p. 55.

233 IN 1998 THE MARRIAGE RATE: Eric Nagourney, "Study Finds Families Bypassing Marriage," *New York Times*, February 15, 2000, p. F8.

234 "HAS BECOME SO COMMONPLACE": Ibid.

CHAPTER FOURTEEN: *Children and Careers*

239 "MONDAY, 1:37 A.M.": Allison Pearson, *I Don't Know How She Does It: The Life of Kate Reddy, Working Mother* (New York: Alfred A. Knopf, 2002), p. 3.

240 "MATTIE WANTED TO DEVOUR HER CHILDREN": Cathleen Medwick, "Present Imperfect," *Vogue,* October 2002, p. 92. Anne Lamott quoted in this article.

240 "DAY SIX OF THE BABY": Sandra Tsing Loh, "The Baby Experts: The High Anxiety of Child-Rearing," *The Atlantic Monthly,* May 2003, p. 118.

240 "I GO GET A TOWEL": Elissa Schappell, "Crossing the Line in the Sand: How Mad Can Mother Get?" in Hanauer, *Bitch in the House,* p. 201.

241 "LOOKING AFTER CHILDREN": Cusk, *Life's Work,* p. 7.

241 "I USED TO THINK IT WAS LACK OF TRAINING": Kristin van Ogtrop, "Attila the Honey I'm Home," in Hanauer, *Bitch in the House,* p. 166.

243 "RESPONSIBILITY FOR HOUSEWORK": Risman, *Gender Vertigo,* p. 61.

243 CHILDREN LIVING WITH THEIR FATHERS ACTUALLY: Ibid., p. 70.

243 WORKING MEN ARE NOW TAKING OFF THE SAME: Lewin, "Men Assuming Bigger Share," p. A18.

245 "LIKE LIFE INSURANCE": Margaret Mead and Rhoda Metraux, *Aspects of the Present* (New York: William Morrow & Co., 1980), p. 131.

246 "MOTHERHOOD IS THE BIGGEST RISK": Crittenden, *Price of Motherhood,* p. 5.

246 THE AMOUNT OF TIME THAT WHITE MOTHERS: Ibid., p. 20.

246 FURTHER GOOD NEWS IS THAT IN INTACT: Lewin, "Men Assuming Bigger Share," p. A18.

246 ONE IN FIVE IS BORN: Victor R. Fuchs, *Women's Quest for Economic Equality* (Cambridge, Mass.: Harvard University Press 1988), p. 15.

246 APPROXIMATELY ONE IN FOUR CHILDREN: Ibid., p. 72.

248 "THE MOST FUNDAMENTAL CHANGES OF RECENT DECADES": Fuchs, *Women's Quest,* p. 47.

248 "THE MORE MONEY YOU MAKE": Richard Bernstein, "An Aging Europe May Find Itself on the Sidelines," *New York Times,* June 29, 2003, p. 3.

248 "WHEN [THE MEN] MARRY, THEY ARE NOT PREPARED": Frank Bruni, "Persistent Drop in Fertility Reshapes Europe's Future," *New York Times,* December 26, 2002, p. 1.

249 GIRLS WITH WORKING MOTHERS: Barnett and Rivers, *She Works/He Works,* p. 98.

250 "THERE WERE NO CONSISTENT EFFECTS": Ibid., p. 99.

250 "CHILDREN WITH WORKING MOTHERS": Kathleen Gerson, "Work Without Worry," *New York Times,* May 11, 2003, p. 13.

250 A STUDY BY RESEARCHERS FROM COLUMBIA TEACHERS COLLEGE: "Help for Working Parents," editorial, *New York Times* July 20, 2002, p. A12.

250 A STUDY BY THE NATIONAL INSTITUTE OF CHILD AND HUMAN DEVELOPMENT: Susan Gilbert, "Turning a Mass of Data on Child Care into Advice for Parents: Four Views," *New York Times,* July 22, 2003, p. F5.

251 IT IS DISTRESSING, BUT CHARACTERISTIC: Ibid., p. F5.

Conclusion

256 "EVEN WHEN THE PATH IS NOMINALLY OPEN": Virginia Woolf, *Women and Writing,* edited by Michele Barrett (London: Women's Press, 1979), p. 62.

INDEX

abolitionist movement, 170, 173–75
accomplished women: attacks on sexual
identity of, 60–62, 144;
biculturalism and, 190–94; denial
of agency in autobiographical
writings of, 24–27; divorce option
and, 167–69; elements of male
identity assumed by, 164–65; even
more accomplished spouse sought
by, 55; father-daughter relationship
of, 119; journalists' preoccupation
with relationship status of, 52–53;
merging of gender roles by, 182;
private vs. public recognition of,
36; remaining single or childless,
165–66; self-deprecation of,
30–32, 192–93; with supportive
husband, 185–86; in
unconventional marriage, 166–67;
women's interest in celebrities vs.,
117
achievement orientation, 83–84
acknowledgments, 127–28
Acocella, Joan, 12
Adaptation to Life (Vaillant), 226
Addams, Jane, 165–66, 175
Adelson, Joseph, 21–24, 28
"adequate aggressiveness," 154–55
Adler, Nancy, 189
adolescent girls, xviii, 195; ambition in
adolescent boys vs., 21–24, 134;
career orientation rising in, 28–29;
femininity notions' impact on, 52;
high-achieving, lack of social

rewards for, 144; relationships vs.
achievement as focus of, 22–24
advancement opportunities, 205, 207,
209; blocked, 135–36
African Americans, 162; feminine ideal
of, 58–60
agency: accomplished women's denial
of, 24–27; femininity and, 148–51
Air Force, U.S., 159
Air Force Academy, U.S., 62, 159
alimony, 28, 202
All the President's Men, 27
ambition, 3–32; in adolescent girls vs.
boys, 21–24; changing social norms
and, 132–33; in childhood, 5–8;
class background and, 24; creation
of, xvi, xvii–xviii, 73; distorted by
women's auxiliary role to men,
19–24; fluidity of, in response to
affirmation, 133–37; freedom to
"choose," 74; as hidden and
emotionally laden subject for
women, 3–5; mastery as
component of, 6–8, 10, 14, 15 (*see
also* mastery); meaning of, 5; in
men vs. women, 5, 15–18;
motivation to pursue, in adulthood,
82–87; parents' impact on
development of, 118–22; by proxy,
115–16; recognition as component
of, 6, 8–15, 72–98 (*see also*
recognition); reshaped throughout
women's lives, 29, 133–37; sexual
attention as substitute for, 111–13;

ambition (*continued*)
    women's downplaying or denial of,
        4–5, 24–27, 29–32, 55
American Association of University
    Professors, 55–56
American Bar Association, 131
American Psychiatric Association, 105
Anderson, Marian, 96
Angier, Natalie, 203
Anthony, Susan B., 167, 174–75
anxiety, 207; in narratives by
    successful contemporary women,
    30–32
art world, 129, 181
Athena Unbound (Etzkowitz,
    Kemelgor, and Uzzi), 210
Atlantic Monthly, 85, 240
attention: deflected by women from
    themselves, 29–32, 35–46; forms
    of, 9; recognition vs., 111; sexual,
    as substitute for ambition,
    111–13; weddings and, 113–15.
    See also recognition
Austen, Jane, 165, 221
authority, 155–56
autonomy, 84, 150; as supposedly
    male trait, 65–69, 231
awards, 130

Baby Boom, 216
Backlash (Faludi), 62
Bandura, Albert, 80, 143–44, 147
Barnett, Rosalind, 206–7, 227–28, 250
Barr, Roseanne, 196–97
Barty, Sandra, 244
Beauvoir, Simone de, 19–20, 199
Bellah, Robert, 15, 84
Bem Sex Role Inventory (BSRI),
    48–51, 149
Benjamin, Jessica, 152
Berlin, Isaiah, 99
Bernay, Toni, 188
Bernstein, Jared, 206
biculturalism, 190–94
Birnbaum, Judith, 207
birth control, 164, 174, 177, 179

bisexuality, 180–81
Bonds of Love, The (Benjamin), 152
bosses, relationships with, 135,
    184–85
Bourke-White, Margaret, 167–68
Boushey, Heather, 231–32
Boxer, Barbara, 189–90
Bradlee, Ben, 26–27
Brady, Lois Smith, 224–26
Breuer, Josef, 86
Bride's, 114
Bridget Jones's Diary (Fielding), 221
Brontë sisters, 165, 252–53
Brown, Denise Scott, 169
Brown, Jane, 113
Brown, Robert, 169
Burney, Fanny, 108
Bush, Diane, 75
business world, 180; research into
    motivation and productivity in,
    87–89; women's careers in, 27, 57,
    61, 131, 132, 135, 185, 191, 207

Cantor, Dorothy, 188
capabilities, 218; gender role
    identification and, 148–51; locus
    of control and, 145–48
career choice, 208–10; contemporary
    culture influential in, 132–33;
    mandates of femininity and,
    57–58
careers, 204, 205–19; abandonment
    of, xviii–xix, 118, 213–15;
    problematic working conditions
    and, 210–15; pros and cons of,
    205–8; unpaid activities and,
    217–19; working for oneself and,
    215–17. *See also* workplace
caretaking role, 228; alternative
    support systems and, 167;
    expanded into community, 170,
    171–72; mandates of femininity
    and, 50, 53–54, 57, 149, 152, 165
Case for Marriage, The (Gallagher),
    229–30
Catalyst, 131, 185

Cather, Willa, 12–13, 76, 165
causes, women's efforts on behalf of, 24–27, 170, 171–72, 188
celebrities, 116–17
Census Bureau, U.S., 28
Center for Women's Business Research, 216
centrality, men's loss of, 69–70
Charles, Eugenia, 189
childbearing, 160, 163, 191, 203, 204; as barrier to women's careers, 204; declining birthrate and, 28, 163, 247–48; delayed for career, 207; social affirmation and, 22
child care, 118, 191, 201, 211, 215, 220, 237–51, 254–55; complementary with ambition, 237–39; as difficult job, 239–41; governmental policies and, 63, 238, 248–49, 250, 251, 255–56; inequality of recognition in, 100–102; men's participation in, xix–xx, 29, 63–64, 222, 227–28, 241–44, 246, 247; pre-nate notion and, 244–46; studies on children of working mothers and, 249–51; by working mothers, media depictions of, 62–64
child care (day care), 206, 250–51
childhood: ambitions of girls in, 5–8; development of mastery in, 7–8; early, preoccupation with impact of, 118, 120; interdependence of learning and recognition in, 79–82; memories of being recognized for accomplishments in, 11–12. See also adolescent girls
child support, 63, 202, 246, 247
Chodorow, Nancy, 69
Çiller, Tansu, 189
civil rights movement, 179
class background: ambition and, 24; choosing "deviance" and, 195–97
Clinton, Hillary Rodham, 49, 182, 189–90
Close, Chuck, 83
Cohen, Abby Joseph, 52–53

Colette, 165
college, 162–63, 178, 203; culturally approved ambitions and, 133; female sexuality and, 158–59; inequality of recognition in, 102–3; lowering of women's career ambitions in, 134; women abandoning math and science majors in, 124–25
collegiality evaluations, 55–56
Columbia Teachers College, 250
combat, women banned from, 159
Committee for the Equality of Women at Harvard, 130–31
community, 164; development of ambitions within, 10–11; expansion of women's role into, 170, 171–72; work as source of, 212, 214
competition: childhood memories of success in, 12; women's supposed distaste for, 45
Conroy, Frank, 8
control, 15, 16, 52, 207, 208, 228, 241; lack of, in motherhood, 149–50; locus of (LOC), 145–48; well-being and, 150
conversations: men's domination of, 36–37; solitary, 106–9, 111
Conway, Jill Ker, 173
Cooley, Charles Horton, 75
corporate careers, 27, 57, 61, 207
cortisol, 90
courtship, 21, 112; weddings and, 113–15, 233
Cowie, Colin, 114–15
Creating a Life (Hewlett), 231–32, 233
Crittenden, Ann, 229, 237, 246
culture, career choices influenced by, 132–33
Curie, Marie, 166
Curie, Pierre, 166
Cusk, Rachel, 149, 237, 241

Darwin, Charles, 81
deferential behavior, deemed "natural" for women, 40–41

Dench, Dame Judi, 77–78, 79
dependence, 155; as supposedly female
    trait, 65–69, 70
depression, 90, 97, 151, 207, 229;
    patient-therapist interactions and,
    92–93
deviance, women who embraced,
    172–78, 194–97; from blatantly
    inadequate or destroyed families,
    176–77, 195; from families of
    political activists, 173–76, 194;
    social class of, 195–97; support
    systems of, 174, 176, 177–78
diary-writing, 106–8, 170
Dickinson, Emily, 84–86, 165
difference feminists, 39, 66–67
Dinesen, Isak, 64
DINS (dual income, no sex), 157–58
discrimination, 207; against black
    men, 58; against women, 27, 47,
    128, 131, 148, 178–79, 204, 215
divorce, 28, 50, 52, 63, 64, 71, 179,
    197, 201, 202, 219, 233, 248;
    alimony and child support after,
    28, 63, 202, 246, 247; financial
    disparity between men and women
    after, 230; as option for earlier
    accomplished women, 167–69;
    pre-nate notion and, 244–46;
    recognition by proxy and, 115–16
DNA, 94, 166
domestic chores, 106, 170; men's
    participation in, 222, 227–28,
    242–44
dominance, 152, 155–56
Douglass, Frederick, 174
Douvan, Elizabeth, 21–24, 28
Doyle, Tom, 168–69
drive theory, 7
Dublon, Dina, 187
Dulbecco, Renato, 41–42
Dweck, Carol, 80–81

education: inequality of recognition in,
    100–103; women's opportunities
    for, 162–63, 178, 203–4. See also

college; graduate and professional
    schools; grammar school; high
    school
"Effects of Sex and Sex-Role on
    Achievement Strivings, The," 49
Ehrenreich, Barbara, 158–59
Einstein's Wife (Gabor), 169, 220
Eklund, Susan, 133
Eliot, George, 164, 165, 166
Elle, 108
Ellis, Havelock, 177
Eminent Victorians (Strachey), 141,
    171–72
empathy, 90, 152; gender differences
    in, 40, 45–46
engineering, careers in, 57
English, Deirdre, 158–59
Ensler, Eve, 35, 125–26
epinephrine, 90–91
epistolary novels, 108–9
Erikson, Erik, 7, 66, 74–78
Estrich, Susan, 37–38
ethnicity, women's roles and, 197–98
Etzkowitz, Henry, 210
Europe, declining birthrates in, 248
Evelina (Burney), 108

facial expressions, 81, 104
fairness, niceness as enemy of, 153–54
Faludi, Susan, 62
Families and Work Institute, 228
family life, 161, 164, 191; part-time
    work options and, 136–37;
    political careers framed as
    extension of, 189; as source of
    identity and satisfaction, 136. See
    also child care; marriage
fantasies: of adolescent girls, 22;
    celebrities and, 116–17; childhood
    ambitions and, 5–6
father-daughter relationships, 119, 184
Fein, Ellen, 46
Feminine Mystique, The (Friedan), 98,
    179
Feminine Psychology (Horney),
    154–55

femininity, 47–65; accomplished
women and, 55, 60–62; agency
and, 148–51; caretaking role and,
50, 53–54, 57, 149, 152, 165;
combining masculine traits with,
180–83; combining mastery with,
162–98; definition of, 48–50;
external locus of control and, 150;
identification with masculine traits
and, 150–51; outside white middle
class, 58–60, 195–98; relationships
as context for, 49–50, 51–54, 58,
59–60; retaliations against
"unfeminine" behavior and,
60–65, 144, 156–59, 253; secrecy
about successes and, 56; self-
promotion at odds with, 129–30;
size of woman vs. man and, 54–55;
socially acceptable careers and,
57–58; stability of ideal of, despite
social change, 164; strength of
older women and, 64–65;
subordinate status and, 151–60,
170–72, 177; supposed male-
female dichotomies and, 65–71;
tenure decisions and, 55–56; white,
middle-class notions of, 47–58
feminism, 62, 179, 247; difference
feminists and, 39, 66–67; as
unattractive, desexualizing label, 48
Fielding, Helen, 221
financial rewards: in high- vs. low-
recognition careers, 94–95; as
motivator, 88–89
Fiorina, Carly, 187
First Wives, 115–16
Fliess, Wilhelm, 86
Flinn, Kelly, 62
For Her Own Good (Ehrenreich and
English), 158–59
Forten, Margaretta, 173
Fortune, 186–87
Frank, Anne, 107
Frank, Jerome, 93
Franklin, Rosalind, 166
Fraser, Kennedy, 112

fraudulence syndrome, 192–93
freelancing, 209–10, 214, 215
Freud, Sigmund, 7, 86–87
Friedan, Betty, 98, 179
friendships, professional, 129, 214
future: difficulty of planning for,
xv–xvi; imagining oneself in, xvi,
xvii–xviii, 73

Gabor, Andrea, 169, 220
gal Friday jobs, 184
Gallagher, Maggie, 229–30
Garrison, William Lloyd, 174
Gates, Henry Louis, Jr., 193
Gellhorn, Martha, 65
gender role identification, 148–51
gender roles: androgynous, in marriages
of accomplished women, 166;
biculturalism and, 190–94;
changes in, xv–xvi, 17–18, 164,
180–83; Mars vs. Venus notion
and, 66–68; more clearly
delineated for men, xix–xx, 164;
stereotypical, marriages slipping
into, 223–26; supposed male-
female dichotomies and, 65–71;
traditional, in past, xv, xvi, 16–17.
See also femininity; masculinity
gene activation, 94
General Electric (GE), 89
Germany, declining birthrates in, 248
Gerson, Kathleen, 121, 208–9, 250
Gibbon, Edward, 109
Gilligan, Carol, xviii, 28, 54, 66–67,
180
Ginsburg, Martin, 186, 198
Ginsburg, Ruth Bader, 186, 198
Gladwell, Malcolm, 153
Goode, William J., 69–70, 201
Goodwin, Doris Kearns, 143, 147
graduate and professional schools,
163, 178, 203, 210; culturally
approved ambitions and, 133;
inequality of recognition in, 103;
mentoring of male vs. female
students in, 128–29

Graham, Katharine, 25, 26–27
grammar school, 203; inequality of
    recognition in, 100–102
Gray, John, 66–68
Guigou, Elisabeth, 62
Guinier, Lani, 61

Hall, G. Stanley, 158–59
Hard Choices (Gerson), 208–9
Harris, Judith Rich, 120–21
Harvard Business Review, 88
Harvard Business School, 180
Harvard Education Letter, 102
Harvard Law School, 37–38
Harvard University, 130–31, 193
Hawthorne Works (Chicago), 87–88
Head Start, 251
Healy, Bernadine, 61
Hegel, G.W.F., 78–79
Heilbrun, Carolyn, 20–21
helplessness, 146, 147, 155
Hennig, Margaret, 135, 184–85
Herzog, Elizabeth, 197–98
Hesse, Eva, 168–69
Hewitt, Nancy, 124–25
Hewlett, Sylvia Ann, 231–32, 233
hierarchies, 153, 156
Higgins, Monica, 127
Higginson, Thomas Wentworth, 85–86
high school, 134, 184, 203; inequality
    of recognition in, 102
Hill, John, 52
Hochschild, Arlie, 136–37
homemakers, 150, 151, 209, 229;
    spheres of recognition for, 97; well-
    being of working women vs., 206–8
homosexuality, 165, 180–81
Horney, Karen, 154–55
household work. *See* domestic chores
househusbands, 186–87, 253
House of Representatives, U.S., 27, 63
How the Mind Works (Pinker), 90
Hudd, Walter, 77

identity, 73, 74–79, 136; definition of,
    75; recognition by highly

respected person and, 76–77;
    responses elicited from others and,
    74–76, 183; sustained by
    recognition, 77–79. *See also*
    sexual identity
I Don't Know How She Does It
    (Pearson), 239
Illinois Valedictorian Project, 134
"Impact of Family and School on
    Adolescent Girls' Aspirations and
    Expectations, The," 120
independence, 15, 150; self-motivating
    aspect of learning and, 79
infants, effects of child care on, 250
institutional support, 86–87, 130–32
interpersonal therapy (IPT), 92–93
Italy, declining birthrates in, 248

Jackson, Robert Max, 163
Jacobs, Harriet Ann, 173
James, Alice, 107
Jane Eyre (Brontë), 253
Jardim, Anne, 135, 184–85
Jenkins, Sharon Rae, 134–35
Jewish communities, 197–98
job interviews, women's difficulties
    presenting themselves in, 37–38
Johns Hopkins Medical School, 61
Johnson, Samuel, 109
Jones, Ernest, 87
Jordan, Judith, 39
Journal of Solitude (Sarton), 111
*Journal of the American Medical
    Women's Association,* 249
journal-writing, 106–8
Jung, Carl, 86

Kagan, Jerome, 80, 119
Kandel, Erik, 94
Kanter, Rosabeth Moss, 88–89, 135–36
Kemelgor, Carol, 210
Kincaid, Jamaica, 14
Kirkpatrick, Jeane, 152
Kissinger, Henry, 55
Kissinger, Nancy, 55
Klein, Donald, 92–93

Kramer, Peter, 91
Krasner, Lee, 169
Krupnick, Catherine G., 195
Kunin, Madeline, 192–93, 194

Lamott, Anne, 240
law school, 195; mentoring of male vs.
    female students in, 128
Lazarus, Shelley, 53
learning: gene expression altered by,
    94; interdependence between
    recognition and, 79–82, 94; self-
    motivating aspect of, 79. *See also*
    education; mastery
LeDoux, Joseph, 128
legal profession, 57–58, 180, 207;
    disparate experiences of women
    in, xiii–xv, 96–97; masculine
    culture of, 190, 191, 193–94. *See
    also* law school
"Letter to a Young Contributor"
    (Higginson), 85
letter-writing, 108–9, 170
Levinson, Daniel, 124, 230–31
Lewes, George Henry, 166
Life Is with People (Zborowski and
    Herzog), 197–98
Life's Work, A (Cusk), 149, 237
Lin, Maya, 31
listeners: imagined "other" as, 106–9,
    110; psychotherapists as, 109–10;
    retreat from role of, 110–11;
    women in role of, 36–37
Listening to Prozac (Kramer), 91
locus of control (LOC), 145–48
Loh, Sandra Tsing, 240
Loring, Karen, 107
Lynch, Mary Ellen, 52

Maccoby, Eleanor, 120
Madonna, 60, 182
Making Connections (Gilligan), xviii,
    28, 54, 67
male identity: women assuming
    elements of, 164–65. *See also*
    masculinity

Mamet, David, 33
Managerial Woman, The (Hennig and
    Jardim), 135, 184–85
Mancini, Patti, 156–57
"marital glass ceiling," 224
marriage, 50, 52, 90, 208, 220–36;
    advantages of, for men vs. women,
    226–30; avoided by women with
    groundbreaking careers, 165–66;
    declining rate of, 233–34;
    financial benefits of, 229–30; at its
    best, 220; as keystone of white,
    middle-class adult female identity,
    220–21; lack of congruence
    between men's and women's
    interests in, 51–52, 201–3,
    221–26; premarriage "plan" and,
    222–23; pre-nate notion and,
    244–46; reformulation of
    relationships and, 234–36;
    rejection of goal of, deemed
    socially deviant, 22–23; reverse
    male-female roles in, 186–87;
    slipping into traditional gender
    roles in, 223–26; supportive
    husbands and, 185–86; two-
    career, lack of sexual intimacy
    ascribed to, 157–58;
    unconventional, of earlier
    accomplished women, 166–67;
    women's achievement level and,
    231–32; women's supportive role
    in, 223, 224, 230–33
Mars vs. Venus notion, 66–68
masculinity, 145, 149, 190; combining
    feminine traits with, 180–83;
    definition of, 50–51; well-being
    and, 150; women identifying with
    attributes of, 150–51
mastery, 6–8, 15, 139–98; adolescent
    girls' focus on relationships vs.,
    22–24; childhood ambitions and,
    6–7; combining femininity with,
    162–98; conditions required for,
    142; contemporary women and,
    178–80; desire to be recognized

mastery (*continued*)
for, 10, 14; developed in context of male support, 183–87; fueled by recognition, 79–82; gender role identification and, 148–51; likelihood of success and, 143–48; motivational paradigm for, 142–44; objective criteria for, 11; pleasure inherent in, 7–8, 79, 141–42; potential rewards for, 143–44; venues for, open to nineteenth-century women, 106–7; women's opportunities for, in present, 142

math, 57; college women abandoning majors in, 124–25; girls' skills in, 148

McCarthy, Mary, 25, 26

McClelland, David, 66, 83–84, 87

McClintock, Barbara, 61

McKenna, Elizabeth Perle, 211–14

Mead, Margaret, 64, 168, 244–45

media: accomplished women's relationship status as preoccupation of, 52–53; negative depictions of working women in, 62–64

medical school, first women students in, 160–61

medicine, careers in, 180, 207, 249

Meir, Golda, 25, 189

Meitner, Lise, 166

Men and Women of the Corporation (Kanter), 88–89, 135–36

Men Are from Mars, Women Are from Venus (Gray), 66–68

mentoring, 122–30; constellations of supporting figures and, 126–30; creation of structures for, 84–86; institutional support and, 130–32; men's careers affected by, 123–24; men's greater access to, 125; primary developers and, 122–26; traditional male-female relationship in, 183–85; women abandoning math and science majors and, 124–25

Mikulski, Barbara, 189–90

military, women in, 27, 62, 159

Miller, Jean Baker, 66, 152

MIT, 130

Modern Bride, 114

money, 217. *See also* financial rewards

Montague, Lady Mary Wortley, 108–9

mood, 229; neurotransmitters and, 90–92, 94; patient-therapist interactions and, 92–93; recognition and, 89–95

Morrison, Toni, 59

Moss, Howard, 80

mother-daughter relationships, 119

motherhood: lack of control in, 149–50. *See also* childbearing; child care

My Brother (Kincaid), 14

My Lord, What a Morning (Anderson), 96

narcissism, 15

narratives of female lives: denial of agency and personal accomplishment in, 24–27; girls as stars of their own stories in, 6; men put at center of, 20–21; selfless, paradigm of, 21, 24; slave narratives and, 173

National Institute of Child and Human Development, 250

Nausea (Sartre), 20

negative reactions, 88, 104

neurotransmitters, 90–92, 94

Newsweek, 62–64, 159, 181

Newton, Ben, 85

New York, 155, 232–33

New Yorker, 12, 65, 77–78

New York Times, 33, 41–42, 47, 52–53, 55, 62, 83, 100, 114, 186, 193, 224–26, 234, 244, 248

niceness, 153–54, 223

niche approach, 40

Nightingale, Florence, 141, 165, 171–72

norepinephrine, 90–91

Nurture Assumption, The (Harris), 120–21

O, The Oprah Magazine, 156
Oates, Joyce Carol, 74, 78
Oaxaca Journal (Sacks), 142
occupational behavior (OB), 87–89, 94
Ogilvy, David, 53
older women: resilience and energy of, 64–65; sexual attractiveness and, 112
Orenstein, Peggy, xviii
"outsider" status, 193
ovum, fertilized, male-female struggle in, 203
oxytocin, 90

Paglia, Camille, 48
Parallel Lives (Rose), 222
parents: desire for retroactive recognition from, 13; father-daughter relationships and, 119, 184; impact of, on development of ambition, 118–22; mother-daughter relationships and, 119. *See also* childbearing; child care
part-time work, 136–37, 214
past: desire for retroactive recognition from important figures in, 13; focus on, in psychological theories, xvi–xvii
pay increases, asking for, 40
Pearson, Allison, 239
Person, Ethel, 192
Personal Attributes Questionnaire (PAQ), 49
personal growth, 39–40
personality, 209
Philips, Katherine, 109
physical assault, 159
physical presence, women's minimization of, 38–39
physical traits, 16, 22, 52, 135; size of man vs. woman in relationship and, 54–55; women politicians' concern about, 189–90

physics, careers in, xviii–xix
Piaget, Jean, 7
Pinker, Steven, 90
Pipher, Mary, xviii
Playing and Reality (Winnicott), 74
political activism, deviance and, 173–75
Political Woman (Kirkpatrick), 152
politicians, female, 32, 61–62; power downplayed by, 188–90
"Politics of Power, The" (Mancini), 156–57
Pollitt, Katha, 152
popularity, adolescent girls' interest in, 52, 134
possessions, prestige, 83
power, downplayed by women politicians, 188–90
praise, 10, 49
prayer, 109, 110
pre-nate notion, 244–46
preschool, inequality of recognition in, 100
Price of Motherhood, The (Crittenden), 229, 237
Pride and Prejudice (Austen), 221
Private Eye, 55
productivity, recognition and, 87–89, 94
professional relationships, 127–30, 214. *See also* mentoring
professional schools. *See* graduate and professional schools
professional women's organizations, 131
promotions, 135, 191, 209; asking for, 40
property rights, 162, 163
proxy, recognition by, 115–16
pseudo-recognition, 106–17; celebrities and, 116–17; literary genres and, 106–9; prayer and, 109, 110; recognition by proxy and, 115–16; sexual attention and, 111–13; solitary "conversations" and, 106–9, 111; weddings and, 113–15

Psychiatric News, 105
psychoanalytic theories, 118, 249
psychotherapy: patient-therapist
     interactions in, 92–93; women's
     desire for another's attention and,
     109–10
Purvis, Harriet Forten, 173

Quindlen, Anna, 213–14

race, 153; notions of femininity and,
     58–60
rape, 159
Reasonable Creatures (Pollitt), 152
recognition, 8–15, 33–137;
     achievement orientation and,
     83–84; ambition sustained by,
     13–14; from *any* respected person
     in child's social milieu, 121;
     attention vs., 111; as basic human
     need, 10, 36, 70–71, 72–73;
     careers high vs. low in, 94–95;
     childhood ambitions and, 6, 8;
     childhood memories of, 11–12;
     constellations of supporting
     figures and, 126–30; constraints
     on talking about accomplishments
     and, 37–38; definition of, 9, 72;
     denial of agency and, 24–27;
     developing reliable sources of, 15,
     84–87, 95–98; disparity in men's
     vs. women's need for, 65–71;
     dissociation from need for, 14–15;
     diversification of sources of, 70;
     femininity and, 47–65; fluidity of
     ambition in response to, 133–37;
     formative nature of, 12–13; for
     group or societal role vs.
     individual accomplishment, 9; by
     highly respected person, 76–77; in
     identity formation and sustenance,
     73, 74–79; imagined "other" and,
     106–9, 110; institutional
     endorsements and, 86–87,
     130–32; internalized sources of,
     14; interplay between past and

present sources of, 13–14;
     learning promoted by, 79–82, 94;
     mastery without, 11; men's greater
     expectation of, 68; men's loss of
     centrality and, 69–70; mentoring
     and, 84–86, 122–30; mood and,
     89–95; multiplicity of roles and,
     97–98; narcissists' exaggerated
     need for, 15; neurotransmitter
     levels and, 90–92, 94; nonverbal
     forms of, 81; patient-therapist
     interactions and, 92–93; personal
     growth and self-fulfillment vs.,
     39–40; potential, for mastery,
     143–44; praise contrasted with,
     10; presence of male peers and,
     41–44; productivity increased by,
     87–89, 94; promotions or pay
     increases as, 40; by proxy,
     115–16; pseudo-recognition and,
     106–17; public, unavailable to
     women in past, 16–17; in public
     arena vs. immediate circle of
     family and friends, 10–11;
     retroactive, from important figures
     in childhood, 13; self-presentation
     and, 37–39; sensitivity to others'
     feelings and, 44–46; social
     approbation and, 132–33; taboo
     against taking pleasure in, 24–25;
     unequally bestowed on men and
     women, 99–105; visibility in
     workplace and, 39–40; women as
     providers of, 50, 54, 73; women's
     deflection of attention from
     themselves and, 29–32, 35–46;
     women's "natural" deference and,
     40–41; in workplace vs. home,
     137
Redford, Robert, 27
reflected self-appraisals, 75–76
Reisman, David, 70
relationships: adolescent girls' focus
     on, 22–24, 52; difference
     feminists' emphasis on, 39, 66–67;
     as focus after career opportunities

blocked, 135–36; masculinity and, 50–51; to men, social affirmation and, 21, 22–24, 221; to men, women's ambition distorted by, 19–24; as necessary setting for femininity, 49–50, 51–54, 58, 59–60; professional, 127–30, 214 (*see also* mentoring); size of man vs. woman in, 54–55; studies of "social supports" and, 228–29; well-being outside of, in men vs. women, 68; women defined by, in past, 16; women depending solely on, for recognition, 70–71; women's caretaking role in, 50, 53–54, 57; women's supposedly greater need for, 65–69. *See also* marriage

Reproduction of Mothering, The (Chodorow), 69
Rethinking the Family (Goode), 201
Reviving Ophelia (Pipher), xviii
Reza, Yasmina, 47
Rhys, Jean, 164–65
Rimm, Sylvia, 30
Risman, Barbara, 242–43
Rivers, Caryl, 206–7, 227–28, 250
roles, multiple, 97–98
Room of One's Own, A (Woolf), vii, 17, 89, 205
Roosevelt, Eleanor, 25, 122–23
Rose, Phyllis, 164–65, 222
Rosenberg, Morris, 75
Rosenthal, Robert, 81–82, 88, 95
Roughgarden, Jonathan (later Joan Roughgarden), 99–100
Rules, The (Fein and Schneider), 46

Sacks, Oliver, 142
Sand, George, 164
Sanger, Margaret, 174, 177–78
Sarton, May, 111
Sartre, Jean-Paul, 20
Sayers, Dorothy, 64
Schacter, Daniel, 127–28
Schappell, Elissa, 240–41

Schneider, Sherrie, 46
School Girls (Orenstein), xviii
Schroeder, Pat, 32, 154
sciences: college women abandoning majors in, 124–25; collegial relationships of women graduate students in, 129; women's careers in, xviii–xix, 40, 41–42, 57, 184, 210
Seasons of a Man's Life, The (Levinson), 124, 230–31
Second Sex, The (Beauvoir), 19–20, 199
secretarial jobs, 171
See Jane Win (Rimm), 30
self-concept, 75
self-consciousness, 78–79
self-deprecation, xvii, 29–32, 35–36, 155, 192–93
self-efficacy, 147–48
self-esteem, xvii, 22, 134, 135, 179, 207, 208, 210, 241; of black vs. white girls, 58–59; serotonin levels and, 91–92
self-fulfillment, 39–40
self-presentation, 37–39
self-promotion, 129–30
Senate, U.S., 27, 63, 198
sensitivity to others' feelings, 44–46, 152
serotonin, 90, 91–92
Sévigné, Marie de, 108
Sex and the City, 113
sexual assaults, 159
sexual attention, as substitute for ambition, 111–13
sexual attractiveness, 134, 144
sexual harassment, 27
sexual identity, 184, 185, 192; in adolescence, 52; of older women, as no longer assailable, 64–65; public attacks on, as retaliation against "unfeminine" behavior, 60–62, 144, 156–59; relationship status and, 50–51, 221; at risk in pursuit of recognition, 48

Seymour, Elaine, 124–25
Shaw, Anna Howard, 175
Shawn, William, 14
She Works/He Works (Barnett and Rivers), 206–7, 227–28, 250
Shields, Carol, 33
shyness, 49
silence, of women in presence of men, 36–37
single fathers, 242–43
single mothers, 246–47
size, of man vs. woman in relationship, 54–55
slave narratives, 173
Smiley, Jane, 50
smiling, 153–54
Smith, Adam, 72, 82
Snowe, Olympia, 188
soap operas, 117
social affirmation: blocked career opportunities and, 135–36; choice of ambition and, 132–33; detached from mastery by adolescent girls, 22; relationship to man and, 21, 22–24, 221
solitude, retreat into, 110–11
Souvestre, Marie, 122–23
Spain, declining birthrates in, 248
Spear, Laurinda, 30–31
spelling bees, 42–43
Stanton, Elizabeth Cady, 167
starting one's own business, 215–17
Stein, Gertrude, 165
Steinem, Gloria, 155, 195–96
Stepien, Carol, 55–56
Stewart, Martha, 60
Stone Diaries, The (Shields), 33
Stop-Time (Conroy), 8
Stowe, Harriet Beecher, 170
Strachey, Lytton, 141, 171–72
Streisand, Barbra, 60
subordinate status, 151–60, 170–72, 177, 255; of accomplished women's husbands, 186–87; dominance vs., 152, 155–56; fear of being desexualized and,

156–59; feminine traits identified with, 152; hierarchies and, 153, 156; in mentoring relationships, 183–86; nonverbal communication of, 153–54
success, secrecy about, 56, 192
suffrage, expansion of, 162, 163
Sweden, maternal and child benefits in, 248

Talking About Leaving (Seymour and Hewitt), 124–25
Talking from Nine to Five (Tannen), 38
Tannen, Deborah, 38, 153
Taylor, Charles, 183
Taylor, Frederick, 87
temperament, 229
tenure evaluations, 55–56
testosterone, 90
Thatcher, Denis, 55
Thatcher, Margaret, 55, 61, 175–76
Thematic Apperception Tests (TATs), 83
Theory of Moral Sentiments, The (Smith), 72, 82
Tilghman, Shirley M., 203
Time Bind, The (Hochschild), 136–37
Toklas, Alice B., 165
trophies, 83
Truth, Sojourner, 173
Turner, Tina, 59–60
"Two Concepts of Liberty" (Berlin), 99

Uncle Tom's Cabin (Stowe), 170
unfavorable judgment, avoidance of, 81
unmarried women: in groundbreaking careers, 165–66; well-being of, 228, 229
unpaid activities, 217–19
USA Today, 59, 189–90
Uzzi, Brian, 210

Vaillant, George, 226
van Ogtrop, Kristin, 242

vasopressin, 90
Verhoff, Joseph, 83–84
vicarious living, 115–16
Vietnam War, 179
visibility, career advancement and, 39–40
Vogt, Marguerite, 41–42
Vogue, 30–31, 114
volunteering, 217–19

Waite, Linda, 229–30
Wait Till Next Year (Goodwin), 143
Washington Post, 26–27
Watergate, 26–27
weddings, 113–15, 233
Weddings (Cowie), 114–15
Welch, Jack, 89
well-being, xvii; internal locus of control and, 145; of married vs. single men, 226; of unmarried women, 228, 229; working outside home and, 206–8
Western Electric Co., 87–88
When Work Doesn't Work Anymore (McKenna), 211–14
Whistler, Sue, 132
White, Robert, 7
Wilson, Edmund, 25, 26
Winfrey, Oprah, 59–60
Winnicott, D. W., 74
Woman Rebel (Sanger), 177
Women in Management, 156–57
Women in Power (Cantor and Bernay), 188
women's rights, 162, 163, 173
Woodward, Joanne, 126
Woolf, Leonard, 166, 198
Woolf, Virginia, vii, 17, 89, 165, 166, 183, 198, 205, 217, 252–53, 256
Words, The (Sartre), 20

Wordsworth, Dorothy, 16–17, 25
working mothers, 179, 180, 205–6, 227; career commitment of daughters of, 120; negative depictions in media of, 62–64; part-time work options for, 136–37; studies on children of, 249–51; time spent with children by, 246
workplace: advancement opportunities in, 135–36, 205, 207, 209; attrition rates for women in, xviii–xix; bad jobs and, 210–15; discrimination against women in, 27, 128, 131, 178–79, 204, 215; inequality of recognition in, 103–4; lack of institutional support for women in, 130–32; painful decisions faced by women in, xviii–xix; pressures leading to women's entry into, 28; relationship with boss in, 135, 184–85; self-presentation of women in, 37–39; structured to fit male life cycle, 202, 211, 254; visibility and career advancement in, 39–40; women's entry into, 28, 163, 170–72, 205. *See also* career choice; careers
World War II, 133, 254
Wright, Robert, 92
writing, careers in, 165; forbidden to women in past, 16–17; as one of first public occupations for women, 17, 109, 170
Writing a Woman's Life (Heilbrun), 21
Writing of Women (Rose), 164–65
Written by Herself (Conway), 173

Zborowski, Mark, 197–98

PERMISSIONS

Grateful acknowledgment is made to the following for permission to reprint previously published material.

AMERICAN ASSOCIATION OF UNIVERSITY WOMEN EDUCATIONAL FOUNDATION: Excerpts from "The Classroom Climate: A Chilly One For Women?" by Bernice R. Sandler, Mary De Mouy, and Roberta M. Hall (*American Association of University Women Educational Foundation,* February 1982). Reprinted by permission of the American Association of University Women Educational Foundation.

AMERICAN PSYCHIATRIC PUBLISHING, INC.: Excerpts from "Where Are the Women?" by Donna E. Stewart (*Psychiatric News,* August 21, 1998) p. 14. Copyright © 1998 by the American Psychiatric Association. Excerpts from "Biology and the Future of Psychoanalysis" by Erik R. Kandel (*American Journal of Psychiatry,* 1999) vol. 156, p. 505–24. Copyright © 1999 by the American Psychiatric Association. http://.psychiatryonline.org. Reprinted by permission of American Psychiatric Publishing, Inc.

AMERICAN PSYCHOLOGICAL ASSOCIATION: Excerpt from "Gender, Language and Influence" by Linda D. Carli (*Journal of Personality and Social Psychology,* 1990) 59:5. Excerpt from "The Measurement of Psychological Androgyny" by Sandra L. Bem (*Journal of Consulting and Clinical Psychology,* 1974) 42:2. Excerpts from "The Socialization of Achievement Orientation in Females" by Aletha Stein and Margaret M. Bailey (*Psychological Bulletin,* November 1973) 40:5. Reprinted by permission of the American Psychological Association.

AMERICAN SCIENTIST: Excerpts from "Career Patterns of Women and Men in the Sciences" by Gerhard Sonnert and Gerald Holton (*American Scientist,* 1996). Reprinted by permission of the *American Scientist.*

CONDÉ NAST PUBLICATIONS: Excerpt from "Of Maya Lin" by Charles Gandee (*Vogue,* April 1995). Reprinted by permission of Condé Nast Publications.

FORTUNE: Excerpts from "Trophy Husbands" by Betsy Morris (*Fortune,* October 14, 2002). Copyright © 2002 by Time Inc. All rights reserved. Reprinted by permission of *Fortune.*

ABOUT THE AUTHOR

Anna Fels has written for *The New York Times Book Review,* the *Times Literary Supplement, The Nation,* and *Self.* She now writes for *The New York Times'* Science Times section. A member of the faculty of the Weill Medical College of Cornell University, Fels is a practicing psychiatrist. She lives with her husband and two children in New York City.